The Real Deal makes clear how to conquer what sometimes feel like overwhelming tasks. Daylle has inspired creative and alternative routes, which help me reach goals in marketing, promotion, business, etc.

—Jenn London, singer/songwriter, New York City

When I came across *The Real Deal,* my quest for information had to be subdued in order to digest the wisdom that flowed from this book. Since reading the book and applying its principles, my musical career has turned 180 degrees and I am now able to assist others and point them in the right direction. This book helped me to be more professional in my dealings with those in the music industry. With consistency and perseverance I continue to grow and have success!

—Richard F. Christie, Jr., CEO, RSC Records, Jacksonville, Florida

Working indie, you need as much professional info as you can get. My copy of *The Real Deal* has a lot of dog ears and pencil notes now, as it has given me more insight into how the music industry works, and what it takes to set up my own indie music business: that it's a business like any other; that the content of a good press kit can make a difference; that's it's essential to get the music mastered; and that it's important to study other great acts to know what's hot today and then find your own way. I did.

—Onno Lakeman, rock duo Red to Violet, Holland

We had been writing songs for about five years when Father Christmas gave me *The Real Deal.* What a revelation! The book had so many new ideas about how to get our music heard. The advice was as relevant on our side of the "pond" as it was on Daylle's and we put it to good use. I was tempted to follow in Daylle's footsteps and set up a record label but that's a big step, one I didn't think I was brave enough to take. I wrote to Daylle and received such a positive and supportive response that we went ahead and set up our own label. We haven't set the world on fire yet but we now have a foothold in the music business. Thank you for your inspiration, Daylle!

—David Yates, director, Loving Monkey Productions Ltd., England

The best way to prepare you for the music industry is to get educated. Go to school, get well rounded. You don't necessarily need to know everything about the music business, but you need to know about how business is done. And be prepared to understand that your music is about to become a business. —Sean "P. Diddy" Combs

kitchen table, mashed potatoes castles, parents droning, bed-time, lights out, silence, thinking, other kids playing late on the street, turn on transistor radio, tinny pressed to ear under blankets, a voice sings, scratchy addresses universe on behalf of 8 year old spirit, recognition of something greater, promise made: "Someday, someway somehow I will be involved with music when I grow-up." and then the challenge, how to hold this contract steady within oneself across the years—serving and protecting it or sacrificing it to the dogs/gods.

—Jane Siberry, on why most people are in
the music business and why there is such variety

THE
REAL
DEAL

★

HOW TO GET SIGNED
TO A RECORD LABEL
UPDATED & EXPANDED EDITION

★

DAYLLE DEANNA SCHWARTZ

★

BILLBOARD BOOKS

An imprint of Watson-Guptill Publications ★ New York

*This book is dedicated to my
parents with much love*

First published in 2002 by Billboard Books
An imprint of Watson-Guptill Publications
A division of VNU Business Media, Inc.
770 Broadway, New York, NY 10003
www.watsonguptill.com

Senior Acquisitions Editor: Bob Nirkind
Editor: Gabrielle Pecarsky
Designer: Leah Lococo
Production Manager: Hector Campbell

Library of Congress Cataloging-in-Publication Data

Schwartz, Daylle Deanna.
The real deal : how to get signed to a record label, updated &
expanded edition / Daylle Deanna Schwartz.
p. cm.
Includes bibliographical references (p.   ) and index.
ISBN 0-8230-8405-1
1. Popular music—Vocational guidance—United States. 2. Sound
recording industry—United States. I. Title.
ML3795 .S244 2002
780'.23'73—dc21

2002000231

Printed in the United States

First printing, 2002

2 3 4 5 6 7 8 9/08 07 06 05 04 03

Acknowledgments

I thank God and the universe for all my blessings. I wouldn't be where I am today without my strong faith. One blessing is Bob Nirkind, senior acquisitions editor of Billboard Books. Thank you for being so supportive and for being a pleasure to work with on every level. Great big appreciative thanks to my editor, Gabrielle Pecarsky, for your excellent editing skills, your pleasant nature, and for working with me to make this book the best it can be.

Many wonderful industry people helped shape *The Real Deal* with their support and knowledge. The music industry is known for being unsupportive and cutthroat. Yet these people make the music industry worth being in. Since there are so many, I'll thank them in alphabetical order.

Thank you, thank you, thank you to the musicians who shared their experiences: Cody Braun, Lester Chiu, Johnny Clegg, Sean "P. Diddy" Combs, Chuck D, Jo Davidson, George Devore, Fisher, Pat Green, Pamela Hart, Terri Hendrix, Sara Hickman, Onno Lakeman, Michelle Lewis, Lezlee, Lucky, Ginger MacKenzie, Nina Mankin, Shirley Manson, Karen Matheson, MC Overlord, Nook, ?uestlove, Chris Rasmussen, LeAnn Rimes, Jane Siberry, Jennifer Smith, Phoebe Snow, Jerry Jeff Walker, Tom Walker.

Thank you, thank you, thank you to the record label people who shared their knowledge: Karin Berg, Jeff Blue, Merlin Bob, David Boyd, Michael Caplan, Angel Carrasco, Monte Conner, Bo Crane, Jeff Fenster, Wendy Goldstein, Tara Griggs-Magee, Jim Guerinot, Hosh Gureli, Bruce Iglauer, Danny Kee, Brian Long, Aldo Marin, Rose Noone, Ricky Schultz, Chris Schwartz, Andrew Shack, Chris Sharp, Happy Walters, Lisa Zbitnew.

Thank you, thank you, thank you to the industry pros who shared their knowledge: Jerry Ade, Tom Baggott, Madison Bedard, Marilyn Bergman, Jane Blumenfeld, Rich Branciforte, Mark Brown, Joy R. Butler, Lois Chisolm, Peter Ciaccia, Richard Dieguez, Marilyn Dukes, Brad First, Janet Fisher, Barry Fox, Jeri Goldstein, J. W. Johnson, Chris Jones, Barbara Jordan, Deonne Kahler, Alex Kochan, Adam Kornfeld, Michael Laskow, Peter Leeds, Micheline Levine, Michael Lloyd, Linda Lorence, Kenny MacPherson, Deborah-Mannis Gardner, Casey Monahan, Joann Murdock, David Nevue, Michael Norton, Shannon

O'Shea, Frances Preston, Phil Ramone, Ed Razzano, Nathan Redus, Erica Ruben, Shani Saxon, Elaine Schock, Harriet Schock, Stormy Shepherd, Peter Slagt, Stan Soocher, Diane Stagnato, George Stein, Susan Walker, Sandy Wilbur. Tommy Williams, Pacal Zander.

Special thanks are in order. I'm extraordinarily blessed to have made so many wonderful friends in the music industry, some of them through my interviewing them. A very big, super-special thank-you to Larry Rudolph and Wallace Collins, for their friendship and for going the distance with me over many years, with continued support. Thank you David Wimble, for always being a supportive friend and for creating the best resource for marketing music on the Internet, *The Indie Bible*! Thank you Paul Sacksman, for publishing *The Musician's Atlas*! I didn't quote you, but I sure learned a lot from you and greatly appreciate your friendship. Thank you Bruce Lundvall, for being so gracious with your time and for showing me how wonderful people at the top can be! Thank you Shawn Mullins, for going out of your way to make time for me to pick your experienced brain and for allowing me to get to know what a terrific person you are! Thank you Terrie Williams, for your continuous support and for showing by example that we can be caring, supportive, and spiritual in the industry. Thank you Wendy Morgan, for enabling me to fall in love with Austin by introducing me to the music community. Thank you Catherine Weir and the staff of Holiday Inn at Town Lake, for making my stay in Austin so comfortable. And last but not least, thank you Ron Stone, for being so generous with your time and for being a mentor to me when I need one. All of these folks show what a wonderful business this can be. I greatly appreciate my industry friends and love you all!

CONTENTS

Part Three
PREPARING YOUR PRESENTATION

Introduction

A record deal is an elusive brass ring in the hearts of many. Some openly go after one. Others yearn secretly. Go to any college dorm and you'll find med students, math majors, law students, and everyone in between, with a guitar, drum kit, mic, or synthesizer in their closets. A record deal seems glamorous and exciting on the surface, with fame and fortune an expected outcome. Are you under the misconception that if you get one, you'll have a zillion members of the opposite sex hanging on you, along with a pumped-up bank account? Hey, that sounds great to me, too! But if that's what you think, put your balloons away—my words will arrive like a pin and burst them.

Having a record deal isn't the answer to most people's dreams. The road to making the dream a reality can be filled with potholes and confusing road signs. Many signed artists find it to be a nightmare. A staggering percentage of recording artists that are signed to good labels don't make a dime in royalties. Some don't even see their records hit stores. I intend to give you *the real deal* about getting signed. But if my words don't scare you, I'll also offer hope, suggestions on how to kick down tight doors, and ways to make money from your music on the road to pursuing that deal. Some people do make money. Some do enjoy being signed. When you finish this book, you'll be much better prepared to find your way to a deal that brings you satisfaction.

Here's *the real deal*. The best way to get a record deal is not to go looking for it. The happiest signed artists are the ones who got their deals because they'd built up a big enough foundation to get a label's attention and to have more say in the terms of the deal. Labels prefer to sign acts that have already created something with their music. Artist development is rare these days. If you don't develop yourself, it may never happen. The bottom line is, your career is in your hands. If you have the talent, you have the power to develop a career. If you're waiting for someone to do it for you, don't quit your day job!

Contemplate this: Which would you rather be—a musician without a record deal who's earning a decent living from your music or a poor signed one? You know the real deal on that! Why be a signed artist who laments that nothing is happening with your music when you can have the career and then the record deal, too? I encourage you to put your energy into your career first. According to Richard P. Dieguez, an entertainment lawyer with an international practice based in Roslyn Heights, New York:

> *When I was a young musician, I tried to get a record deal—so I understand how that long-term goal becomes the mark of success. Some clients think I'm crazy, but, as an experienced music lawyer and artist manager, I actually challenge them to consider other options. Why? Because the odds of getting a good deal and becoming commercially successful are against you. Instead, build your career now by pursuing achievable goals. Aspire to become the most commercially successful independent artist in your community—promote, build your fan base, perform, sell CDs and merchandise. Your local or regional success might just lead to the great worldwide deal everyone is chasing. Flea, of The Red Hot Chili Peppers, summed it up best when he remarked that being a true artist is about living like one now and not about waiting for that "big break."*

In this new edition, I want to help you turn your focus away from making a record deal your primary goal and put more energy into finding ways to make money from your music. I've seen too many artists lose their passion for doing the music they love when getting a record deal becomes too important. Do you love your music? Are you trying to get a deal because you love music or because of your ego? In my opinion, the best way to get a record deal is to pursue your music career with passion. Get as much exposure and make the most of your talent as possible to give you the strongest foundation for getting a label's attention for a deal. I've added new chapters with that goal in mind. I encourage you to sharpen your skills and work on ways to develop a career in music. A record deal can be fleeting; a career lasts a lifetime. As you develop as a musician and create success as one, it's easier to get a record deal. I've included interviews with an assortment of musicians who are finding success in many different arenas. Learn from their experiences and suggestions.

People come to me for advice on how to get signed to a record label. Sometimes they're so confused by what others tell them that they can't make good decisions for themselves. Everyone in the music industry has an opinion. Ask five different people how to approach a specific situation and you may get five conflicting points of view. It's hard to know whom to listen to. Trying everything sets you up for what I call the *yo-*

yo effect, being yanked back and forth as you grab at all suggestions for getting ahead. You're advised to "do this" and rush to try it. Then someone presents another option and you hurry to try that, too. Heeding everyone's advice gets exhausting and frustrating, as little gets accomplished. You can burn yourself out.

How can you know whom to listen to? As a teacher of music business classes and a consultant for start-up labels and artists/songwriters, I regularly hear misconceptions about the music industry. I was hampered by them myself when I broke into working in music. While there's no formula for getting a record deal, the wrong advice can keep you from trying all options. The bottom line is, there's no one way of getting music to the attention of record labels. What works well with someone at one label may bomb with another. There are endless possibilities for someone with talent who is willing to work her butt off in pursuit of musical success. This book tells you the real deal about how you can maximize your chances of attracting the best record deal possible.

How do I know what I'm talking about? My entry into the music industry came from a very different place than most. I was a schoolteacher in New York City, and I guarantee that anyone reading this knows more about music than I did in the beginning. I didn't even know what a CD was! There were few female rappers back then, and no white ones to speak of when my students dared me to make a rap record. They laughed at me, saying a white woman couldn't rap. I became determined to break their stereotypes, to show them they shouldn't let things like gender or race stop them from doing what they believed in.

I eventually learned how to rap by hanging out in the streets, going to clubs, listening to rap radio shows, and literally living and breathing hip-hop. I got ripped off big time, swayed by everyone's promises. In the streets, where my lessons began, there were many misconceptions about the industry. At first, I believed everybody because I wanted to believe the exciting things I heard. My passionate highs dropped to disheartening lows as I went from excitement (when someone souped me up, inflating my bubble) to downright depression (when someone else burst it). It was an emotional time—of much learning, growing, and toughening my stance. But I survived.

When I made my first rap cut, the kids in school were sold. I got nicknamed "The Rappin' Teach" and picked up lots of media attention, but still no deal. I had no clue then what I was doing. The kids thought I was good and were furious when people took advantage of my ignorance. This is a heck of an industry. Many insiders tell you anything you want to hear at that moment so you'll kiss up to them. At first I kissed, so desperate was I to get the deal I wanted. But no one in the industry believed a white woman could succeed in rap, even though they knew I was good.

The kids decided I should get revenge against those who'd done me wrong, suggesting I have the offenders' tires slashed, their houses spray painted, and more. If I wouldn't do it myself, there were volunteers to do it for me. However, I truly believe it's healthier to use the energy behind your anger to do something positive for yourself. So instead of slashing tires, I opened Revenge Productions and through it, Revenge Records—a vehicle for me to put out my own material. That was the beginning of my positive revenge! And positive revenge is definitely sweet!

I learned by trial and error, and got taken advantage of many times. My knowledge was so limited back then that I had to depend on others for everything. But I worked very hard, determined to prove my point. At music seminars, I felt like a nonentity but continued to network like crazy. People read my tag and walked away with their noses in the air. What a lousy feeling! But that's the way it can be in this industry. Be prepared for it. It may never get better. A strong belief in your talent and a thick skin helps you get through those times of feeling like a nobody.

My efforts began as a lesson to my students about not letting stereotypes stop them from achieving goals. But all of a sudden I had a viable record label—signing artists and selling lots of records! Major labels were making deals with me for my artists. Best of all, I finally earned one of the hardest commodities to attain in this business: respect. Respect needs to be earned and the dues are high. In the beginning, I was humored, but not taken seriously. Ignoring skepticism, I focused on making a success of my label. After my first major deal, people saw me in a different light. When I got asked to speak at national music seminars, the respect was there. I began writing songs and getting artists to perform them, which increased respect. Then people not only talked to me at seminars, they coveted me so much that I almost wished to be back in anonymity.

I learned from my mistakes, and you can learn from my mistakes, too! Since I'm a real teacher, people came to me for advice about making it in the music industry. Former students sent me their friends and relatives because they believed, as one put it, "Schwartz will tell you the real deal about the music business." Some of the informal advice I gave came from what I learned while running Revenge Records, and from information I picked up from seminars and books. The rest came from *on-the-job training*. I was the paid manager of an alternative rock band for two years. I successfully shopped material. I learned from my successes. I learned from failures as well. It's said that experience is the best teacher. Mine were certainly lessons you can't learn in school.

In 1990, I put together a formal seminar called "How to Start & Run Your Own Record Label." After receiving pressure from satisfied students, I started teaching an assortment of classes, including "How to Get a Record Deal." I still teach these sessions regularly and people attend my private, full-day seminars in New York from all over the country, as well as from overseas. I also travel to other cities to lecture in educational programs. Everyone wants to learn from the former "Rappin' Teach."

I put this book together because there's a need for simple, qualitative facts about getting your product heard and marketed. It's an offshoot of my popular classes, which are known for starting with the assumption that nobody knows anything and working up from there. People are often embarrassed to ask simple questions, assuming they should have the answers already. Most seminars I attend and books I read assume that people know the basics. But there are no sources of getting them. Thus, I've put my classes in a book. I've tried to include everything that comes up in my classes and during consultations. And, in this edition, I've included more information on touring, marketing songs, and finding various avenues for making money with your music. If you're going to knock yourself out for your music, you need all the help you can get.

In order to survive, a musician must develop a coat of armor. This industry is tough. Promises take you on an emotional seesaw ride. The high is exhilarating when success is dangled in your face. Anticipation raises adrenaline. But lows come quickly when promises are unfulfilled and your calls aren't returned. That ride destroys. Musicians burn out when disappointment makes them lose heart. When I first started rapping, someone would pull my chain and get me excited, promising a deal shortly. I'd scream with anticipation. Then they'd disappear, and my excitement turned to depression. Luckily, someone pointed out that I'd crash if I continued on that seesaw. Now I stay mellow through the good and the bad. I only get excited when a deal is signed. You can't take people seriously until they come through. Take everything people say lightly.

There are plenty of things you can do to give yourself the best shot at achieving success in the music industry. Time and time again I hear young musicians speak with misconceptions as to how to go about getting a record deal. In this book, I've included and dispelled many common ones that I've heard regularly from people in my classes. These are myths that people hear and believe that keep them from exploring every possible avenue to getting a deal. Having learned this industry the hard way, I'd like to share the knowledge I've gained, both from my own experiences and from the numerous industry professionals and successful musicians I've interviewed in order to present different perspectives. Take the tools in this book and apply them to whatever genre of music you're working in. The rest is up to you!

PART
ONE

THE
BUSINESS
OF
MUSIC

TAKING CARE

of

BUSINESS

Myth:

Creative people shouldn't have to deal with
the business end of the music industry.

● ● ●

Do you want to make money from your music? If you do, put on a business cap. This is called the music *business* for a reason. It would be lovely if you could just create and have someone with good business sense take care of yours. But why would someone like that want to handle your business before you're making enough money to pay him? When you're making lots of it, you'll get help. Even then, have enough business panache to make sure that your money is handled properly. Pianist David Nevue, who took his biz very seriously and is making money from his music because of it, cautions:

> *Prepare yourself for long hours and hard work. Up to now, I've spent much more time working on the "business" than I do on the music. But that work has paid off, and very soon I'll have more time to focus on my music. You have to treat your music career*

like a business if you want to bring in the income to allow you to do what you really want to. If you are a talented musician and have something unique to offer, I believe my own success proves that doing music full time is within anyone's grasp. You just have to be willing to work for it, be patient, and keep going no matter how discouraged you feel.

DEVELOP A BUSINESS ATTITUDE

In your own eyes, your music is a special creative endeavor. But, in the larger scheme of the music industry, you're a product. It's not a great thought, but accept it if you want to make money from your music. If that offends your ideals, consider doing music as a hobby. If you want an income from it, start seeing it as a business, like marketing shoes or fruit. Music involves different strategies, but it's still marketing a product—your music. You don't have to sacrifice creativity, but you do need to incorporate a business attitude. Ron Stone, president of Gold Mountain Management, applies this concept to managing his clients. Until you get good management, it's *your* job. Stone explains:

> *I'm the CEO of my artist's company. I manage the business end—the legal, accounting, publicity, research, development, manufacturing, marketing, and sales departments. Just like any company, it has the same components. The unique aspect of it is that the product is also the client. The client is the chairman of the board of directors. I'm only the CEO. I serve at the will of the chairman. I go to the board of directors and present my plan of how we're going to do it. And I regularly report in, analyzing all the different divisions of the company. The most difficult part is the conversation with the artist, who is the chairman of the board, because you're talking about marketing them as a product.*

It sucks to think of your music as a product, but that's the bottom line. Either work with that or bitch and don't make money. The bands I interviewed who are earning a living from music take business seriously. If you think like a business now, you'll have the best opportunity to quit your day job. Folk singer Terri Hendrix makes a full-time living off of her music and even has employees. She says:

It's hard, but I love to play, and I can't play where I want to play without doing my business. Music is a business. "Music business" doesn't have to be a dirty word. It can be creative, too. You can look at the world and figure out where to sell your art. It's a good thing, not a four-letter word.

LET THE DEAL COME TO YOU

Too many musicians chase a deal and end up dissatisfied when they get it. I want to help you keep your dream from turning into a nightmare. A record deal CAN be a wonderful commodity if it's a vehicle for advancing your career. But it rarely gives you one if you haven't started it yourself. Recording artist Shawn Mullins recalls:

I think what kept me going was not waiting on a record deal. I thought, "Hey, I can do this!" Before I got signed to Columbia [in 1998] I did it for ten years as an independent. I was pretty sure I wasn't going to sign with a major label; I didn't think they got what I did. Early on, I'd shopped a couple of times and it didn't work out, so I decided to put out my own records. I had a good enough following in a few places to build on and keep going. When my song "Lullaby" was on the radio a lot, there were many label calls. At that point, it was probably smart for me to go with a label because I needed help. I could steer my own deal, and it worked out well. I had to be talked into getting a deal.

If your music doesn't fit into one specific genre, it's harder to get a deal without bending your style. You've got to *show* labels how to market you. Recording artist Pat Green got an offer he couldn't refuse from Republic/Universal. A & R people began checking him out a year before he got signed. He eluded them as he developed his career in order to get a deal on his terms. He says:

I turned previous offers down or placed myself out of negotiation because they were the wrong people for me. You don't ever want to put yourself into the position of working for somebody. You want to work with them. Some bands don't develop a relationship of give and take. If you let them take the reins, they're gonna take them and whip you. I'd rather earn what I get than do what they want. I do what I want even if people put my music down.

With our band, it became clear to me that I couldn't go to Nashville. We're kind of country music, kind of not. We're not easy to pigeonhole and have no desire to be polished. I couldn't see myself in a video wearing a cowboy hat, even though I play country music and love the fiddle. We wanted to go with a rock label—somebody that would take us as a band. I want to be a band. We'd sold 150,000 records or more. I had the ability to sell, but knew that if I had more dollars behind me, with more marketing and better spacing on shelves, I was in a spot to have some leverage. We were selling a shitload of tickets in at least ten markets just in the state of Texas and at least seven markets out of the state.

Before talking seriously to labels, Green demonstrated that his music could sell well. He proved that the most satisfying way to get signed to a label is to put your energy into developing your career instead of chasing a deal. There are four advantages to this:

1. A record label is more likely to sign an artist who is working to get exposure for her music and who has a fan base. Labels prefer you to have a core of buyers for the first round of records. The days of artist development are history.

2. Labels don't know what to do with music that doesn't fit into molds. Their marketing formulas are insular. If your vision isn't in their face, they'll pass. If you play one genre with a bit of this or that genre, labels will make you choose between this or that. Why be at the mercy of folks who might rule you at a label when you can first prove that your music can sell your way? Show them why they want to sign you by working hard to get gigs, press, radio play, placement in film and TV, and CD sales!

3. The more you do yourself, the better the chance of attracting a deal on your terms. Don't settle for any deal. Labels are notorious for ignoring their artists. Why sit on a shelf or endure the frustration of no support once your record is out? If you develop the foundation of a career first, you have something to build on, despite them. Shawn Mullins says, "I learned so much about the business by doing it myself. I had prepared myself for a strong record deal. I ended up with seventeen points, not common for a first-time artist. I got a very, very large advance."

A record label is a vehicle that provides radio and retail promotion, distribution, tour support, and publicity, if your engine is

already running. Get into the position of choosing to si̶g̶
only if it can bolster your career, because you have one eit̶h̶
Don't be at a label's mercy!

4. A record deal can be very short lived. A career can last a lifetim̶e̶
If you want to do your music for a living, go after the career!
Then you can keep doing music if the record deal ends.

Brian Long, senior director of A & R at MCA Records, confirms, "There seems to be a real movement from A & R departments in major labels to have research departments seeking out the unsigned artists who are being played on the right radio stations and are selling at record stores." Put yourself in a win/win situation with your music: You win if you get a good record deal, but otherwise you're still a winner because you've got a music career without one. Recording artist Jo Davidson marketed her music herself before getting her deal with Edel America. She explains:

> *I don't pretend that I wanted to do this indie thing, because I didn't. What I did like was that nobody in this process was getting in the way of my creativity. I made my record myself because I wanted to keep the integrity intact. I think a lot of record people make a complete living just interfering with the creative process and disrespecting it. I wasn't trying all that hard to get a deal. I focused more on getting group shows. I'm very proud of my record. I got a record deal because I wasn't desperate to get a deal. I don't feel that much more secure with a record deal. I do feel good because now there's a team of people who are interested in having my record succeed. And it really reaches a lot more people.*

DEVELOP A MARKETING PLAN

Make a plan to market your product properly, however informal. Think about how to market your music most effectively. Target your audience and figure out the best ways to reach it. Everyone may love your music, but you can't market to everyone. Pat Green says, "I was very driven to find that core audience and exploit that. For me it was college-age kids—frat kids—who liked to party and have fun." Choose the most likely audience—college students, young adults, high schoolers, etc.— even if others may buy it, too. Then create a marketing plan that identifies how to expose the audience to your music. Identify the best venues and magazines for reviews. If you're not sure how to ascertain who your cord labels won't bother to do so either. They want t. Targeting your audience defines your direction, er shot at success.

ness plan, include specific goals to help you stay nes. Note the word *realistic*. Don't set yourself up nachievable goals. Map out small weekly goals for shing each is progress. Write down whom you shop you'll attend, which artist to catch live, what song to work on, which rehearsals to schedule, etc. These all get you one step closer. As you accomplish goals, pat yourself on the back instead of focusing on what hasn't happened yet. At the end of the week, keep a journal of every little thing you did for your music to motivate you to persevere and keep you on a positive track. On a spiritual level, that attracts more positive contacts and avenues.

Network to find out which labels are appropriate for your music and which A & R person at each label handles your genre. Get the names of managers and agents who might eventually be right for you. Whenever you do a mailing, include them in it. Whether it's a gig announcement, a press release, or a newsletter about your music, keep these industry people in the loop. It makes your name more familiar to them. Those who pay attention will see that you're getting out and doing things with your music.

MAINTAIN PRODUCT QUALITY CONTROL

You can't just have a decent product. Develop your talent until it shines like a jewel. Too many musicians get jaded and think that since people come to their shows and buy CDs, they're good enough. If you're satisfied to stay at that level, let your ego rule. But if you want to make real money and get a good record deal, always assume you can improve. Stop chasing record deals and hone your craft! Do everything you can to get so good that people can't ignore you. Jazz singer Pamela Hart says:

> *I've been working on myself and my performance. Everyone told me that I was ready for a record deal, but I had to decide for myself. Now I'm ready. I'm not scared anymore. My musicianship is ready. It wasn't before. I had good vocal quality but not as much control as I would like to have had. I'm confident now that I won't have a big crack in the middle of my song. I feel professionally*

ready and my voice is ready. I had a high standard of what it would take to be thought of as good by those who know what good is. Now I'm acceptable to that level. I have a reputation.

Practice as much as possible! Find ways to get critiqued by professionals. Get a good producer to work with you. Improve your songwriting by going to crafting classes. Study with a reputable vocal coach or master musician to sharpen your skills and develop your talent fully. Do whatever you can to polish your music to a level that works in the big leagues, if you want to be in them. It takes patience to wait until you're developed enough to go after your dreams. But that's how to achieve them.

EDUCATE YOURSELF

One of your strongest qualities, in my opinion, is to know your weaknesses. Too many people shoot themselves in the foot because they think they know it all. No one does. A good businessperson finds resources to compensate for knowledge or skills that he is lacking. Educate yourself about the industry by reading as much as you can, going to seminars, and picking people's brains. Learn to take care of your business. Industry people consistently advise educating yourself about all aspects of this business.

Some artists opt for a quick deal—a lump of cash at the beginning—leaving the label with most of the money. Why? Ignorance. Many musicians who get ripped off are hungry for a deal. A label might offer what seems like a huge chunk of change as an advance. To a kid desperate for a deal, even $10,000 can seem sweet. Often without the benefit of a lawyer or manager, artists sign contracts on their own, clueless about what they're giving away. By the time they see how much money the label is making off of their album, and how little they're getting, it's usually too late to do anything about it. Mind your own business!

Learn as much as you can about the business end of the industry. You don't need to be an expert, but basic knowledge empowers you. I've taken auto mechanics classes, with no intention of working on my car. But my knowledge saves me money when I discuss my car's problem with a mechanic. As a result, I know what to check first before going for a major overhaul. The same is true with a record deal. It's useful to talk to your lawyer with some understanding of what's being said. It helps you to ask good questions and challenge evasive answers. Why give someone else the power over your decisions because you don't know enough to make them yourself? It's also important to understand the basics of deals so you don't market your music with too much idealism.

WATCH YOUR ASS

Decide on a lawyer first (see Chapter 5). That's what a business does! This doesn't mean paying before it's necessary. It means shopping for a lawyer while you're not under pressure, which gives you the best chance of finding one you feel comfortable with. Musicians often wait until an A & R person, manager, or publisher offers a contract before beginning their search for a lawyer. Why settle for whomever you get quickly? Have your representation in place before approaching anyone for a deal. Once you find one you like, tell her you'd like her representation when you have a deal. Establish her fees. Ask if you can give her name as your representative. You shouldn't have to pay anyone at this point. Some attorneys want a retainer up front to cover any quick representation you may need or to cover expenses. Policies vary from attorney to attorney. Shop around.

Have written agreements for any arrangements you make that involve money or committing yourself to someone. Handshake agreements are out, period! Many of you are thinking, "But wait . . ." Too many people get in trouble because they think they're the exception: "But she's a good person," or "He's my best friend," or "I trust him with my life." Trust him with your life but not your career! When you work with someone, keep it on a business level and leave the personal stuff at home. Things happen.

People forget promises when a deal is imminent. They may not purposely want to screw you, but they're going to look out for their own best interests. They may actually not remember what was agreed to and think that their way is best for everyone concerned. But where you're concerned, take responsibility for your best interests and be careful! Your best insurance policy is a written agreement. This industry changes people. Don't take chances. *Put everything in writing.*

If there's more than one member of your act, create a written agreement between you. You may be friends now, but this is business. Entertainment attorney Joy R. Butler, from the Washington, D.C., metropolitan area, advises:

Any act seriously pursuing commercial success should have a written agreement. In addition to establishing how the business of the act will be managed, a written agreement outlines what rights each member has in the name, the songs written by members, and the act's recordings. These issues can become crucial when the act begins achieving some degree of success—or when a member leaves. That's when a member may wonder, "Should I get a larger share of the income for group songs that I wrote?" or "Can I continue to use the group name even though I no longer perform with the act?" Having a written agreement encourages the members to find solutions for these and other potential disputes before they arise. That way, there's less chance that a dispute will lead to the breakup of the act or to a costly lawsuit.

People get greedy when money is in the picture. Protect yourself by establishing all the details in writing. It minimizes unnecessary conflict later on. Joy R. Butler is also the author and producer of the audiobook *The Musician's Guide through the Legal Jungle* (see Appendix 2). She has seen many people get screwed—so take her advice and watch your ass!

CREATE YOUR BUSINESS MATERIALS

You don't need many materials, but I recommend having a nice business card. It gives you a more professional front. A business card is easier to give out than a piece of paper with your info. I put thought into my design because it gets me mileage. Foolishly enough, a card that stands out impresses people. It's amazing how many people say to me, "Nice card. You're doing well, right?" Right! Doing well at having a successful front. Get a card that shows you take yourself seriously.

A great tool for promotion is color postcards. As of this printing, 1800postcards.com offers 5,000 small color postcards for $250 if you provide camera-ready art. Otherwise, for a reasonable fee, they'll prepare the artwork for you. (Say you read about the company in *The Real Deal* and get 10 percent off your first order.) Put a photo or a CD cover, if you have one, on the front. They'll print whatever you want on the back. I recommend placing near the top general contact info, the address of your website, quotes, if you have any, and information on how to order merchandise. Leave most of the card blank. If you do a mailing or want something to hand out at events to announce a gig or some other event, print the info on labels and paste a label on each card. They're more professional-looking than homemade mailings. If your info is generic, the cards can be used for years. Even if you mainly do e-mailings, send cards to your targeted industry list.

PREPARE TO WORK YOUR BUTT OFF

Work to get a deal! Rarely will someone come to you before there's been an effort on your part. Talent isn't enough. Great material isn't enough. Dynamic image isn't enough. The artists who make it are those with talent, material, and image, who want it bad enough to do almost anything it takes to get the attention of someone who can be instrumental. Sitting home waiting to be discovered won't cut it, no matter how much talent you have. Doing all you can to reach as many people as possible offers the best shot at success. Hone your craft and develop your music career if you want to attract a *good* record deal.

I meet musicians who've written loads of songs. When I ask what they do with them, the replies are variations of, "One day someone will discover me." They stay in their home studios continuing to write. Then there are musicians who jump at chances to play live, even for free; who run to open mics; and who cultivate contacts in the industry at every opportunity. They want a deal so much that they'll hustle and network and keep paying dues until they get there. IF they have the talent to match their drive, they'll get it. This attitude served Jo Davidson well, even after getting signed. She says:

> If you don't have a deal, and especially when you do have a deal, you can't get lazy about creating opportunities. At first when you sign a deal, you think that other people will take care of things. They do to a point, but you have to remember that you're the center of the wheel and they're the spokes. The second you totally stop, it won't be long before everything stops.

CARRY YOURSELF LIKE A WINNER

If you want to get taken seriously, take yourself seriously first! The way you treat yourself reflects on how others see you. People treat you as you allow them to. Once, while I was speaking at a music conference, a woman got on the mic, complaining about how hard it was to get people to come to her gigs. She began by stating that she knew she was a nobody. Hello! I told her to eliminate the word nobody from her vocabulary. If she thinks she's a nobody, why should others take her seriously? You're a somebody whether your career is hot or not, as long as YOU know it.

If you act apologetic, like you don't have a right to ask for things, people won't take you seriously. A confident, courteous approach helps people notice you in a positive way. Respect yourself and expect to be treated as a professional. It reflects in your attitude. Believe in yourself and others will follow your lead! Develop enough confidence in your talent to carry yourself with pride. Getting better at what you do improves self-image and boosts confidence. Own the talented person you are! That's where your career begins. When I decided I wanted to write, I got a business card that said "writer." From then on I was one, and I gave it out proudly, though it took years to get published. You can be a great musician with or without a deal or a big following. As René Descartes said, "I think, therefore I am." Live by that!

CREATE YOUR FOUNDATION

Don't market your music until you're ready. Develop your marketing package. Create a demo and press kit, and have photos taken. Do as many live performances as possible. Be prepared for whatever opportunities come your way. A band once came to me for a consultation. They'd invested tons of money in pressing up a CD with a great recording and beautiful artwork and sent it to various labels. They actually got four responses. But the labels didn't want to sign them. They wanted more. That's how it works. Labels can be pigs. You do it all and then they add fuel to the fire you've set. These guys were asked for a press kit and photo. They had none. The labels wanted to see them perform. They had no following and no gigs. Their credibility went out the window. Singer/songwriter Sara Hickman wasn't prepared when she signed with Elektra and recalls:

> I would sit in a club in Dallas and play for maybe fifty-five guys who would stare at me in the dark. The next thing I knew, I was on the Tonight Show, my record was everywhere, and there was a huge poster of me in the window of Tower Records in New York. Nobody said this would happen. All these things start hap-

pening like a freight train, and you're supposed to know how to deal with them. I really felt like I was taken off the farm and put at the top of the Eiffel Tower and told to fly. I was flying by the seat of my pants.

Labels want you to have your act together. Don't approach them too soon and risk blowing an opportunity or settling for a bad deal. Wait until you have together as many pieces as possible. Jo Davidson says, "The key to success for me is versatility—still doing music but various aspects of it—having your hands in a couple of different things." Create a foundation that shows you're serious. Be patient until you get there. Don't lose yourself in a record deal. While signed to a big deal, Shawn Mullins says:

I do smaller things based on fans and my love for the actual music. I also do the stuff I'm asked to do from the label. They don't know what you had before you were signed with them and the relationships you built. It's important not to forget. I ran from deals for three years. I felt I'd been busting my balls doing this and didn't want them to take my thing. Sometimes it still creeps up. I spent ten years working, working, working, but it all comes down to a single when you're in this line of work. But I still get to tour and connect with the audiences.

Develop your product as well as you can for the best chance of a GOOD deal. I'll provide loads of ways to do that throughout the book. For this edition I interviewed many musicians who've created a good foundation and are in that win/win situation. Most of them have their own websites. (Because of the constantly shifting nature of the Web, I'm not including the addresses in this book. You can do an Internet search to locate each musician's official site, typically the artist's name followed by ".com.") I encourage you to check out their sites to get a feel for how organized these artists are. They're all self-made, and more of them may be signed to record deals by the time you are reading this. Many of them don't care about a deal anymore. They're too busy making more money than they'd make from most labels!

THE REAL DEAL ABOUT RECORD DEALS

When you become proactive about your career and take responsibility for it, you give yourself the power to make it happen! Feeling powerful really helps you to have the balls to work your music! Jennifer Smith, of

Naked Blue, was signed to Viceroy Records. She appreciates the support she got from them, but says:

> *Each year that we grow on our own indie label, a record deal seems less attractive. There was this great sense of freedom when we realized we didn't need a label. When we kind of let go of that whole brass ring idea, it changed the way we do business and opened us up to having fun marketing ourselves and realizing we were doing okay and still have the potential to grow on our own.*

Hip-hop artist Nook states, "I want a business partner. I don't want to sign to a record company and be just another artist on the roster." Ideally, that's what a label deal should offer you—resources for working together to advance your career. But unless you have enough going for you to call some of the shots, a label deal may hold you back. Pop artist Ginger MacKenzie says, "I would love a record deal, but only under the right circumstances. If you chase a record deal and don't have anything else, you're going to be like a lot of my friends who are with majors and just wait for something to happen." Ginger had a record chart in Texas and supports herself with music. She's doing better than some of her friends who have label deals. Hip-hop artist MC Overlord adds.

> *Most of my peers have been in and out of label deals and had negative experiences. I don't want a label deal just to say I'm signed. I want one that will benefit me. Otherwise, I'm content to stay on my own. I have the benefit of learning from people who have been down the road and have made mistakes concerning labels. A bad deal can take the wind out of anyone's sails.*

A record deal is good if the label provides tour support and helps you produce a better album. Rock artist George Devore remarks, "Until I get what I want, I've got my own record company. I pay my bills with music and nobody tells me what to do." Waiting for a label to do the work for you holds back your career. They may ignore you, and then what? Lester Chiu, of Schrodinger's Cat, says:

> *We're not actively seeking a record deal. We're an independent label now. So we'll do our best to build up regionally and get ourselves out there. We certainly have had label interest, but no deals that we were happy with. So we court and keep building because if one comes, there's more behind it. If you keep building*

and there's a buzz, eventually they're going to know you're doing it on your own and they can jump on the bandwagon or miss out. There's no artist development anymore.

I'm honestly not trying to discourage you from signing with a record label. I just want you to understand that settling just to be signed is shortsighted. Wait for a deal that adds value to your career, unless you don't want one! Tom Walker, of Friday's Child, says:

I think there are good labels. But I haven't been super impressed by the label people I've met. I won't give up ownership of my material to people who have no intention of promoting it. If we find a label that appreciates that we bring a ready fan base, won't try to screw us any more than they have to, and will add public relations and radio promotions machines to what we already have, we'd do it. Until then, I won't take a deal just to say I'm signed to a label when I'm doing a good job myself.

Jerry Jeff Walker got his start when Bob Fass, a DJ at WBAI radio in New York, played his version of a song he wrote, "Mr. Bojangles," over and over. It became the buzz of New York. He had a gold album in '73, when he was signed with MCA. In the '80s, he asked his wife, Susan, to work with him. He'd just recorded a new CD, and they went to Nashville with the intention of signing a new contract with MCA. Susan recalls:

I told the head we had a CD completed and wanted to see if he'd like to release it. He said, as he sat pompously with his feet up, "I'll take it home, smoke a joint, and see if I can figure out a formula." I was furious. It was so insulting to Jerry's artistic integrity. He'd already been in the business for twenty-five years. But that's the way labels are. I told Jerry Jeff, "That's it. We're starting our own label." I want to thank every one of them for not signing Jerry Jeff because it's been very lucrative for us.

When an indie has big sales, the artist can make a lot more money than he would with a label. Sara Hickman feels stronger after being signed to Elektra Records. She now has her own company and is more successful than ever. She says:

Record companies have become these monolithic gods that take your soul. It's like being married and being locked in a castle. Why would you want that? When you're your own person, you see the *product going into the fans' hands and they're handing you the money. You can sell 100,000 CDs at a label and not see a dime. Even with my teeny label, the first album I put out earned about $50,000. I realized the power of doing it yourself. There's always this promise at a major label of fame, glory, and money, which less than 1 percent of their artists get to. Here, after I pay myself back for the investment of making my CDs, I get five to eight bucks for selling my own. I never got anything from record companies. All I did was accrue this huge debt that I'm never going to pay off, and they have my music in perpetuity.*

● ● ●

Let a deal be the means to the end. Get your career going first, wait for a deal that supports the career you already have, and let the end be longevity in the music biz.

2

UNDERSTANDING
What It Takes to
MAKE IT IN THE
Music Business

Myth:

You need a lot of luck to get a record deal,
and that's not in my control.

• • •

There are no pat rules for getting ahead in this crazy business. Success is often attributed to *luck*. I believe we make our own luck by working our butts off. Networking, getting exposure, and working hard increase your probability of *good luck*. When I began in the music industry, I created luck by talking to everyone I met, showing respect to everyone I encountered, and never taking "no" for an answer. I worked hard and owned any luck I earned. If you have what it takes, work hard and earn it, too! Learn the rules and then break them! Of course, industry protocol can't be ignored. You don't want to alienate folks you want help from. But stay on your own path. Many factors enhance chances of attracting luck. Take an active role in getting you and your music out on as many levels as possible. Don't wait for luck to come to you. Below, I've laid out what I consider the keys to getting a record deal.

MY RULE OF ONE

You may get turned down by dozens of labels. Potential managers and booking agents may ignore you. Be careful. Rejection kills even positive spirits. Kick it in the teeth if you're serious! Those who don't recognize your talent and potential don't have to affect you. I know it feels lousy to be turned down. Beating your head against closed doors isn't fun. But that's the music industry. Musicians can get turned down by dozens of labels before finding the one that appreciates their talent. And that person is the only ONE who matters!

Never forget this: You need only ONE good industry person to work with you. The others don't count. The important person is the ONE who signs you. You need only ONE person at ONE label to give you a record deal. You only need ONE manager and ONE agent. Those who pass on you are meaningless. Chuck the word *rejection*. Think on a more positive and spiritual level. Feeling rejected is bad for attracting success—it brings you down. Concentrate on attracting the ONE person who recognizes your talent enough to work with you. You need only ONE! Remember that if you're feeling defeated by those who don't recognize your talent! Focus on the ONE.

BUZZ

Buzz is the catchword of the music industry. You'll hear it at seminars: "If you want a record deal, create a buzz." Record labels listen for the buzz. But what does that mean? It means people are taking notice of you, for any of a number of reasons: your act is getting radio play; you're doing lots of gigs to large turnouts; you have good press; you're doing well on the college circuit; your privately released CD is selling well, etc.

Having a buzz means that something is calling attention to your act and people are talking about you. Labels are looking for your ability to get attention. Throughout this book, I'll present various tactics for generating that all-important buzz. The more directions a buzz comes from, the stronger your foundation for a music career and the more seriously labels take you. And the more money you make on the way!

PATIENCE

I've decided that patience is the attribute that's most important if you want to make it in the music industry. Be prepared to wait until the time is right for you to get that deal. It could take many years. Those with patience get deals. Time makes a smart musician more savvy about the industry. It allows you to develop your act to perfection and to learn from your mistakes. Be prepared for the long haul or don't waste your time.

You need patience to hone your craft well before plowing forward. That's hard for many of us. Once you get your act vaguely together, you'll want to rush out and do your stuff. That's okay if you can accept the level of musicianship you're at. While friends and family may love your music, you may not be ready for the big time. At least be patient enough to finish this book before going too fast. If you want to make money from your music and attract a GOOD record deal, have the patience to develop your music, your performance, and your press kit. Don't let your ego rule. There's enough rejection in this business without setting yourself up for it. Shawn Mullins encourages, "It takes a long time, but that's okay because you get better and better."

Patience helps you deal with characters that don't keep promises. Even people who mean well keep you dangling. People in this business are busy and may take longer to get to you than you'd like. Sitting tight is hard but essential while waiting until the time is right and people help you. Don't allow your spirits and belief in yourself to falter. When your act is developed fully, your songs are perfect for the current market, and people are noticing you're ready for a deal, there'll be one if you've stuck around for the long haul. Patience is the truest virtue for a musician!

VISIBILITY

Visibility helps create a buzz. The more people you meet or who see you play, the more familiar you become to industry people. Being lucky enough to be in the right place at the right time is easier if you get to as many places as possible. It's logical. The odds of meeting people are more favorable if you're out and about a lot. The more times you perform in public, the more people hear it. Sitting home complaining about no deals is counterproductive. Having a great act isn't enough. Opening yourself up to the most possibilities creates the most opportunities for luck to work with you.

Develop visibility by going to industry functions. Perform or hang out at clubs that play your genre, attend seminars, crash industry parties, etc. Showing your face around helps industry people get familiar with you. It's the beginning of networking. It keeps you in the thick of music-related socialization. You may not meet the people you want to, but you become a known entity. As you develop your presentation and get closer to being ready for a deal, you won't be a total stranger in music circles. Even a little visibility helps. Each time you perform live or schmooze about your music is another opportunity to find that ONE person who can help advance your career.

RELATIONSHIPS

Success in the music industry hinges on developing relationships. A consistent piece of advice given by industry pros is to *build relationships* with people you work with and with those who can advance your career. When they know and like you, there's a greater chance of receiving help. Getting friendly with as many people in the industry as possible can't hurt. This is a people-oriented business. Technology helps it function, but people make the decisions.

What does building a relationship mean? It doesn't mean becoming buddies with everyone you meet. It does mean building a level of confidence and trust between yourself and others; developing a good rapport; creating a comfortable interaction between yourself and the other person. You can establish a good relationship with someone you've never met in person. I've built great ones by phone. My favorite definition is establishing yourself as someone who isn't a pest!

When you build a relationship, people *may* take your calls. It creates productive and successful interaction between you and others. It's the ground level of working your way up in the music industry. It's the top level of being successful. Building a good relationship establishes boundaries that make interactions more comfortable. People prefer dealing with someone professional and reliable. People who know I don't abuse their courtesy respond when I call. If someone can't help me, I thank them anyway. Don't make people avoid taking your calls because you're too pushy or abrasive.

Good relationships help get your foot in the door. People may keep you in mind for activities that can further your career and introduce you to other people. If a person knows you're cooperative and pleasant to work with, you may get chosen over someone else for something. After you get a deal, good relationships attract more cooperation at the label. If you work well with everyone, you'll get more support. It can mean the difference between a label giving your CD a halfhearted nudge when it's released or working it hard. I've had artists on my label whom I didn't feel motivated to work with. I went the greatest distance for the most cooperative and professional ones.

How can you build good relationships? One important factor is showing respect for the other person's time. When you call, be prepared. Say what you need to and don't keep the person on too long. If you finally get to someone big, it's tempting to bring up a zillion issues. That's a great way to make that your last contact with the person. Prioritize your needs and ask only for what's necessary. Say "thank you" whether you get what you need or not. "Thanks for trying" makes them more amenable to try again.

PERSEVERANCE

Prepare to persevere! The harder you work, the more luck you'll attract. If you have the talent and don't quit, you'll get there! Be prepared to hang in or don't waste your time. Hosh Gureli, vice president of A & R at J Records, recommends, "Only pursue your dream if it really is your dream. There are a lot of people out there doing it, and people who really want it the most get it." You can't let criticism stop you from going for it. Folk singer Terri Hendrix says:

> Negative criticism is probably the most underestimated weapon. Every time a person said I couldn't do something, I put it in my craw and made a pearl out of it. When I see people getting bitter, I feel sorry for them. Criticism has to be used to make you better. It takes a determined spirit.

As I've indicated, this isn't a business consisting of only sweet people. You may hear promises up the wazoo and see nothing materialize. You must persevere. People aren't good at returning phone calls. Persevere! Someone may be your best buddy today and then forget you tomorrow. Get used to it! There will be many disappointments. Persevere! You may be ignored, disrespected, or kicked in the face. Welcome to the music industry—home of the stoutest of heart! Persevere! Or, choose another career. The music biz ain't easy. Ricky Schultz, president of Zebra

Records, worked at Warner Bros. in the late '70s and recalls his memories of Christopher Cross:

> *Despite the fact that some people say Christopher Cross had a short run, it was a pretty spectacular one. This guy believed in himself and was tenacious. He was turned down by every record company of note, multiple times. He had a particular desire and passion to be hooked up with Warner Bros. I think they turned him down three different times before he was finally signed. He kept working on it. He channeled his focus and energy and kept crafting his tunes. He had one of the biggest, most successful debut albums in history and swept the Grammys in the early '80s. He did it because he was tenacious and didn't give up. He didn't become discouraged by getting turned down.*

TALENT

A & R people say, "The cream always rises to the top." Unfortunately, many musicians don't have enough talent and good material to make that trip. Most demos and CDs given to me in classes don't have what it takes, in my opinion. I admit I'm not an expert and refuse to critique music because my ear isn't great. But I've never heard a buzz on any of these artists, ever, yet they all think they're IT! I've been told that well over 90 percent of hopeful artists don't cut it. It's not a happy thought. Throughout the book, I'll emphasize this: *You have to be very good to have the best chance at a deal.* I don't just mean good! I mean, THAT GOOD! There are plenty of good solid musicians, but few have that special something that sets them above the rest. If you have the goods, someone will eventually find you if you don't give up. Shawn Mullins says, "You have to be so damn good that they're coming after you. There's nobody these days that's so damn good and no one knows about them."

There are many acts I enjoy very much. But it's rare that one jumps out at me. When that happens, I know they'll get a deal if they hang in. A & R people want hit singles. Songs are the most important aspect of an artist in their eyes. They want something that sounds better than all the good solid musicians they hear. You can't just have *some talent* to have a good shot at a recording contract. The talent, including your songs, must shine like a neon sign to people at record labels. Polish yours and be the best you can be. Never stop working to get better.

Make sure your material has hit singles. You can do it if you work hard. (Chapter 9 goes into more detail about hit songs.)

BELIEF

You have to believe in yourself! No matter what others think, you have to know your material is the absolute greatest. If you don't have 1,000 percent faith in what you're doing, it's not worth the effort to market it. Your own enthusiasm attracts attention or provokes curiosity. A subdued pitch won't excite anyone. I have little interest in those who describe their music as "okay," "pretty good," or "see for yourself." The ones I want to hear are those who sound enthusiastic and proud of their work. Jo Davidson didn't wait long for a manager. She says, "People always ask, 'How do I get a manager or other people to help?' I never asked that question. I always assumed that I'd get it. If you're constantly asking that question, maybe your songs need to be crafted better."

Believing in your music shows confidence—a quality that industry people like. If you find yourself apologizing that you could have done a better job in a better studio, wait until you get the quality you want. Don't sell yourself short by not putting your best foot forward. Respect yourself and your music by setting high standards. In the long run, this earns respect. It's easier to get people excited about your music if you are.

KNOWLEDGE

No matter what kind of music you're working with, apply the information in this book. You have to know your own genre well. I'll tell you about doing live performances, but *you* have to know what venues are appropriate for your music. I'll tell you how to get press coverage, but *you* have to know publications that cover your genre. I'll tell you to hang out and network in clubs, but *you* have to know which ones. The more you live and breathe your genre, the better your chance of finding an open door. The more you read about it, listen to radio stations that play it, go to live shows, join organizations, etc., the more contacts you'll make and the more knowledgeable you'll be.

When I was working with rap music, I listened to rap shows as much as I could. In private I listened mainly to rock. But my focus was on the music I was marketing. I went to rap shows and rap clubs to develop an ear for exactly what style was popular and to make valuable contacts. I read magazines that focused on rap and knew the names of the reviewers, writers, and editors. I went to seminars with an emphasis on hip-hop. I knew it so well that I was asked to speak on hip-hop panels. I did the same thing when I was working dance music projects and with my alternative rock band. Immersing yourself like a sponge in your genre gives you an edge.

BALLS

Develop balls. It takes balls to ask for what you need or get up on stage and perform for an audience that doesn't know your music. It takes balls to speak highly of your music when others doubt you. Take risks to get ahead! Few people make money from their music if they hover inside of their safety zone. Recording artist Pat Green says:

> I never took no for an answer. I waited and was very patient. If someone said no to me about a gig, I'd catch them next time. And if I didn't catch them next time, I'd bug them till I did. There were times that I'd show up to be the opening band when I wasn't actually booked to play. I'd show, say, "I'm booked," and set up all the gear. If they had gotten really mad I would have taken it down, but they didn't. I'd go to little honky-tonks, opening up for Merle Haggard, Jerry Jeff Walker, and anybody else.

Play in a city where you have no following! The worst that can happen is people won't show. But you could do well! Press your own CD and believe that people will buy it. It takes balls to hang in when the going gets tough. Not quitting can be the hardest thing you do. Shawn Mullins says, "Artists are lazy people, and there are just a few of us who have the audacity to want to prove something, and we work really hard." You're never a failure if you don't quit. Balls keep you from failing. Either develop balls or do music as a hobby.

PART
TWO

FINDING
THE KEY
PLAYERS
FOR YOUR
CAREER

3

SEEKING THE RIGHT
Personal Manager
AT THE RIGHT TIME

Myth:

It's important to have a manager right away,
even if it's not someone with lots of experience.

• • •

Some call a manager a glorified baby-sitter. When artists on my label opted to wait to hire management, I informally assumed that position. They called with personal problems, too, and I often did feel like a baby-sitter. But a real manager does a lot more than troubleshoot. A good one can develop your career to its potential. A bad one can end your career. Choosing an appropriate manager is a very important career decision.

Artists act like they're unique when they say a version of, "I've got things going on. If ONLY I could find a manager, I'd be set." That's a very big ONLY. It often means you don't want to work yourself. Get rid of unrealistic goals about managers. They don't wave magic wands and get you a deal. They take what you already have going and build on it.

Managers make only a percentage of what you earn, so a good one won't touch you unless you've created the foundation I spoke of earlier. If you have it, managers will be open to representing you. According to manager Michael Norton:

> *An artist must have something that's marketable, and that doesn't just mean a good look and cool music. A lot of people have that. They also need a spark going, however small it is, in a market; then a manager can help them throw as much gasoline on it as possible. You have to find the spark and fuel it.*

THE ROLE OF A PERSONAL MANAGER

A manager orchestrates all aspects of your career. I asked manager Peter Ciaccia (PC Management) what his definition of a personal manager is:

> *Someone that can take the client who they're working with and cover a lot of ground for them. A manager winds up being everything to the acts: the A & R person, the publicist. A manager has to make good judgment calls for the band. He is the liaison between the artist and the record company. When a band is unsigned, he works with them from the beginning to find a home for them. He's out there selling the band, selling the image and music of the band. He has to have a good sense of what the market calls for, what would interest people, and how to get to the people. He creates a realistic buzz about the band. He has to be tied into the street.*

A manager is the person who shops your tapes for a record deal. She also advises you about the direction of your career, which label to sign with, etc. Once a deal is signed, a manager acts as liaison between you and your label, making sure the terms of your contract are met. In addition, a manager stays on top of your label to give your record good promotion and marketing and, in general, to make sure the label treats you right. Ron Stone, president of Gold Mountain Management, has a poetic explanation:

> *The manager is kind of the conductor of the orchestra. The artist is the composer. The record company is the string section. The publicity department is the first four violins. The sales department is the oboe section. They are all pieces of the puzzle, including the legal, research and development, merchandise, and recording parts. All these pieces get blended together and everybody has to start on the same page. They have to understand what the music*

is about and where it's going. The manager has to know every-
body's part. A conductor knows everybody's part. He rehearses
with everybody and works out all the details so that at the perfor-
mance, he just reminds them where to come in and what they're
supposed to do. So, if I'm doing my job correctly, I have everybody
turning the pages at the same time. And hopefully the promotions
department is in sync with the sales department, which is in sync
with the press department, and the artist knows what's going on.

A manager advises you on the production of your songs and on your team (producers, lawyers, agents, etc.). If you're lucky, your manager will have a good ear to give you creative guidance with your material. Finally, a manager is responsible for contacting talent agents to get you booked into live appearances. He makes sure the arrangements are fair and that everything else goes smoothly. With all of these roles, it's best to have a manager with enough experience and contacts to do all of the above properly. The manager will be the CEO of your business. If you want to make money from that business, make sure that person can run it properly. According to Ron Stone:

A manager's job is to get the artist to choose the right things to
do based on the best information available and to provide that infor-
mation. Hopefully, a manager will educate the artist well enough so
that he makes the right decisions. Management is about patience,
listening, and understanding. A manager must never lose sight of
the fact that it's his job but your life. There has to be a special lan-
guage between management and artist that takes into consideration
that they're talking about your life as if it were a product.

WHAT TO LOOK FOR IN A PERSONAL MANAGER

If you're considering a manager, see how you get along and what her game plan for your career is. Pay attention to her enthusiasm (or lack thereof) for your music. She doesn't have to love it, but it helps. Interview a potential candidate as you would anyone who might work for you. Don't act like she's doing you a favor. If you believe in yourself, others will, too. Your manager should see you as a good source of future income.

Many people want to be managers, but fewer know what the job entails. Being a manager is not just about trying to make appointments with A & R people. It's more than hanging out at clubs to schmooze with industry people. The best managers carry themselves in an appropriate manner, are familiar with industry protocol, and know as much about your genre as possible. According to Jim Guerinot, owner of Rebel Waltz Management, managing bands such as No Doubt and The Offspring:

Ultimately, you want someone honest that you can trust. You don't need the biggest name, the biggest hotshot, someone who has worked with the biggest people. If you use someone who's smart and honest, they're going to figure that stuff out. You can have someone who's really smart, aggressive, and well-known, and who's worked with a lot of big bands. But if he's not honest or he's working off his own agenda, he'll ultimately bury your career. I would rather see a kid get someone who's close to the band, who's honest and sharp, and who will ask questions—not act like they know everything—and come up with the group. A lot of artists want the manager of bands that sell ten million records. Well, guess what? If you find that guy, you're going to be working with an intern in his office because he himself is occupied with the person selling ten million records. It happens all the time. People sign with big managers but they don't work with those managers. They work with their neophyte, and they can pick their own neophyte.

Being a manager is a big commitment. Many folks expect it to be fun, but it's stressful and hard work. A manager must be available. Sometimes there's nothing to do. Other times it's a never-ending, thankless job. Decide if you trust a potential manager with your career. If you don't have confidence in him, should he represent you? An artist must have enough respect for a manager's judgment to go along with his decisions.

It's important to assess a candidate's personality and attitude. One A & R person at a top label said that if an artist's manager rubs her the wrong way from the beginning, she's less likely to sign the artist. She told me about a group she signed with a manager who's annoying, and said she'd do a lot more with them if she could bypass him. She admits that, to avoid dealing with the manager, she passes over the band with opportunities. She hates neglecting the group, but can't be bothered with the manager. Your manager deals with the record label, so if her personality annoys you, think again. And if she doesn't know exactly what she's doing, think how that will look to label people.

A manager presents an image of you through her representation, so it's best to have a professional, knowledgeable, and experienced person working on your behalf. Getting just anyone willing to represent an unknown artist won't help. Ron Stone advises, "Look for a manager when the record companies start buzzing around. From the manager's point of view, you have to believe that the act is going to pay off fairly substantially. Even if they're successful, the process takes two to three years." Wait until you're in a position to attract a deal or are making real money before approaching good managers. If you sign a long-term contract with someone just starting out, you may be stuck with someone who can't help you. Patience is essential.

WORKING WITH AN INEXPERIENCED MANAGER

In a perfect world, it's better to have a manager with industry savvy and contacts, and who knows his way around. But in reality, finding the "perfect" manager may not be easy. Ron Stone says, "An entry-level artist will end up with an entry-level manager." Be careful! In an effort to prove themselves on your behalf, inexperienced managers may try too hard. They can blow a deal by being too pushy. A manager guides his act and needs their respect to do this properly. You must able to take your manager seriously.

An inexperienced yet driven person who wants to manage you should not necessarily be passed up. Someone who wants to work with your band because he believes in your music and who seems ready to work his ass off for you should definitely be considered. You just have to be more careful. Jim Guerinot began this way:

I started managing when I was nineteen. I was hanging out, going to shows. My buddies were playing and I asked, "Why don't I help you?" so I could get in for free. I wasn't a nineteen-year-old with a plan. I wanted to get in for free. They said, "Carry this." I said, "Okay." When they didn't get paid one night because the guys stiffed them, I offered to talk for them. I offered to make flyers to get more people in. All of a sudden, in a very organic fashion, they said, "Why don't you manage us? Seems like whatever you're doing is working." I said okay. That's where it started. Then I thought they should have a CD, so I did that. I started doing it by doing it. You really can do it.

It's possible for a manager to learn the business by working in it. Manager Shannon O'Shea (SOS Management), who manages the band Garbage, says, "The problem with management in general is there is no training process or it's very difficult to get training. A lot of bands may find a young manager with not a lot of experience but . . . who has the hunger and drive and is prepared not to see a huge amount of income initially." If your act takes off and your manager feels out of his league in handling details, Ron Stone says that it's possible to go to a large management company and have your manager work with them, preferably if the act first gets signed to a label:

> *If a new manager hooks up with an artist and something starts to happen, if they're smart, they'll realize they need a support system to get better access in the industry—at the record company level, at the radio level, at the concert level. A management company that's been around for a lot of years has done all the networking. If you can get behind somebody else's connections, you'll save yourself three years of trying to figure all of that out and serve your client very well. If a young manager has a hot young band that gets signed, if he has something worthwhile, the judgment is made on the act, not the manager. Somebody young and inexperienced, who has the right act walking in the door, makes it easier for me to give them the benefit of my experience, particularly if they're smart.*

I found it a relief to know that this option exists, although it isn't as easy as it sounds. But if you have a green manager who does work with you to get things happening, and management companies approach you, try to get your manager placed within that company. If you're a manager, keep an eye out for this possibility.

If you have a potential manager who's inexperienced, ask lots of questions: Why do you want to be a manager? What do you see as your responsibilities? What contacts do you have? How will you use them? Set up various scenarios that may arise and ask how he'd handle them. Make sure that you respect his judgment.

HOW TO FIND A MANAGER

Most managers tell me that they'll find you. Ron Stone says, "An artist has to be really, really good and a manager will find them. That's how it works. If there's a hot band in town, there's a bit of a word of mouth that zips through the business quickly. If the music really is powerful, people will find you." Those who are looking to pick up new acts have feelers out. They go to clubs looking for artists to manage. If you're playing live and getting attention, managers may approach you. In that case, they'll want more, so have a press kit ready. Shannon O'Shea says:

> *I would try to gain as much local press as I possibly could . . . reviews of what you're doing. Try and get radio interested, even if it's local college radio. Get as much local support as you can get so you get a nice package together. Maybe you can get quotes from a radio station. Then you have something to go to management with. Management is going to want to know that the band is willing to work, and if they can do this on their own, well then they've got what it takes. If you've been doing gigs, include a list ing of those, too. Mention the size of your following, if you have one. Anything showing activity in your career would be of interest to a potential manager. Managers want to see that you are working hard. They want to work with acts who have already developed a foundation.*

Ask around for names of managers working with artists in your genre of music. When you go to clubs, get names from other artists. If you want to know the manager of a signed artist, call the public relations department of the record label and ask for the name of that artist's manager. Sound professional and you'll often get what you've asked for. Also, check out directories of managers that list whom each manager represents (see Appendix 2). If you're out and about in the industry long enough, you'll find a manager. Rather than calling or sending a package, a concise pitch to a potential manager can show how hard you're working. According to Shannon O'Shea:

> *What I would do is send a fax through to . . . someone on a mid level who's going to be less busy and more open to what you have to say. Send them a short fax. Attach a one-page summary of your best reviews and just bullet-point it. Tell them what you've accomplished locally. Do a short, hard pitch that's the bottom-line stuff, that's really positive. Say that you'll be sending a package shortly. On the envelope, you want to put "expected material," unless you happen to get lucky and speak to the guy on the phone*

who does request it. Then you put "requested." Remember that everybody has this big box in their office, particularly labels but managers as well, and it's full of tapes they've got to listen to. So you need to separate yours by [what you write] on the envelope so the assistant knows they're expecting it and pushes it through. Otherwise it can sit in a pile. And be a little patient. Appreciate that people are busy and it may take time for them to get back to you. Don't hound people, because they'll think, "The artist is going to be driving me crazy." Pursue the manager as you would work with them.

Be patient about finding a manager. It may feel better in the short run if someone who knows more about the industry than you do could manage you right now. But in the long run, waiting for the right one to represent you is the way to go. If you still think, "If ONLY I had a manager," write down what you think a manager would do for you. If you're waiting for the "fairy god-manager" to create your career, either prepare for a long wait (is forever long enough?) or get out the list and do it yourself now. Begin a list of reasons why a good manager would want to represent you. Keep adding to it as you have more accomplishments. When you're earning money from those reasons, it's the right time. If you get a career in gear, you'll get the right manager without a hassle.

SIGNING WITH A MANAGER

Most management agreements are for a three- to five-year period. How can you tie yourself up for that long to a person who may not do the job properly? Protect yourself to some degree by having a clause in your contract stipulating a minimum amount of money you must earn in the first two years or a time frame for a record deal. If the goal isn't reached, you can terminate your management contract. But that's still two years of dealing with someone who may keep you from getting ahead.

Sign a contract for the shortest amount of time possible. If nothing has happened with your career during that time, you may want to get someone else. I've heard musicians say they'd rather have their managers committed to longer agreements to give the managers more time to develop the acts to their fullest potential. But that won't guarantee they'll work on your behalf. If you're doing well at the end of that period, your manager will want to renew anyway.

PAYING A MANAGER

Managers get paid only when you do. Depending on the contract, they're entitled to reimbursement of expenses made on your behalf. Personal managers get between 15 and 25 percent, and, on rare occasions, 50 percent, of your gross earnings. Having spoken with many artists, I've found that 20 percent is most common. With few exceptions, managers get their percentage off the top, before expenses are paid. In the case of a recording advance, managers who are fair, and artists who are smart, agree to the manager taking their percentage after recording costs are paid. Your lawyer can work out the finer points and include reasonable exceptions and deductions from this *gross income* for you. Always make sure you have everything in writing and use a lawyer to check the agreement. Ron Stone says, "Lesson number 1: Protect your ass!"

UTILIZING THE
Skills of a
TALENT AGENT

Myth:

I don't need a talent agent if I have a manager.

• • •

A manager and an agent work together. Talent agents focus on help-ing you to earn an income from live performances. Managers orches-trate the entire picture of your career. Therefore, you may have a man-ager before you sign with a talent agent. As a result, a manager often assumes both roles in the beginning. But once your potential for paid performances develops, an agent should be added to your team. Your manager should concentrate on managing your career while your agent gets you paid appearances. A manager works with an agent to get the best bookings possible. A talent agent books you for live appearances. Playing live helps on all levels of a career. When you're starting out, it is instrumental in building your following. When you're signed, live performances are both a great source of income and a big help in selling records.

THE ROLE OF A TALENT AGENT

A good agent has strong relationships with the various people who bring talent into clubs, as well as with tour promoters. At the beginning of your career, a regional agent gets you into smaller clubs where your following can grow. Once you have a huge following or a record deal, an agent who works with name artists in your genre can book you as an opening act on a tour. Check with different agencies and see what acts are on their rosters. Jerry Ade, president of Famous Artist Agency, representing talent such as Salt-N-Pepa, Toni Braxton, and Jay Z, says:

> *I tell every artist to choose somebody to be on your side. You have one record company, you have one manager, you have one mother, you have one agent. When you put a cohesive team together and they all work in unison with one another as a team, you are more apt to be successful than if you are fighting a variety of different influences in a variety of different ways. You've gotta be consistent to present a unified force.*

Your team should work together toward your best interest. The main goal for everyone on your team should be furthering your career. When you reach the level where larger agents are interested in representing you, Alex Kochan, president of Artists & Audience Entertainment, representing a roster of acts such as Nine Inch Nails, Live, and Paul McCartney, advises that you:

> *Look for somebody that you can trust, because essentially the agent represents you and not the manager. Although the agent will do all of the work through the manager, you want to have somebody that you actually trust to do the right thing for you, the band, as opposed to the right thing for the manager. When there's success, staying on track and being able to present an opinion about what's right for the band becomes awfully difficult. You want to have an agent that has an independent view, that's not the record company's view, that's not necessarily rubber-stamping the manager's view. That way, they're a real member of the team as opposed to somebody's yes-man. If an agent is the expert for the live touring business that you hire, then you want to get what you're paying for. You want to get their expertise. You don't want to just have it blocked, suppressed, or written off by some prepackaged formulaic idea of artist*

development that the record label may have—because the record company is selling records, not tickets.

DIFFERENT TYPES OF AGENTS

Talent agencies come in all sizes, ranging from larger operations, such as Famous Artist Agency and Artists & Audience Entertainment, to small regional agencies that book acts into clubs and other local venues. Regional agencies, which exist in every corner of the country, run the gamut in size. Which type of agent would be right for you? Jerry Ade says it's critical to be selective about choosing your agent. "Agents have specialties. . . . It's important to find somebody who works in the area you are working with."

Unless you have a record deal, signing with a large agency is unlikely. Ade says, "Bigger companies can't afford to take no-name artists who don't need to be moved around the world. That's where a regional agency has significance. It has the ability and lack of expenses to go out there and work." He points out that large companies in major cities have a big overhead and need acts that can bring in money to offset their expenses. Regional agents work out of their homes or in small offices. Their expenses are kept to a minimum, so they can afford to work with artists who aren't bringing in the big bucks and to take more time developing those who show potential. Adam Kornfeld, a booking agent with Artist Group International, representing acts such as Billy Joel and Metallica, books venues that range in size from clubs to stadiums. He says:

> *If it's a regional band with a regional CD out locally, meaning like in a four- or five-state region, I would definitely [recommend looking] for some of the regional booking agencies around the country, who know every little nook and cranny and every little Main Street bar that does shows. Once the record goes national, picked up by a national label, [the artist] will want representation on the national or international level, which is what I do.*

There are regional booking agents who can help a young artist on a grassroots level. A small regional one is more effective to you at the beginning of your career. Regional agents know their region and have those all-important relationships with people who book the venues. Once your career warrants it, you can move to a bigger agent, who'll get you into venues more appropriate to the next level of your career.

WHAT DO AGENTS WANT?

Ideally, your manager should help you choose your agent. Most large agencies aren't interested in signing an artist without having a good reason—such as having a record out on a good label or having an indie CD that is selling well. Until you get a following, even regional agents won't work with you. They have to know you're getting exposure and developing yourself and your profile. Joann Murdock, who runs Artists of Note, an Illinois agency that books folk artists, says:

> I can't sign an artist until they have a demonstrated following at least in certain regions in the country. I can't call a club owner and say, "Here's someone you've never heard of before, but they're really wonderful." You have to first do it yourself. Get something to radio stations. Try to play opening sets. I have to be able to tell a club owner that you're doing something. I can't book people in the very starter level. Once you've built a little circuit for yourself, you can go to an agent and say something like, "I've been playing all these places but don't have time to do the booking business. I need someone to do that for me."

Diana Stagnato is an agent with Cellar Door Entertainment, based in Washington, D.C., with an office in Virginia Beach. She books bands into a variety of venues, from college-type bars to blues restaurant bars, from large to small clubs, from original rooms to cover rooms. Stagnato says:

> A lot of bands that do original music and that want to play a lot need to do some covers. The bands that become very popular right away doing all originals are the ones that come out of colleges, because they have a following. It's very difficult for a band to get together and do all original music if they don't have a fan base. They often will do covers as well. Once they become popular, people will listen to their originals, too. Bands have to understand that. Sometimes they can get a good gig opening for someone or in a small room where they can build a following and not make a lot of money, But agents are looking for bands that make money, since their income is a percentage of what the bands make.

Some bands do covers for money and originals for their fans. Stagnato says it's not easy to put a band from out-of-state in a local club, as the club wants bands that will draw a crowd. "It depends on the club," she says. "Some clubs are healthy clubs, and there are going to be people

there no matter who plays because the club is fun and does well."
According to Stagnato, the only bands that aren't from the region who
do well are those who do covers for an audience that wants a lot of mod-
ern rock or party music.

When is the right time to approach an agent? Agent Tom Baggott,
owner of thebookingagency.com, in Colorado, says, "I look for a client
who shows willingness to go out and bring their music to an audience,
and to support that effort." He advises:

> *I don't think that artists should start looking for booking*
> *agencies until they have developed six to twelve markets to the*
> *point where they are worth 150-200 people and are making at*
> *least $1,000 in each market. They need to have established a*
> *grassroots following in a region so they have somewhere to make*
> *the money to support further/extended touring and so that they*
> *have experience about what goes into it.*

Since Adam Kornfeld works for a large agency, longevity is a big issue
for him. Whereas regional agents have a larger turnover, larger agencies
want acts that are signed to national labels and that can be developed on
the touring circuit. Kornfeld says:

> *In a business sense for signing new acts, [I assess] the poten-*
> *tial of an artist to have a long touring career. I always have to be*
> *into the music, because that's what it's all about to begin with.*
> *That's why I'm in the business. But of course, since I am a book-*
> *ing agent, [I am looking for] the viability of this artist to have a*
> *touring career that will hopefully climb the ladder and move*
> *from the club circuit up to larger venues.*

Although Alex Kochan also finds it preferable to sign an act that already
has a major deal, he'll occasionally consider a band that has put out its own
CD, and is "already in the track to sign at a major label but doesn't have
the deal yet." Kochan is motivated by a great live performance. He says:

> *A few bands come along that are just such compelling per-*
> *formers that you have to get involved immediately. Whether*
> *there's a deal or not in place is irrelevant. You just see these bands*
> *as incredible performers and it's just a matter of time before they*
> *get a record deal. We've had a few like that. We look for incredi-*
> *ble performers who have that something magic that happens*
> *between them and their audience; we look for that at every level.*

You often don't have a choice as to who will represent you at the beginning of your career. Most artists are happy to work with an agent who will get them gigs. It's not as critical to be selective when you're dealing with small regional booking agents, because you can always go to another if you're unhappy.

ACQUIRING AN AGENT

If you begin touring on your own and your press kit reflects success, agents are more likely to work with you. They're not hard to locate. *Billboard International Talent and Touring Directory* is a great source for U.S. and international talent. It includes booking agents, facilities, services, and products. *Pollstar* is a terrific resource if you want to learn more about touring. You can get it by subscription only, and it's filled with a plethora of concert business information, covering activities both in the U.S. and abroad, including up-to-date news briefs, box office statistics, an extensive listing of tour schedules for all genres of music, and much more. In addition, they publish directories, including one with booking agents, cross-referenced with the artists they represent (see Appendix 2).

How do you find regional agents? Ask people in venues where you'd like to play who books for them. Ask artists who are further along in their careers than you which agents they use. It may take research, but the rewards are worth it. Call or drop into the student-activities offices at colleges to see if anyone has the name of an agent. Stormy Shepherd, of Leave Home Booking in Hollywood, California, booking bands both unknown and well-known, such as L7, recommends trying to get booked on a bill with bands represented by an agent with whom you might want to get signed. Offer to play for free, if necessary. Joann Murdock says:

> *If someone is interested in using me as an agent, they should put me on their mailing list and keep me apprised of what they're doing. If they have the opportunity to meet me, try to cultivate a relationship before asking me to book them. It's nicer to know them personally a little bit first.*

Diana Stagnato likes bands to send her a promo kit with a good bio and photos. If a band has a CD, that's a plus. If it's an original band, it needs a following. Stagnato says:

If I feel what they've sent me is good, and they're polite and have a good attitude, I'll put them in a few rooms. If they do well and the clubs want them back, I'll keep working with them. I'm looking for bands that have a professional attitude, that are realistic, that will try to promote their shows, that will do a good job, and that realize that agents are people, too.

Every agent has her own way of choosing bands, but those bands that are easy to work with seem to be a favorite choice. Working with agents involves building those all-important relationships. Agents like working with acts that have proven reliable and that are pleasant to deal with. Prima donnas don't go over well with agents (or anyone else, for that matter), unless they're making so much money the agent has little choice. If you make a good impression, there's a much better chance the agent will remember you if she has an opening later on. Tom Baggott says:

This is an intensely relationship-driven business. Relationships are more important than the deal. Deals come and go, but relationships are what will keep you working. Be nice to people, be honest. Understand what a venue has to do. When a venue puts a particular artist on in a particular time slot on a particular night, they're doing that rather than putting another artist on. Artists aren't created with entitlement. They have to earn gigs and should be paid based on what they're worth.

Let an agent know about any publicity, radio, club play, etc. that's creating a buzz for your act. In addition, an agent should be kept informed of any specific regions where your record is doing well. If you have a following somewhere, let her know about it. While she might not book you on a national tour so fast, she may at least book you in the area where you're getting a response. Joann Murdock says:

Agents and club owners have their ears to the ground. If someone calls and I've never heard of them before, it's highly unlikely that it will be a good match at that point. If I've heard of them, I may have an interest. I may have seen their name on schedules for venues. I may have heard of publicity that they've done on the Internet—a review of their recording or radio DJs playing their song. I'm always watching what's playing on the radio or in clubs.

Work your way up with regional agents. Start by booking your own tour. Once you've got a following, approach a small agent. After you've proven yourself with successful gigs, ask for a reference to agents who book larger venues or gigs out of their region. If you've developed a nice relationship, your first agent may help you, if it doesn't conflict with her gigs. When your act gets bigger, don't forget the agents who gave you your start. It cements a long-term relationship and shows appreciation.

AGREEING TO TERMS WITH AN AGENT

Most national agents want an exclusive commitment to handle all bookings for you. Then, if someone calls you directly for a gig, he must call your agent—even if your agent had nothing to do with attracting the booking. Sometimes you can avoid signing an exclusive; the more the agent wants you, the greater the chance that you can negotiate for a deal that's not exclusive. If you're signed to a big deal with a major record label, you can call more of the shots. In the case of agents who work only regionally or in one specific area, such as the college circuit, you can generally use more than one agent.

Most agents require a commitment of at least three years. Try keeping it to a maximum of one year. The hotter your act, the more flexibility you'll have in terms and length of commitment. If you must sign for more than a year, have a clause added into the agreement stipulating that if your agent doesn't generate earnings of at least x dollars in a year, you can be released from your contract. Why be stuck with an agent who isn't booking you? Most agents won't object to a reasonable bottom-line figure, because if they aren't making money, they won't want you anyway.

Finally, it used to be that agents took 10 percent of your concert fee, but now it can be 15 to 20 percent. They aren't entitled to anything else, in most cases. Don't sign away any of your publishing or record income either, because it isn't ethical. Some regional agents will ask for a flat fee if you're doing low-paying gigs to build a following. Otherwise, they may get only a few dollars for their efforts.

BEFORE YOU ACQUIRE A TALENT AGENT

When you haven't yet found an agent, your manager can represent you in booking gigs to get you exposure and build your following. If you don't have a manager, a friend who knows how to hustle and has some street savvy can speak to the clubs on your behalf. If circumstances merit your manager representing you because you don't have an agent, it's a conflict of interest for him to take an agenting fee as well—he's already getting his percentage as manager.

How big a following do you need? Joann Murdock recommends, "If you're just known in a 100-mile radius of your home city, you'll still have to branch out to get into a 300-mile radius at the very least. Then an agent can look at what you're doing." An artist with talent who is willing to work hard should be able to eventually find a good agent. The more you perform live, the more your career develops. As Jerry Ade says:

> *I have found no artist who couldn't grow if they kept working. It's very hard to understand that, but I find a rock band or a jazz band or a black band can find their way in this business and have a career if they're willing to never quit working. They have to be talented, and I take for granted that's there. But if they're willing to work hard, they can build some kind of life for themselves and make a substantial living. There are hundreds of jazz artists that most people wouldn't be familiar with who can go gross a million dollars a year and tour the world and have a pretty nice lifestyle because they never quit. I've found rock bands with substantial regional followings that can gross an enormous amount of money and maybe never make it to that next level. Because they are willing to keep trying, they keep working. Hard work pays off in this business, and it's rarely forgotten.*

FINDING

the Appropriate

ATTORNEY

Myth:

Someone I know isn't a music attorney but wants to
represent me. She'll be good because I trust her.

● ● ●

You absolutely, positively, unequivocally should not be represented by
anyone who is not a music/entertainment attorney. NEVER! Unless an
individual specializes in this field, he'll rarely understand the specifics
of a recording agreement. People get screwed in deals all the time
because they allow a well-meaning friend or relative to represent them.
Most of them aren't capable of handling music contracts, which are
quite specialized. I've had many artists complain after they got screwed
over by a label because of a bad contract. They couldn't understand why
their father/aunt/best friend, etc. let them sign such an unfair agreement. It happens all the time.

REASONS FOR HIRING
AN INDUSTRY PROFESSIONAL

Many attorneys attend my seminars. They want to work in the music field BUT don't know enough about it. It takes years of learning, plus on-the-job experience. According to Larry Rudolph, Esq., of Rudolph and Beer, an entertainment law firm in New York City, "A lawyer does not learn how to be an entertainment lawyer in law school." He says classes in entertainment law are general and don't train anyone as a music attorney. The field is learned through practice.

Beware of any person who says she's *sort of* a music attorney. That usually means she isn't one but wants to be. The music business can seem exciting. Practicing other kinds of law can be tedious, even boring, according to some lawyers who come to my classes with the intention of switching to entertainment law. These "nouveau" entertainment lawyers need practice and seasoning before they can represent you effectively.

Don't be someone's guinea pig, even if he gives you a better rate. An act on my label had a litigator who had limited experience in entertainment law represent them when I was getting them a deal on a bigger label. This lawyer continuously botched the negotiations, causing us to lose one deal and almost another. When someone I respect recently recommended this lawyer to be on a panel, I winced. She asked why. When I told her, she laughed and said he told her he was awful at first. Now he's excellent. It took years for him to get there.

There are so many conditions in a music-related contract that it takes a lawyer devoted full time to music to understand all the ins and outs. While most attorneys understand the basic contract, they won't know which figures are considered favorable by record industry standards. There's a lot of give-and-take in negotiating a record deal, and certain concessions are expected—if you know them. There are things that a label can remove from the contract as a trade-off for something else. To a seasoned music attorney, these are routine. To an attorney inexperienced in the music business, it can be a foreign negotiation. An artist contract favors the label. A lawyer must know what a label will typically give in on and what you'll have to accept.

I had a client who needed to draw up an agreement between him and an artist he was going to be working with. I implored him not to use his local lawyer, who reassured him that he did at least thirty music contracts a year. That's not a music attorney! We were consulting on the phone, so I couldn't wring his neck when he said his lawyer left out important factors because he assumed the artist's own lawyer wouldn't go for them. That's what negotiations are for! A good lawyer doesn't concede at the gate. My client was trying to save money but lost the deal. According to Wallace Collins, Esq., a New York City-based lawyer specializing in entertainment, copyright, and trademark law, "An entertainment lawyer will navigate you safely through the minefield that is the music business. Recording and publishing agreements can be extremely complicated, and proper negotiating and drafting requires superior legal skills as well as a knowledge of music business practice."

It's hard enough to negotiate an equitable deal, even with a music attorney. Don't sell yourself short by using someone who will not give you the best possible representation. As Larry Rudolph says, "If you need brain surgery, would you go to a foot doctor? So if you need a music contract negotiated, don't go to a real estate attorney." Get one who specializes in what you need.

HOW TO SELECT YOUR ATTORNEY

The best way to find an attorney is through recommendations. Ask around. Don't settle for the first one you meet. See if you can get a low- or no-cost consultation to feel him or her out. Get the right attorney for your needs. Wallace Collins, who was signed to Epic Records as a recording artist before he became a lawyer, recommends meeting with several candidates to see which one you feel most comfortable with.

What do you need to know about a potential legal representative? You need to know how she bases her fees; what her attitude is like; how she feels about your music; and if you're comfortable with her personality. After all, you don't want an attorney who rubs you the wrong way. Some attorneys are more into music than others and know what's happening in the music scene. They actually go to clubs to see bands and network as much as possible. Others prefer sticking to business, reading trade magazines to keep abreast of what's going on. They don't worry as much about the music, as long as they know the going rates for an album deal. Neither approach is right or wrong, but you may feel more comfortable with one or the other.

It's nice to find an attorney who believes in you. She may work harder for you or perhaps help get to an A & R person you want to reach. Enthusiasm goes a long way, and especially helps when your legal counsel deals with a label. Larry Rudolph recommends finding one "whom you vibe with, whom you feel comfortable with personality-wise, who will work with you on fees, and who believes in your talent."

In selecting an attorney, find out what your prospective legal representative thinks are the most important conditions of a contract when negotiating a deal, i.e., where her priorities lie. Some attorneys may be more concerned with an advance, while others may focus on a video, a large promotional budget, etc. See if her intentions are the same as yours. Also, find one whose fees you can afford.

Attorneys who believe in you may be more flexible about getting paid. If they feel you have strong potential, they may take you on as a client as sort of an investment. They'll keep track of their time but not charge you for everything at the beginning, assuming they'll make it up when you hit big. Having your attorney behind you is motivational. It's always nice when your lawyer likes you enough to come to your gigs.

ATTORNEYS' FEES

Attorneys' fees vary widely. According to Larry Rudolph, the average is anywhere from $175 to $350 an hour. You'll find top attorneys charging more and younger ones with less experience willing to do it for less. Many lawyers now charge a flat fee of 5 percent of the advance on your first album to negotiate an artist agreement. There are also variations in how they bill; you can use two different people for the same amount of time at the same hourly rate and pay one a lot more than the other, as some are more flexible than others as to what they'll bill you for. That's one reason it's important to shop for the right lawyer for you and your budget.

Find out whether you'll be on the clock every time you speak with your attorney or if she's flexible about billing for her time. I've actually used a lawyer who, when I called to see if he received something I'd sent, charged me for the few minutes it took to look. Many music attorneys aren't like that. As I've already said, if they believe in you, they may be more agreeable to working within your budget. If they feel you have a good future, they may be realistic in the present, hoping you'll still retain them when your career is doing well. This doesn't mean they'll work for free. But your bills might not be as high.

Don't expect as much flexibility from a well-known attorney with lots of celebrity representation. Generally, the more well-known the attorney is, the higher the fee. Shop around. You don't have to settle. If you believe in yourself, make them believe, too. Always remember, your legal counsel is working for you.

CHANGING YOUR ATTORNEY

If you don't like your attorney, get another. Lawyers don't have contracts saying you must exclusively use them for a given amount of time. Unless you're in the middle of a negotiation that needs the continuity of the same person, or it will cost too much to have a new lawyer start proceedings all over, get a new one if the old one isn't working for you. You'll just have to make a financial arrangement for the time already put in.

PUT EVERYTHING IN WRITING

If you can't afford a lawyer, prepare a letter of agreement between yourself and the other party, spelling out specifically what they'll do for you in exchange for specifically what you'll do for them. For example, if you promised a friend three points for producing a song, be specific about what it's three points of. Is it only for what he worked on or the whole album? Write it down. Be as specific as possible about whatever he's going to do for you in exchange for what he'll get from you. When you have your letter of agreement ready, make two copies that both of you sign. Each of you should keep one copy. I'm told getting it notarized isn't necessary, but it can't hurt.

According to Wallace Collins, "A simple contract may not necessarily require extensive involvement by lawyers. A contract can be as basic as a letter describing the details of your arrangement, which is signed by both parties to the agreement." While Collins acknowledges that an oral agreement is binding, he emphasizes how much easier it is to prove if all the terms are written down. Handshakes don't usually stand up in court, although technically any agreement is supposed to. But you can't prove a handshake. Words on paper are less likely to be misconstrued. Of course, while a formal contract is the best way to go if you can afford it, a letter of agreement is still written proof. Please, put everything in writing!

If all this legal stuff sounds very expensive, be aware that in many cities there are organizations that offer a variety of legal services. If your income is low enough, some offer free or low-cost representation. Many will answer legal questions on the phone. Most can recommend music attorneys, and offer seminars and other resources. There are organizations like this all over the country. Each has specific services offered. I've listed most of them in Appendix 2.

● ● ●

You don't want to just get a record deal. You want to get a deal that gives you the greatest potential to make money and have a good career doing your music. Having the right attorney watching out for your best interests helps you reach that goal. Having everything written down in a legal and binding manner will protect your rights and give you the best chance of getting what you're entitled to.

6

USING A
Producer to
ENHANCE YOUR
Recording

Myth:
I don't need a producer. I can write my own songs.

• • •

Many artists say they don't need a producer. Some make the mistake of letting their egos convince them they can orchestrate the whole recording process themselves. Some don't trust anyone else to make decisions for them or don't want the expense of paying a producer. Many musicians think that they don't need a producer because they don't fully understand the role of a producer and its importance. That's why I have a whole chapter to explain it. Do you want the best shot at succeeding with your music? A well-produced recording is critical to making that happen. Don't let your ego limit your production! A good producer can make the difference between a song that doesn't get noticed and a hit record.

THE PRODUCER AS PROJECT DIRECTOR

A producer is not necessarily a songwriter or engineer. A producer oversees the production of a recording, making sure all the players are in place, the studio is right, the song works, and the budget is adequate. He or she manages the recording session, directing the players of a production. A producer works with the songwriter and artist, making sure the project flows. In the purest sense, a producer sets up the budget; organizes the project; chooses the studio, engineer, editor, and session players; and makes sure the recording is finished properly. Producer Phil Ramone says a producer's role is "to understand like a director what is musically going on in front of you."

In reality, with the influx of small and, often, in-home studios, a producer may be all of the above. For smaller projects, producers may work for a flat fee. They get from two to four points on the record when it's released (more about points in Chapter 25). A producer with an impressive track record gets more. Arrange this before going into the studio. If you hire a producer, make sure everything is in writing from the get-go.

A producer must have a good ear in order to work with the creative people. Producer Michael Lloyd says, "If an artist writes, there are certain qualities that a producer brings to draw out certain elements of the compositions, to make sure they're defined and focused, and then to try to interpret the artist's vision, to make them the very best they can be." He or she must be objective in making suggestions for revisions of a song, and know when it's finished. A producer usually has final say on a project.

THE PRODUCER'S ROLE IN PREPRODUCTION

A producer plans what goes on in the studio before getting there. A good one meets in advance with the artist, songwriter, musicians, and other members of what should be thought of as a team, and specifically decides what to do in each session. The producer makes sure everyone is prepared. Figuring out your next step in a studio that charges by the hour isn't economical. Planning ahead saves time and money.

Essentially, these are the activities that a producer traditionally is responsible for:

- Preparing a production budget
- Making most decisions about production

- Having a good ear for music and taking responsibility for knowing when the project is finished
- Knowing how to choose a good production team
- Being a diplomat when there's a dispute, e.g., the engineer and the artist disagree on something or the songwriter wants to add something that just won't work
- Letting the engineer know what needs to be done and what his limitations are (for example, not giving creative input if it's not asked for)
- Knowing where the trends in music are going and being ahead of them
- Motivating everyone to be as creative and productive as possible
- Understanding the artist's needs when doing the vocal tracks, knowing when he has had enough, and finding the best way to get a good vocal

THE EXECUTIVE PRODUCER'S PART IN YOUR PROJECT

An executive producer is the person financing the project. When I do a project for my record label, I'm the executive producer because I'm paying the expenses. The executive producer usually has the final say as to whether a project is finished, since the money is coming out of her pocket. Sometimes an executive producer suggests a musician she wants to use or an engineer for the mix. But usually, the producer is in charge of most things and the executive producer doesn't get too involved.

WHY YOU NEED A PRODUCER

You need a producer because a project needs objectivity, and it's hard to be impartial about your own music. Another set of trained ears hears things you might not. Kicking ideas around with an experienced pro leads to more creativity. It's hard to produce your own material. Phil Ramone agrees, "I highly recommend an independent producer. Billy Joel and Paul Simon are perfectly capable of producing themselves. . . . But you need one soul in the room who can say 'no.'" A producer is more detached. Michael Lloyd says each player listens mainly to his own part in the production:

You do benefit from having someone with an unbiased attachment. A producer tries to get the best out of everyone in the group. He or she is listening to the whole picture. The producer is listening to everything collectively and how it interreacts. That type of dynamic is critical to making good records. Otherwise, you'd have people just listening to their own thing and not get that overall perspective.

Ramone says a producer can also take the role of a heavy—making decisions that are right for the project but uncomfortable for you. For example, a producer can ask that your friends leave the studio. Once when I was producing, I had to insist that a close friend of my artists leave because he was clowning around. The friend was angry and my artists acted annoyed. When he left, they thanked me—he was distracting them, but because of their personal ties they couldn't throw him out. A producer needs to intervene in all situations where decisive action must be taken, whether the decisions are well received or not. Michael Lloyd says:

You need someone that is not afraid to have an opinion and voice it quickly, and not afraid to listen to suggestions. While you need someone in charge, a producer has to react quickly [with specific suggestions], not just, "You have to do that better"—if they don't know what that means, they will keep doing it the same way. A producer must be able to take suggestions and deal with them— by trying them or saying they're not a good idea and why. Too many times, people feel that they're never listened to and have no say in what's going on. It's a fine line. If you had no one in charge you'd have anarchy. But you do have to have the other elements.

A good producer decides what's working and what needs to be changed, so she should have more skills than you do, yet be compatible with you and the team working on the project. A producer should appreciate your music and be experienced with your genre. She is responsible for recording your project properly. You can't be everything. If songwriting is your forte, focus on that and bring a pro in to produce. A good producer can take an okay song, add the right production, and turn it into a hit.

Many producers have label contacts. That's something you might consider when you're choosing one. When your project is done, she can pass it to A & R people if she likes it. If it gets a deal, she stands to make money on royalties. Recording artist Jo Davidson recalls, "Edel America heard the record through my producer."

PART
THREE

PREPARING
YOUR
PRESENTATION

7

USING

Constructive Criticism

TO GET WHERE

You Want to Go

Myth:

Everyone tells me my music is fantastic,

so I know it's a winner!

• • •

Practically every musician who called my label prefaced their pitch by saying that *everyone tells them their music is fantastic*. They also said they were sending a demo that would blow me away. Sadly, most of these demos were rated G for "garbage." A & R people say a large percentage of material they receive isn't worth listening to. Yet artists insist they're getting positive feedback. Some put a lot of money into packages they send to labels, filled with their hopes and dreams. What a shame that *everyone* didn't help them by telling the truth.

My A & R staff for Revenge Records was the general public. I'd bring my boom box to school yards and play material for the kids there, since they bought the music I put out. While I recognized that the quality of many of those demos was poor, the kids identified samples that were played out, beats that weren't happening, and vocals that were unintelligible. So how come *everyone* didn't know the tracks weren't working?

It's important to get constructive criticism. How can you grow as a musician otherwise? I love to get suggestions for improving my work from people I respect. Why not create the best recording possible? In getting input from others, go to people who will give you truthful, objective feedback. Being objective about your own material is difficult, especially when *everyone* is souping you up. Learning not to get carried away by the enthusiasm of those who aren't the best critics is harder. So whom can you turn to for an objective analysis of your material?

WHERE NOT TO GO FOR AN OBJECTIVE CRITICAL EVALUATION

When seeking opinions, we naturally approach those who like us— friends, family, neighbors, etc.—people we know on a personal level. But most people don't want to give negative opinions to someone they like. As a result, they don't always tell the whole truth, or they sincerely want to like your material because they like you. Usually, we approach friends with enthusiasm about our latest work, expecting enthusiasm in return. Asking a friend, "So, do you like it?" does not encourage an objective critical evaluation.

This doesn't mean your friends are liars. They just may not want to criticize your music, figuring that if it's really no good, someone else will tell you. After all, we don't always like friends who aren't positive about our work. I'm that way. As a songwriter, I too ask for feedback. But deep down I want only praise. When I play a song for someone who starts to criticize it, I don't like that person anymore. It's just human nature. I won't hate the person, but I will have some resentment for them, if only for a little while. I (unfairly, I admit) find myself asking, "How dare this person criticize my wonderful material?" It must come across in my attitude, because friends say they love everything I write, even when they may not. I go elsewhere when I want honesty.

There are also times when people sincerely think that what they hear is good—coming from *you!* Often friends and loved ones just don't see you first as a musician. So when you produce something that's not half bad, they honestly are impressed, since they may not have expected anything. They praise you to the hilt for a song that isn't going to cut it in the same way with an A & R person who doesn't know you at all. Manager Peter Leeds calls it "The Emperor's New Clothes" syndrome:

Artists take their music, and they play it for their mother and their sister and their best friends, none of whom know the difference between a good and a bad song. More importantly, even if they didn't like it, they would not tell them because they don't want to hurt their feelings. In "The Emperor's New Clothes," they were afraid of what the emperor would do. In this case, it's more like, "Maybe he or she won't like me if I tell them this song sucks." The artist is bolstered into thinking that something that's not good is good. That creates a vicious circle.

When I started rapping, I was proud of what I was doing. My first tracks sounded great to me. I played them for my high school students and they raved. Now nobody can pay me enough money to listen to them. I'm embarrassed remembering how awful they were, yet I proudly played them. The kids responded with sincere enthusiasm. Teenagers are very critical, yet my students were really excited. How can that be? Because they expected a white woman to sound like a total fool, and I didn't. I was far from good, but for their teacher I was fantastic. So off I went, playing my awful tapes to everyone. Eventually, with the help of a new producer, I got better. That's when I realized how bad I'd been and how hard it is to get an objective opinion.

WHERE TO GO FOR AN OBJECTIVE OPINION

Before mixing your demo, get objective opinions from people who know music, such as DJs, people working in record stores, etc. They love music and are usually gracious if approached nicely. If you're friendly, you'll get cooperation. Sometimes you have to play up to people's egos to get them to listen and to give their "expert" opinion. But these individuals usually know what's selling and in what direction music is going, so their advice is helpful. When your record is out, thank them for their input (which may make them want to push your record more). If it becomes a hit, they can brag that they gave you advice at the beginning.

The best way to get an objective opinion from anyone, especially an industry person, is not to tell them it's your material. Say it belongs to a friend, someone you may work with, etc. Get rid of the personal obligation attached to the tape. The person will be a lot more honest. Also, criticism is easier to take when you're anonymous. It can be embarrassing to have your music put down. I can accept criticism when the evaluator doesn't know it's my material.

I always equate creating music with a pregnant woman: the future mother is carrying life just as you're carrying the life of an idea, which you give birth to in the studio. Having your idea come to life is euphoric. It can, especially for an unseasoned artist, sound fantastic, even when it's not. That happened to me. Just hearing what had once been only in my head sound like real music was incredible, perfect. When a mother gives birth to a baby, she always thinks it's beautiful, perfect. I see more babies than not that are red, wrinkled, lopsided, or funny looking. Yet I always tell the mother what a beautiful baby she has. It's the same with your music, which in a way is your baby. Your idea comes to life, and while you proudly wait for a response to it, no one wants to tell you your baby is ugly. So if you want honesty, don't tell those whose opinions you seek that it's your baby until it's a hit!

LEAVE YOUR EGO AT HOME

It's impossible to know it all. Be open-minded to criticism and suggestions. This doesn't mean changing whenever someone criticizes you, but it does mean accepting that you may not always be right. If the same suggestions are given by several people, at least consider them. It might make your material even better. You may not have noticed something obvious because you were too immersed in your original ideas. It's hard to be objective about your own material. Even managers and others working with an artist fall so in love with the music that they lose their objectivity.

It's easy to get so caught up in an idea that you lose sight of the market. Trends change so fast it's difficult to keep up. What was working when you were in the studio may not sell today. It's something you have to accept. Listen to what others tell you, whether you like what they say or not. Don't act on everything you hear, but accept that others may have a better idea. If one person after another tells you the music isn't current or cutting it, pay attention. Play it for more people in stores, and if the opinion is the same, be prepared to make changes. If you're working on a trendy style of music, work fast, or it may not be happening by the time you finish. Try to stay on the cutting edge of what's selling so you can get in at the beginning.

8

PREPARING
a Demo That Gets
YOU NOTICED

Myth:

A & R people will act as visionaries if they hear a song
that has potential, even if the quality isn't good.

• • •

Put your expectations in your product, not in an A & R person. A & R
people get huge numbers of tapes each week. It would be nice if they
had time to use their imagination to recognize the potential beyond
the poor quality of a demo, but it doesn't usually happen that
way. They may work to make a great product sound even better,
but often can't be bothered with something that doesn't strike them
immediately.

I've heard A & R people, especially those dealing with urban music,
say that they do listen past the poor production of a demo and can hear
if there's raw talent. Some say that a vocal track with a simple piano or
guitar accompaniment is enough for them. But it's a matter of luck
whether you get to an A & R person who appreciates raw talent. Don't

leave your fate in someone else's hands. Make sure your demo is produced well enough for the A & R person to hear your vision.

RECORDING YOUR DEMO

Give A & R people as finished a product as possible. A great majority of tapes I've received for my label are of very poor quality and are not pleasant to listen to. I often get accompanying notes explaining what could be done with the material if I sign the artists. But even if I see their vision, how can I know they can follow through? I've signed to my own label only artists who provided quality demos that make their talent clear and their vision almost complete. I may remix or edit, but the end needs to be in sight before I invest money in it. Jeff Blue, a vice president at Warner Bros. Records, advises, "The production should be decent. It could be a four-track. Macy Gray was a four-track demo, yet it was clear that she could write and there was a great voice there. If you're going to make a four-track or boom-box tape, make it at least sound good."

Some will disagree, but I believe that if you make a demo as clean and well produced as possible, it has a better chance of making a good impression. Competition is bad enough without defeating yourself. It's hard to sound positive about your music if you're apologizing for the quality. Give yourself the best shot by enabling the listener to hear your vision, not imagine it. According to Lisa Zbitnew, president of BMG Canada:

> *If an artist is submitting something and it's not the best music they can create, they should think about whether they're ready to put something forward. A lot of things that come forward are unfinished. Obviously, an independent talent can't necessarily afford brilliant production on a record, but they should make it the best they can. They should put their best foot forward and have their package represent who they are. They need to give the experts in the field reasons to be compelled to see the artist perform and to solicit more music. Something has to jump out as outstanding.*

No matter how good and clean and produced to the best of your ability your material is, present it as a demo. Don't call it a finished product. Let A & R people envision how much better it can be with money behind it!

Mixing Your Demo

Use a reasonably good studio to record your demo. If you can't afford to do your whole project in a good studio, at least do your mix in one. When I did synthesized music, I'd lay the tracks down in a small room with MIDI (in layman's terms, this means that what you program in one studio can be transferred to equipment in another). Before the mix, we'd copy the tracks onto a twenty-four-track tape, record the vocals in that room, and then do the mix. It saved money, yet the quality was there.

Don't leave the studio until you're happy with your mix. You can get very psyched when the music is pumping loud and everyone is into it. Everything sounds wonderful. A common problem when you get home is finding that the mix doesn't sound like it did in the studio. The music levels may not be where you want them. I know the feeling. After a major high in the studio, you can be on a major low when the music doesn't sound right the next day. It's terrible to have to either do another mix—if you have the money—or settle for one that's not what you want.

Here's a suggested insurance policy for getting the mix right the first time. Bring to the studio as much playback equipment (Walkman, boom box, car with stereo, etc.) as you can. After the mix is completed, leave the board as is in case you want to redo something. Your ears need to cool down; they can get almost numb after a long session of listening to loud music. Make a copy of the tape that was made during the mix so you're not listening to a first-generation copy (one right off the mix). After ten or fifteen minutes of cooldown time, play the tape in the different systems you brought. See if it sounds the way it should. If the bass line isn't up enough, do another pass with the board still up. This way, you're not wasting the time and money to remix the levels at a later date.

An engineer can "EQ" your music when you play it back in the studio. This means he can adjust the levels of the tracks to make it sound better than it will on an average stereo. Sometimes, when he's in a hurry to get you out, the engineer might do this. A studio system is probably much better than an average one. Playing it on your own system gives you a more real picture of whether the mix is what it should be. And the few dollars more you'd pay for extra time in the studio is a lot less than the cost of doing another mix from scratch after later hearing yours isn't working. Get it right the first time!

One common problem found after a mix is recorded is that the vocals aren't up high enough. If you already know the lyrics, you hear them in your head, even if they can't be heard clearly on the tracks. Anyone familiar with the lyrics, including the writer, artist, producer, engineer, etc., will silently sing along, so it's hard for these people to be good judges of the vocal levels. Play the song for someone who's never heard it before. Bring your tape in a boom box to the studio secretary, to someone in the pizzeria downstairs, to anyone around who has never heard it. Ask if they understand the lyrics. If the answer is "no," do another pass with the levels higher on the vocal tracks until that person understands them. Don't go home until everything sounds good on your Walkman.

It's good to master your demo. Mastering fine-tunes the sound, making a good mix cleaner. Although some say it's not necessary, it puts a better foot forward. A good mastering engineer can greatly enhance your recording. The better the quality of your demo, the more you may be taken seriously as an artist. Manager Lois Chisolm, with Thor Enterprises, advises, "Take the time and expense to get a quality production done. I can't tell you how many productions I've listened to and couldn't get past the sound. Record it in a proper studio with the right microphone and a good engineer."

Giving Your Demo the Best You've Got

Although there are no concrete rules about exactly what should be on a demo tape, the industry standard seems to be three songs. It's always best to start with your strongest cut, because it may be the only thing an A & R person listens to. Bruce Lundvall, president of jazz and classics at Capitol Records, adds, "I prefer three to four of your best songs rather than a dozen or more. That waters it down. No one can write that many good songs."

What do you include with your demo? The preferences vary with the A & R people. Michael Caplan, senior vice president of A & R at Epic Records says, "I like a three-song CD and pictures if available. It depends on the kind of music. If it's alternative rock, they have to have a charismatic-looking front guy. With pop, the picture is almost more important than the music." Jeff Blue likes to receive three to four songs. He says, "I don't like bios. Photos are okay, but they can work against you. I'd rather receive a CD—absolutely no tapes. If I want more, I'll ask for the photos and press kit. It's good to have a website so if I want [to find out more about] them, I don't have to wait for the bio and the photo." Most A & R people I asked said they prefer CDs. While some will listen to a cassette, many won't. Happy Walters, CEO of Immortal Records, says:

> *I don't look at press kits. I want the music and maybe a picture. If I like it, I can check out the press. The most important thing to me is the music. These days, I'd advise CDs. They're so cheap, the quality is better, and many people don't have cassette players in their cars anymore.*

Choose your songs carefully. It's said that a ballad can be the kiss of death in this industry. For some reason, most artists break on more up-tempo songs and then release their ballads. Therefore, avoid putting a ballad first on a demo tape, no matter how good it is; it can be second or third. Make sure all three cuts are strong. You may have just one shot at getting a deal. Make your presentation as good as possible. Don't trust an A & R person's vision when presenting your material. She may not have enough!

PACKAGING YOUR DEMO

You don't need anything fancy packaging your demo. However, a neat, attractive, professional-looking package has a better chance of catching someone's eye. Since competition is stiff, anything that makes you stand out can be advantageous. I've gotten demos with information scrawled in pencil or that was plain illegible. Assumptions are made about you based on how you present your material. No matter what their rules of thumb, most A & R people prefer working with artists who take themselves seriously. I've actually gotten tapes without phone numbers on them. What kind of message does that give? If you had a choice of working with one of two equally talented artists, would you pick the one with the neatly labeled package or the one with a package that looked thrown together? Having sloppy labels is not worth the risk of being passed over. Some A & R people may not care, but more do.

Don't spend a fortune, but at least be aware of your presentation. In most cases, it's the first impression anyone has of you. Put your best foot forward, or the best one you can afford, at any rate. It doesn't take a lot of money to have a typed label. If you have a computer or have access to someone with one, print your labels instead of writing them by hand. If you have the money, you can have the information printed right on the demo. It will make it look even more professional, and it can also be sold at gigs.

Attractive inserts for the cassette or CD can be made with a little creativity. Some people use as an insert an actual photo that's been folded. Someone in one of my classes had the names of the songs and the group superimposed on their photo. Clear computer labels can also be used on photo inserts. A nice photo insert catches the eye and gives an A & R person a glimpse of what you look like. Attractive packaging may set your demo apart and get you listened to faster. If it has a professional-sounding recording inside as well, it can lead to getting a deal.

9

MEASURING

the Marketability of

YOUR MUSIC

Myth:

As long as my music is good, I can create

my material in the style I choose.

● ● ●

In any business, you'd be concerned with knowing the market in order to make a profit. Trends come and go in all businesses. Certain restaurants are considered trendy one week and are empty the next. Bell bottoms used to sell like crazy, then you couldn't give them away. This is a world of fickle people who love and dislike in one breath. It's the people who understand the marketability of products who end their day with a bank full of dollars when they figure out what's commercial.

The music business works the same way. People follow trends. They buy what's on the radio. If you want to make money from your music, worry less about what's good music and more about what's commercial. Whether you like it or not, if you want a record deal, your music must have a niche or such a huge foundation that labels have no choice.

Otherwise, they may not know what to do with it. It has to be commercial in today's market. Highly marketable music will get you a deal in this business. Having great music without showing concern for its marketability will keep you in your day job.

KEEPING CURRENT WITH THE MUSIC MARKET

For the best chance of getting signed to a record label, keep up with trends in music. Know what's selling and what's popular. There's a distinctive sound that's currently popular in each style of music, so be familiar with it. This doesn't mean you should copy music that's hot. Imitation is a bad idea. Trends change quickly, and it's better to stay ahead of them. Be aware of what's working today and see if your music can follow it tomorrow.

Many musicians give me demo tapes with outdated music. They're creating music without a clue as to what's selling, what's being played on the radio, or what's gathering a following in the college market. This doesn't mean you shouldn't write from the heart. But if you're also writing for your wallet, think like a business, too. Despite their quality, some things sell and some don't. You've got to be flexible about your music. Otherwise, call it a hobby and play it your own way. Share it with your friends and relatives, but forget about making money from it. It's your choice. Jeff Blue, vice president of A & R at Warner Bros. Records, used to be in song publishing. He recalls:

> *I'd get these wicked songs, but they were dated. I would ask if they wrote them ten years ago. They were great, but there was no way they could hit the marketplace. That's part of your job. Listen to what's going on and do my job, too. Think about whether your song will be dated when it gets into the A & R person's hands and when you make the album. You have to look a year down the line.*

FINDING YOUR STYLE

Many artists jump from one style to another. It's nice to be versatile, but it makes you harder to market. A label wants to know where to slot you when they hear your music. The audience for your album should be obvious after hearing three songs. Choose your strongest genre and stick with it, saving other styles for later. If you like R & B the best, just do

R & B and save the reggae and rock for your personal pleasure. Your demo should be consistent in style. Don't confuse a label. The songs don't have to be similar, but whatever the variations in your music, they should appeal to a specific group of music lovers so a record label will know how to market your album.

I've heard demos that jump from blues to hip-hop to classic rock to country and more. The artists say they can do it all and want to show it. Most people who hear one genre of music assume the whole demo will be like that. Why risk losing people who might love the rest of the demo? Artists hear me out and then argue, "But you don't understand. I do great rock but also have killer country tunes, and even blues. I know labels will be impressed." "Everyone loves my versatility." That's not how the industry works. Everything is classified. So if you want a record deal, choose your genre.

Sometimes, deciding what specific music to record is the hardest task for an artist. Ask professionals which one you do best. Or choose the genre you love the most. Concentrating on one direction may go against your creative instincts, but you have to do it if you want a deal. Focus on the best avenue to your success. Later, when you're famous, you can experiment.

WHAT IS A HIT RECORD?

Essentially, record labels are looking for hit songs. It's the combination of vocals and strong commercial material that makes a hit. Hearing a great voice singing a mediocre song won't capture a label's attention nearly as much as hearing a great song by an average vocalist. A great singer without great material isn't appealing to a label. But a mediocre singer with great songs can be made to sound great in the studio. When people at labels listen to demos, if at least one song doesn't grab them, they'll go on to the next one. Jeff Blue says:

> *"Hits" to me means that you go to an album and don't want to skip a song. It doesn't have to be a radio hit. I believe that both Macy Gray and Linkin Park broke because they had this. When people buy a record and every song is good, they're not used to that. They're used to having one smash, one song that's pretty cool and the rest they skip over. When you have an artist that has twelve great songs, you want to go buy the album. To me, that's*

how word of mouth spreads. If people are talking about your whole album being amazing, an artist will have a lot longer life.

Hooky melodies, dynamite beats, and memorable choruses set certain songs above the rest. That's what labels listen for in a demo. Having to acquire songs for an artist is more effort and more costly for a label. They'd rather sign artists who have strong material of their own. According to Hosh Gureli, vice president of A & R at J Records:

> *It really all comes down to hit records. You will get the most amount of attention if you come up with a hit record. What is a hit record? There is a formula. Most of the time, it's a very strong melody that sticks in one's head, which usually includes a multi-line chorus, not just a one-line chorus, verses that are very descriptive and do not say things like "I love you" over and over in the same general way. Say something using double entendres, or in ways you've never heard it before, so when the listener hears it, it makes them think, and it affects the listener and is not pedestrian. It's something that's special. Everybody can identify with a special relationship-oriented song because they've gone through love and pain. But if you can say that in a way that's not been said before, and you can do it with a chorus that's really penetrating, you're on the road to what's described as a hit record.*

Because it's more convenient for a label if great songwriting and vocals come in the same package, they prefer artists who write their own material. Labels want it all when they can get it. If you're not a good songwriter, find someone to write songs with. An artist with great songs has a much better chance at getting a deal than someone without commercial material. Hosh Gureli adds:

> *I had a hand in signing Dido. Dido is an artist who is self-contained. It took a long time to break her. But when an artist like that does break, the rewards are multi-platinum. She's great—an artist's artist. She knows what she wants. She is willing to take feedback, but she's the final decision in whatever happens. Only an artist who writes and really has the talent and stage presence can have the final say. Very few artists can. A lot of artists who write don't write hits. Some do write hits and are smart enough to know that they can't write all of them. You can tell the artists that are savvy enough to know what they need.*

Good Seller Vs. Good Music

Material that isn't commercial enough may still be great, but just not right for today's market. There's a big difference between great music and marketable music. The trick is creating great music that's also marketable. No matter what the style, a great song stands out. Unfortunately, if it doesn't work with what's selling today, it may not get recorded. There's tons of talent trying to get a record deal. If your great material doesn't hit a person at a record label as commercial off the top—NEXT!

Manager Lois Chisolm advises, "The first thing you need to decide is what your goal is. Is it to make money, or is it to express yourself as an artist? People don't ask themselves that." The bottom line is, if you want to make money from your music, you may have to sacrifice some artistic integrity. Marketing your product means making it commercial enough to be a worthwhile product. Chisolm adds:

> *If the goal is to sell records, you have to do some commercial tracks. People want a hook that they can sing or rap along with. It has to be at least that commercial. I can't tell you how many rappers tell me they want to keep it real. I tell them to keep it real and stay poor!*

LEARNING WHICH MUSIC IS MARKETABLE

To understand what's marketable, live, breathe, and eat music. When I was doing dance music, I checked out as many dance radio shows and clubs as I could. It's imperative to know what's popular. Listening to the radio can't be a once in a while thing. You've got to know what's getting airplay and which songs are charting. Read the trades. Talk to DJs to find out why certain records are so popular. Talk to record store employees to find out why certain records are selling. Then find your own way.

A woman once came to me with an R & B dance track for a consultation. I asked her if it had the same flavor and format of others in the clubs. She kept telling me she knew it was a great song but finally admitted that she rarely went to clubs and didn't feel it was necessary if the song was good. I wanted to shake her. She was clueless and refused to accept that her song might not be right for today's market.

When I marketed dance tracks, I studied them. It took many moons before I could listen to one without looking at my watch to count BPMs (beats per minute). The above-mentioned woman didn't know what they were, yet this is crucial with dance tracks! When DJs mix from one song to another, the beats should be at the right speed so the flow is smooth. Since BPMs change, I followed them like a weatherman follows high- and low-pressure systems. For years, when I heard a new dance track, I'd automatically look at my watch and count beats. Become aware of critical factors for your genre.

Go to clubs where your style of music is playing live. Live music venues give you the best flavor for what's working. Watch how people respond to different acts. What turns a crowd on? What turns them off? Get the hang of your music scene. See what gets a crowd moving. Absorb everything you can so you can grow as a musician. Living outside of the music scene makes it harder to succeed. From hip-hop to dance to jazz to rock to reggae to country and back, there's a culture in live music clubs. You've got to be part of it to have the best shot at success. There are a ton of contacts to be made while hanging out. And you'll get the best education possible about your music.

CREATING

a

WINNING IMAGE

Myth:

If my music is good enough, I don't have
to worry about my image.

● ● ●

Great commercial music should triumph over everything, but that's not always the case. To the music industry, you're a product. Until you reach success, you're a generic one. Often, packaging is what sells a product. A generic tube of toothpaste in a plain box won't sell nearly as much as a generic one in a package that's nicely designed. It's worse in the music industry, since we're among the only products that can be too fat or short or nerdy-looking or have the "wrong" hair. Businesses put money into packaging to make it as appealing as possible. In the music industry, your image is your packaging, like it or not.

It's a shame that talent isn't the only thing record labels seek. But that's the way it is. If you don't care about a deal, hold fast to your ideals. Perform and write songs for fun. But if you want to make money, you may have to bend.

IMAGE COUNTS

It would be great if image wasn't important in relation to selling records, but it usually is. Stunning, hot-looking artists sell more records in genres that appeal to young buyers, who care how an artist looks. If you're very attractive or have personality to spare, it attracts attention. More people want to see you perform if they like your looks. Publicist Elaine Schock, owner of Shock Ink, says that beautiful artists still sell the best. A top A & R person whom I interviewed said he called an artist after just seeing her photo, without even listening to her music; she looked so hot he had to check her out. Schock says a great photo can get you in magazines, but adds:

> *Ultimately, what really matters is the music. It's just the image is going to be a hindrance. It doesn't mean that you aren't going to be successful, but you've got to think about your image. Even if you're a bit overweight, you have to look great. And you can look great if you're a little overweight.*

Schock feels that you can work with what you have and advises getting the best-looking picture possible. She insists that by investing in hair, makeup, and clothes, *anyone* can be made to look good in a photo. She elaborates:

> *Get a good hair person and makeup artist, even if it's just for that one picture. Have someone you trust help you pick out your clothes. [Press and A & R people] are inundated with stuff, so it's easy to ignore you. Don't give them a reason to ignore your press kit.*

Image is particularly important for female artists. Men can get over the image hurdle by looking "different." Beauty is more of a requisite for women. Fat is out. It's a terrible but true double standard that female vocalists are expected to look good and be slim. This is a glamour-oriented business, and that's not going to change because it's what record buyers want.

For younger markets, hot and gorgeous still sells best. But in many genres, women with a *look* are working it. Independent, offbeat women are selling records, too. While some women have broken stereotypical image patterns, they haven't eliminated the need for a look. I doubt there will be a time when artists don't have image standards, even if beauty isn't the only factor. The new wave of female singers is still attractive, slim, young, and sexy. Guys must also appeal to the eyes. Sometimes, an interesting or funky look may be enough. Great looks or a terrific body are assets for guys, too.

Let's face it: labels want artists with the whole package. There's nothing wrong with having an attractive image, as long as it doesn't feel demeaning. If you think you look good, your confidence rises and you perform better. It's human nature to want to be around attractive people. When music lovers watch a performer, it's as much visual as auditory. The visual provides enjoyment for the viewer.

I once had a band approach me to develop them for a nice price. I found three members awful to look at and told them they'd need serious changes in their image. They got defensive, saying their great music was enough. They refused to try. A year later, I took a friend to one of their gigs. Halfway through she whispered, "They're great musicians, but I'd enjoy the show much more if someone could put paper bags over three of them." An artist who looks good is more pleasant to watch. Decide for yourself. It can happen without looks, but the chances are slimmer.

While there are plenty of artists who've made it by just being themselves, it's easier to get a deal if you give labels what they want, at least at first. When I managed an extremely talented rock band, two members wouldn't listen to suggestions that went against their creative beliefs. Their music was terrific, but their image was the pits. Two made their living as word processors and looked it at gigs. I asked them to just wear jeans and T-shirts to gigs. They wouldn't, because "all that should matter is our music." So they held their ground, refused to change, and eventually broke up. Their standards were maintained, but now they don't do music at all.

DEVELOPING A MARKETABLE IMAGE

Now that you've decided to do whatever it takes to get that deal, how do you actually develop a marketable image? If you're not sure what's right for you or your band, check out acts in your genre. Study what works for them. There's enough latitude for you to see the range of looks from act to act. Go to clubs that feature live music. Get a feel for what's successful. Try different styles when you perform. Ask people in the business for suggestions. You don't have to do what they say, but find a common denominator that's worth trying.

Find your unique approach that sets you apart from others. I know this sounds hard. I just told you to fit in and now I'm encouraging you to stand out. You need to walk that fine line between not fitting in at all and fitting in with something different and special. Labels, writers, managers, and music fans are all looking for the new act that has ALL THAT in a fresh way. Manager Lois Chisolm suggests:

> Look at all the products out there and figure out how to be different—whether it's something you wear, the sounds you use in your music, the flow of your rap. You need something that makes you stand out among the others. I can't tell you how many times I've seen hip-hop artists perform the same exact way on stage. They all look the same—walk across the stage, hold their crotch, and put their hand in the air.

The looks that work today are those that appear most natural, as if the artists aren't trying at all, even if they've spent hours at it. Live and breathe your music and develop your image as you go. Jane Blumenfeld, president of In Media Publicity, believes that "Looks don't matter—style matters." Often, image is more about developing a sense of style. And style can work for anyone. No matter what you look like, look your best. Wear clothes that suit you. Being well groomed can enhance your image. Find the style that's good for you and work it. Dressing attractively, taking pride in your appearance, and having a great personality go a long way toward creating an attractive image, especially for live performances. Ultimately, great music prevails if you develop a following so big it can't be ignored.

DEVELOPING
Your Presentation
PACKAGE

Myth:

It's not important to do any more than make
a demo tape to get signed.

● ● ●

In order to show an A & R person or someone in the media your marketability, information about your act should be presented in a press kit. A professional-looking one shows an A & R person that you're taking yourself seriously and marketing yourself.

A press kit provides a picture of who you are. It's a vehicle for effectively presenting your image, credentials, and marketability, all in a small package. People are more likely to read your material than listen to a long spiel from you or your manager about what you've done. Press kits are used to get label interest, media coverage, gigs, and more.

When presenting yourself to a label or the media, provide as much *quality* information as possible. I emphasize quality because you want to offer selling points for your band. This means gathering the most impressive materials—such as places you've performed, radio play, interviews, etc.—and packaging them as concisely as possible.

THE ELEMENTS OF A GOOD PRESS KIT

Press kits are put together in various ways. The most common components are a cover letter, bio, and photograph. Include press clippings if you have them. A good press kit contains as little as it takes to make a positive impression while getting the information across. Don't overload it with unnecessary words or too many papers.

Good writing skills are essential when developing your presentation package. A poorly written one turns people off. Use your letterhead (name, address, and phone number) at the top of everything since things get separated. Someone might see one of your sheets and need to contact you. If there's no contact info, forget it!

The Bio

A bio is a good vehicle for getting an editor's attention for a story or attracting A & R people. It contains pertinent information about you or your band. A synopsis of your story, it should be a well-written, interesting presentation of facts. Spice up the facts with description about the artists. Hiring someone to write your bio is a worthwhile investment.

Shani Saxon, music editor of *Vibe*, suggests, "Keep bios short. Don't make them too flowery. Get to the point." Get the essence of you and your music across clearly. The first paragraph should present a good taste for who you are as an artist and what kind of music you do. Don't make people have to figure it out. They want to know the basics up front. Let your bio speak well for you.

An effective bio attracts interest. Put your music accomplishments first. If you as an artist haven't done anything special, find something unique or interesting that might perk up what you've done. Mention a hobby or charitable activity, for instance. Being an artist who attracts media attention makes you more desirable. Play up anything you can think of, even if it's a wee bit exaggerated. Keep in mind that a bio shouldn't sound like a resume. Graduating from a good college or being an excellent musician won't set you apart from others, even though they're admirable qualities. Include fun facts to give an editor more concepts to pick up on. Descriptive words bring you and your accomplishments to life. You don't want to be too flowery, but a bio shouldn't fall flat.

A bio should be limited to one or two pages in length—the shorter the better. While a top star may need several pages, publicist Elaine Schock says, "A page is enough for somebody who is unknown." The shorter your material, the more likely someone may read it!

Photos

A photo can catch someone's eye when opening a press kit, creating the initial impression of the band. It can attract major interest or turn someone off. Be selective in your choices. Personally, I don't like photos depicting a band posing like a family group. Shani Saxon says, "I prefer when the photo reflects the artist—whatever their style is. Personality has so much to do with it." Capture the essence of your music or performance in the photo. A fun shot is fun to look at; an interesting one grabs attention. As Elaine Schock said in Chapter 10, lack of beauty or a perfect body can be camouflaged in a good photo. Do what's necessary to have a photo that makes you look terrific! If you don't have a great one, leave it out. A "not great" photo hurts you.

Press photos are usually in black and white and shot vertically. They can get separated from the press kit, so contact info is important. Have this information printed at the bottom, use stickers with the appropriate information, or stamp or write it on the back. The most common size photo is 8″ x 10″. Color photos are expensive; if you have them, add a note stating that they're available on request.

While some photographers disagree on what reproduces best in print, glossy pictures are still the most popular. They're the choice for a record label package. Some photographers say that matte works better in print, but glossy photos are still in most press kits. Publicists say glossy looks nicer and reproduces well enough for publications.

Cover Letters

A cover letter is a brief introduction. It's also known as a pitch letter because it's used as a sales pitch to the recipient. It tells what you're interested in, such as a record deal, a review, a write-up, etc. Describe why the person should consider signing you or doing a write-up. Be specific about your selling points in as few words as necessary.

Your cover letter should be well written. If you've already spoken to the A & R person or journalist, give the letter a personal touch. You might remind the person about when you spoke and that they requested the material. Elaine Schock recommends, "Write an incredibly passionate letter about your music and why it's important." She also says that a handwritten note can get someone's attention. If you have a good press clipping and want the person to come down to your gig, write a note directly on the clipping inviting him. It's a nice personal touch.

Press Clips

Elaine Schock says good press clippings are the most important items in your press kit. They show the media has acknowledged you. Good clips are free advertising. Neatly cut out articles and reviews. Paste the publication's name or logo at the top of the page or down the side, and the article or review in the center. If it's a long piece and the columns are uneven, cut and place them so they look neat. Once you have a collection of clippings, mount several short ones on one page. Don't make it too cluttered. If the name or logo is too large, either shrink it or type in the publication information above the piece.

Don't send too many clips at one time. There's a limit to how many sheets someone will read. Send a specific clipping to each media person only once. If you have several current ones, put some in your press kit and include one in each subsequent release. Keep in mind that A & R people are more interested in greater detail than the media are.

Fact Sheets

A fact sheet can be included in your press kit as well, though it's optional. This is more of a resume type of presentation of the specific facts about your act. Full sentences are not required. Used as a reference by the media or by an A & R person, a fact sheet usually lists, in a concise format, the name of each member of the band, what he or she plays, where each of you are from, whether you have a CD released, and other pertinent information. It can include specific facts about the act in bullet points. The name and number of your contact person should be included.

Gig Sheets

If you're doing live performances, a presentation of your gigs on a sheet is helpful. Gig sheets illustrate that people are coming to see you or that clubs like you enough to have you back. Since labels want you to have a following, presenting a list of the gigs shows you're getting exposure. Journalists, too, pay more attention to an act that's performing a lot.

When you tour regularly, a gig sheet should indicate your upcoming venues, with dates and times. One way to present your gigs is to simply list the clubs you've played in during the last year or so. Put dates next to each club so it shows you played in some venues many times.

Quote Sheets

A list of quotes from reputable industry people about yourself is effective. Consolidate the best of those comments published about you onto one sheet. Take a sentence or two from various publications, put quotation marks around each, and write the name of the source underneath. Space your quotes evenly down the page so it looks attractive.

Quote sheets function as a quick summary of your press material. If laid out nicely, they can enhance your press kit. I've seen bands with no clippings get quotes from industry people such as DJs, club managers, talent agents, and industry pros for their quote sheets. Get permission to use quotes from such industry figures; quotes from the media don't need permission.

PUTTING IT ALL TOGETHER

Press kits look nice in a folder. These days, folders are reasonably priced. You can do a press kit with or without them. Some publicists swear by them and say they increase chances of getting attention. Elaine Schock doesn't think they're that important. Shani Saxon says, "I actually detest folders!" This one is your call.

Folders keep the components of your press kit together. Print the artist's name on the cover or label it with a sticker. Folders can be decorated with logos, stickers, and other creative things. Include a business card. Tapes and CDs (with contact info, please) go in the folder, too. I've seen Velcro tape used on the back of a CD so it could be mounted on the folder and easily taken off when someone wants to play it. Stickers that indicate "Recommended Tracks" are helpful.

When organizing your folder, put the photo on one side and the papers on the other. I've always recommended that the cover letter be on top or clipped to the outside of the kit. Next comes the bio, then press clippings and other sheets. But Elaine Schock recommends putting the clippings first. Since she feels they're the most important component, she says, "You have to put them up front. I have everything behind the press clippings, including the photo. It gives people a reason to pay attention because they have a billion reasons not to. They get inundated with stuff. It's all about competition." She feels that good clips get more attention than anything else, and I agree with her logic. Just don't overload your folder.

If you don't use a folder, the cover letter is usually on top, but here, too, Schock suggests putting the clippings first. Since a photo is the most eye-catching element, it should be near the top. Written material is behind it in the same order as described above. Put a big clip at the top and insert your business card underneath. No folder saves postage, too! I always address by hand whatever I send to give it a more personal touch. Some journalists say they're more inclined to open those packages first.

DEVELOPING
YOUR
MUSIC
CAREER

12

HUSTLING
for
MEDIA EXPOSURE

Myth:

You can't get media exposure until

you have a label deal.

● ● ●

Getting media exposure is work, but it's worth the effort. Reviews or articles about you enhance your chances of getting signed. It indicates to an A & R person that there's an even greater potential for getting media coverage once your album is released.

USING A PRESS RELEASE
TO ATTRACT ATTENTION

A press release alerts the media to something very specific. It announces a gig/tour, a CD release, a fund-raising event you're participating in, etc. You can't just announce that you exist or that you have good music. To be effective, the press release should be brief and to the point, providing concise, concrete details about a particular event or news item.

Your press release should be double spaced on $8\,{}^{1}\!/_{2}{}''$ -x-11'' paper. One page (two at most) is best. Make it appealing, using boldface and larger types to emphasize key information. Include contact info in the letterhead. Below it, write PRESS RELEASE. You should indicate whether it's for immediate release or to be held for a later date: at the upper left side of the page (under your letterhead), print either FOR IMMEDIATE RELEASE or FOR RELEASE ON MARCH 1, 2003. Contact persons are listed underneath or in the upper right corner. A headline emphasizes your main announcement.

Your first paragraph is critical. It's usually three to four lines and provides the basics—who, what, when, where, and why, like a newspaper article. If you're announcing a gig, for example, include specifics up front—who you are, time, place, cost, what's happening, etc. Develop that information in the rest of the release. A professional press release ends with either three number signs (###) or "-30-" in the center.

TARGETING YOUR MARKET FOR MEDIA EXPOSURE

Decide where to send your material. Check out all magazines relating to your genre and local free papers. There are publications all over the country that write about music. An excellent source for local publications by region can be found in *The Musician's Atlas* (see Appendix 2). Make sure each publication you target is appropriate. If you're not sure about a magazine, call them to find out more about them. You don't have to identify yourself.

Keep a record of appropriate publications—some specialize in reviews, while others do feature stories, have sections about new artists, or review gigs. Shani Saxon, music editor of *Vibe*, says that in her magazine there are few spots for unsigned acts. Saxon wants artists with national record distribution. Wait until then before going to bigger magazines. Publicist Elaine Schock advises, "The locals will bring on the nationals. You take one step at a time. You can't bypass. You have to really work at it." Know what you're after before sending anything. Is it a human-interest angle, a review, or promotion for a show?

Newspapers and Magazines

Many publications review independent music. If you entice writers, they might come to your gig. Barry Fox, entertainment writer with the

Patriot-News, in Harrisburg, Pennsylvania, says, "Hundreds of newspapers have a 'Best Bet' kind of column—art, a little bio, the cover of a CD can all run with that. A story is one thing, but there are a number of ways to get into newspapers." Keep sending announcements of your events and someone will eventually come. Elaine Schock advises working the hometown angle (if you live in a tough city like New York, look to the burbs):

> *If you're local, someone will review your gig. It might not be the first time. It might be the sixth time. But if you keep playing, someone will come. Write them a note. Say it's a hometown angle. If my band is from Boston, I have it all over any band that's not from Boston. That gives me an in. Hit them up! And they're always looking for stuff on the local news. If you have a hometown angle, you are in. Send out a press release announcing the gig. Tie it in to the local angle.*

Don't give up if a publication doesn't respond immediately. Keep sending stuff. Most writers pay attention if you don't let them forget you. When sending material for review, the music with a cover letter is sufficient, although some reviewers want more. Target an appropriate reviewer and address the material to that person.

When pursuing an article about your act, call the publication for the name of an appropriate editor or writer, making sure to get the correct spelling of the person's name. If possible, call or e-mail first to ask if the person prefers a full press kit. There are no rules and everyone is different in their preferences. Shani Saxon says she'd be thrilled to only deal with CDs and get written material by e-mail. She thinks big packages are a waste of money. But Rich Branciforte, editor of *Good Times Magazine,* in Long Island, New York, emphasizes:

> *I want a full press kit. I absolutely want a bio. If it's someone we're not familiar with, the writer of the review isn't going to just listen to the music. The better the press kit, the more these guys look semi-professional. We get a couple of hundred CDs in a month. A lot won't get reviewed. The reason, half the time, is just visual. If the stuff doesn't look attractive, you assume the music isn't good. The more you put into a press kit, even if it's not read, the more impressive it is. When you see that a lot of other people have written reviews, it validates that maybe this is somebody we should listen to.*

Branciforte won't visit bands' websites. Yet Mark Brown, popular music critic at *Rocky Mountain News*, in Denver, Colorado, says:

> *What I like, rather than a long bio, is a Post-it note stuck on the front of the disc listing the three best songs and maybe a short explanation of why the act thinks so. If you're smart, instead of sending a press kit, just include your website. If I do like it and want to do a write-up, I'll have all your biographical information there. Tell me what to listen to—what you're most proud of. The simpler the press kit the better. I get boxes and things that I can't open without a welding torch!*

When in doubt, send a press kit! It can't hurt. In terms of photos, action or fun poses are advantageous. I've had a photo with a blurb used several times in magazines because they needed a filler and liked the photo. Barry Fox says that every photo in his paper is in color. But you can e-mail him one or send him to your site. Rich Branciforte says, "A picture is good. If we're going to run an article on them, we might want to run a picture to illustrate it. Graphically, it's always good to have a picture with it." Mark Brown adds:

> *Always include a photo or have a good one (print quality) that's downloadable on your website. People send me to their web-site and there's this tiny little JPEG that isn't going to reproduce in a paper. Sometimes the photo can be enough to make me give [the CD] a listen—if it looks like an interesting lineup. If you're coming to town and get a listing, a photo could run. We pull three every week, almost at random.*

Independent touring artist Jeff Tareila, known as Lucky, adds:

> *I always send a band photo and they put it in the paper. If you get the perfect picture to represent the image you want and attract the type of people you want, it's the only weapon you have in a town where you don't know anyone.*

Television and Radio

Besides airplay, radio stations offer opportunities for live interviews to promote gigs. I'll elaborate in Tour Support (later in this chapter) and in Chapter 19. Television exposure is harder to get. But TV programs always need stories. If you send material when they're looking to fill a time slot, something can happen. Producers need a reason to bring you on a show. Few beginners provide that. However, there's no harm in trying. Sometimes a local news show may be interested on a slow news day. Recording artist Shawn Mullins says:

> *I got myself on a lot of local TV when I was working early on, just by sending in a CD and calling. The first time I was on, I put out a good-quality CD. I had enough buzz in Atlanta playing around a lot that they had probably heard of me. I really worked it network-wise and built up a fan base. It was doing it and persistence. I did a bunch of syndicated radio shows that were broadcast across the nation—like* Mountain Stage *and* World Café—*before I had any kind of support. I just called. After ten years, people started to remember my name.*

Television talk shows want more than interesting people. I know, because I've been a guest on them. They're looking for a story, topic, or concept to explore. If you come up with an angle, send the producer of a talk show a press kit. Cable TV shows can provide initial exposure. Producers on these shows are easier to approach and may be more receptive to having a newcomer on their show. Research to find shows on smaller cable networks.

If you get on TV, no matter how insignificant the show, view it as an opportunity to get a performance video. If you do at least one full song on the show, ask everyone you know to tape it, yielding you instant free copies. Then you have a videotaped performance when approaching larger stations. If nothing else, learn from watching the tape to improve your next appearance. When shopping your material, say you have a performance video, available on request. Taping a TV show is an inexpensive way to get a visual.

FOLLOW-UP

Follow-up calls boost your chances of getting press. Elaine Schock says, "You have to follow up on it or I guarantee they'll throw your materials out. Call. They'll answer the phone. And if they don't answer, hang up and keep calling back until they do." Yes, I recommend not leaving messages. Mark Brown explains, "My voice mail holds thirty messages and fills up every day. There's no way I can get back to all of those [callers]. I prefer an e-mail, with facts about the dates so I can at least get a listing in, . . . or call back and get me live." Follow-up calls give you personal contact with writers so you can begin media relationships. Recording artist Sara Hickman has gotten tremendous press support and says:

> *You have to learn to work the press. You have to dance with them, date them, and woo them. I've found that once you get one on your side, they become a lifelong advocate for you, especially if they move up in the press corps. Back in the days when they didn't know me, I tried to be different. I was homey about it. I'd call and invite them to my show. I'd acknowledge that they must get lots of requests and say why I was different. I'd say, "I'd love it if you could come down, even for a half hour." Your enthusiasm will get other people enthusiastic. That's really all it is. When you're bubbling over with something, everybody wants to be with you.*

Find out the best times to call—when the writers are not on deadline. Although all have different preferences, a general rule is to touch base about a week after you send them material. Rich Branciforte says, "Wait two weeks and then call to see if we've received the stuff. A call makes us aware that the artist is interested enough to call. The next time a writer comes in, we may suggest they check them out." For larger publications, e-mail is best. Shani Saxon says it's the best way to communicate with her. The first call or e-mail is to see if the person has received your package; if you get an assistant on the phone, ask if he can check. Then call to see if the writer will write something about you or your music. Be friendly. Your personality can determine whether a relationship is born.

Good manners are critical. Rich Branciforte advises, "The most important thing is to be polite. Everybody isn't going to want to review your CD just because you put it out. Sometimes if someone calls and they're pleasant, they go to the head of the list. They're interested enough to call." Persistence and a positive attitude pay off big time with the press. Even if they don't return calls, don't EVER show your annoyance. Be patient until people pay attention. They will if you keep at it. Sometimes you have to send them quite a few press releases before they come to a gig. Elaine Schock says:

> *Play at your local club. Keep hitting people up to come and see you and eventually they will. It's a matter of perseverance and*

determination. Once you've got that first clipping, Xerox it, make it pretty, and send it to everybody.

TOUR SUPPORT

When you break out of your hometown and go on the road, give yourself tour support. That means notifying local outlets and publications in order to get press. Press is the best way to let people know about your gigs. If you get something written about you, it entices people to come see you. Elaine Schock recommends sending press releases six weeks before a tour. "Hit all the local outlets—all the newspapers, all the weeklies, all the shopping giveaways. I start phoning a month into it because I want to beat everyone else out." Barry Fox adds, "Timeliness is important. Make sure the info is correct."

Call local publications for the name of the appropriate person to send a press kit or release to. How do you find publications in places you've never been to? Schock advises investing in Bacon's newspaper and magazine directories. "It has all the publications you can ever want. You can find the books in the library, but it's a good investment." Ask the promoter to send you a local press list; he will if he has one. Ask what he needs from you to promote the gig and for suggestions as to which writers you should send a press kit to if you can't afford to send to every one. Call each writer and invite her to see you perform. Writers for local papers say they appreciate when you keep in touch before you arrive; it shows you're serious about getting PR. Use e-mail when you can. Barry Fox agrees, "An e-mail helps. I can just cut and paste the info off the e-mail. A piece of paper gets lost."

Will they really write about an artist whom they've never heard of? I've been told a big fat "yes!" Except for those in very big music cities, music writers are happy to support acts coming to town, IF they like the music or find the story interesting. Mark Brown says:

> *If it's an interesting story and there's a local connection, if they're coming to town I might do an article. The review is whether I like it or not. Some of my favorite music is stuff that never even made it onto a CD or into stores—people's demos and that stuff. I get a million phone messages. Give me a quick call. If you get the machine, don't leave a message. Keep trying until you get me.*

Don't get discouraged if you don't get any press at first. You might have to return to the market several times before the print media pay attention to you. In Chapter 19, I'll go into more details about touring. Most artists emphasize you must go to a market three to four times to get press and attract people to your gigs. That's how you build a career. Each time you return to a market, remind the writers who you are in your press release. There's a lot of competition for getting into publications, but patience and perseverance will give them no choice but to write about you eventually, IF you have the goods.

13

GRASPING

the Importance of

PERFORMING LIVE

Myth:

Playing in local venues won't do me any good.

• • •

The best way to create a buzz is through live performances. Bands argue that doing gigs isn't worth the effort. I agree that it's hard to make money when you're unknown. You might even lose money. Doing gigs is frustrating. People may not show up. The club management may be rude. When I was a manager, we played clubs where the band didn't even get a free drink! So why do it? You play live because it gets you exposure. In Chapter 19, I'll have more resources for getting you to the next level of touring, once your foundation is intact. A majority of A & R people say that touring and developing a following is essential for getting signed. Many bands tour for years before getting a record deal. But if you're good, you'll make money long before that. You *can* make money touring, with or without a deal.

THE IMPORTANCE OF LIVE EXPOSURE

Anything in this business is a gamble. A & R people, managers, and other industry people go to clubs to look for new talent. Erica Ruben, producer of Central Park SummerStage, says she frequently checks out talent in clubs for her popular venue. Managers, agents, producers, etc. go to clubs when they need acts to work with. I know a band that got the attention of a top music publisher because his daughter went to a club and liked the band. She raved to her father and he came to their next gig. Every time you perform live, there's a chance someone who can help you will be there. The chances of your number coming up on the roulette wheel aren't in your favor. But the more gigs you perform, the greater the odds of there being someone in the audience who can help you. Some do beat the odds.

Gigging gives you the opportunity to hone your craft. It's practice—rehearsal space you don't pay for. No gig is wasted if you play your heart out for your audience, no matter how big or small. A true pro plays to the two that came out in the snow as if they were a full house. Those two people may come back with loads of friends the next time you play, if you wow them. Artists don't start at the top in real life. Success has to be earned. Tom Walker, of Friday's Child, says:

> *Be a professional. Every gig you do—we can do Webster Hall one week and a Borders show the next week—show up to that gig with the same attitude for them all. Don't treat booking agents like crap, like you're doing them a favor to show up. And don't suck. Concentrate on your craft first. Every gig counts. If you have two people in that audience, stand in front of their table and play for them. Don't disrespect anyone. That's how you build a following—treat everybody like they count.*

Performance Marketability

Regular gigs provide opportunities for someone interested in your act to see you live. Many A & R people won't sign an act without first seeing them live. Technology enhances sound in the studio; some acts don't sound good outside of the studio without it. Some acts are stiff on stage, which doesn't sell CDs. Labels want to see you please an audience. An act with good on-stage personality and that sounds as good if not better than their recording is marketable. That's what labels want. From a record label's point of view, a good live performance translates into sales. That's a good incentive to sign a band that tours.

If you keep playing and no one comes to see you, find out why. Be honest with yourself. If you're with a group, powwow to figure out why you haven't gotten fans. Are you too lazy to announce gigs? Or perhaps your music needs work. Many bands play smaller clubs where they bring their own audience. To break out of that and get an increased fan base, you have to be very good. I mean VERY good. You may not be— yet. That's the real deal. Ask club promoters for suggestions for improving your performance. Even the bartender may have ideas. Ask people at gigs to fill out anonymous feedback reports: What did you like about the performance? What can we do to make the performance stronger? What improvements do you feel are needed?

Chuck your ego and pay attention. If you want to make money and get a record deal, you need to get VERY good. If people aren't coming to see you, work on your music or performance. Be flexible about doing what's necessary to get good enough to build an audience and keep them coming back.

Developing a Following

Having a following means people come to your gigs. Some artists play in local clubs for what seems like forever. But as more and more people come to see them, their following grows. So does interest from record labels. It won't happen right away. Musicians say they see the same label people at many of their gigs, checking out their numbers. As they see your musicianship get stronger, your fan base increase, and your touring cover a wider area, they'll be more likely to take you seriously and ask for a package.

How do you develop a following? By persistently playing clubs, open mics, festivals, and any gig you get. Have good material and a well-rehearsed set so people want to come again. You can't count on friends all the time, but they're the start of a following. When you have a gig and need bodies, send (preferably by e-mail) or hand an invite to EVERYONE you know. Being in a band can be an imposition to friends, but hopefully they'll like your music enough to want to support it. Tell friends to invite friends. Invite coworkers, neighbors, and anyone you met in your lifetime. Ask them to spread the word. Have a mailing list for people to sign at the gig. I prefer using cards (index cards or 3″-x-5″ pieces of paper), as people don't want to wait behind others to sign a list. Create a template on your computer and print the following on each card:

```
┌─────────────────────────────────────────────────────────────┐
│                                                               │
│   NAME _____   │
│                                                               │
│   ADDRESS _____   │
│                                                               │
│   E-MAIL ADDRESS _____   │
│                                                               │
│   COMMENTS _____   │
│                                                               │
└─────────────────────────────────────────────────────────────┘
```

Pass the cards out at gigs. If you can get miniature-golf pencils, have them handy. (People don't return pens, but few want to keep a small pencil with no eraser.) Have someone (a friend or your manager) hold onto it all. Announce the opportunity to get on your mailing list several times during your gig. Followers of other bands playing that night might sign up. The friends whom your friends brought might now be fans. Next time, they can bring friends. As your mailing list grows, so does your following.

Thank fans for coming. Let them know how much it means to you. Be friendly and stay in touch. Metallica built their following by staying to sign autographs no matter how many wanted them. Loyal fans stay loyal and spread the word. Never take your fans for granted! They're the number-one reason you get on bigger tours and attract record deals. The Internet makes it easier to keep in touch with fans (more in Chapter 18). Once you have an e-mail list, do regular mailings to keep your fans posted. Answer all letters. Recording artist Fisher says, "Once you connect with your fans, don't let them break. If someone writes, answer them. Reach out and shake the hands that shake yours."

Network with other bands to share information and help each other. Don't think of them as competition. There's room for many good musicians. Go to gigs for other acts and get friendly with them. Offer support. Share your mailing lists. Attend their shows and invite them to yours. Ask them for constructive feedback for improving your performance. Swap gigs. Ask other acts to open for you and hopefully it will be reciprocated. Jo Davidson says, "A really good thing to do is [to] try to tap into other people's fan bases by doing double bills or booking with other artists. The truth is, this is a slow process."

A showcase is what the name implies—an opportunity for people who may be interested in your act to see you perform live. If industry people are interested in you, do a showcase at a club. Make a special effort to develop this gig and invite as many industry and media folks as possible. Try extra hard to have it go well. Choose a good venue with a great sound system. Do whatever it takes to get your following to attend. Send announcements to everyone on your mailing list, and call everyone you know. Explain it's an important gig and you need a massive turnout. Hopefully friends will come through. Industry people like seeing lots of enthusiastic fans.

You can also apply to do showcases at music conferences. Many have shows in a variety of clubs for all the days that they run. Some conferences are easier to break into than others. Don't expect miracles, but it can be good exposure, if people come. Many bands have played at a seminar showcase and gotten a record deal.

Some conferences cover music in general and some focus on one genre. Choose one that would be right for you. For example, if you have a band that works well on the college circuit, the CMJ Music Conference (see Chapter 14) in New York is a good venue. Many participants are involved with college radio stations, so appearing there could lead to airplay or a gig. There's a list of conferences in Appendix 2. Follow the *Billboard* calendar for more.

Many organizations host showcases. Performing rights societies (ASCAP, BMI, and SESAC), songwriters' groups, and other formal and informal groups put on showcases for unsigned artists and songwriters. Sometimes you have to be a member to participate. The best way to learn about them is by networking with other musicians. Call some of the larger organizations and see if they host showcases or can give you suggestions. Persistence pays off here.

BOOKING GIGS

At the beginning, you'll have to book yourself. Be prepared to perform for free or for chump change at first. Once you've discovered which clubs are appropriate for a live performance of your style of music, call and ask who does the booking and when they're available. Many times you'll be told to mail a demo. Send it with a cover letter and press kit. Sometimes you can deliver it in person. Rarely will the booking people listen to it on the spot, or even after you've called several times to remind them. It's a frustrating chore, but never let them feel your annoyance.

Do the legwork. Nobody will come to you in the beginning. Loads of musicians are looking for gigs. You have to hustle to get those you want. Send in a professional demo. Get friendly with people who work in clubs. DJs have influence, so get to know those who play in clubs where you want to perform. Give your demo to them. If they like it, ask them to put in a word with the right person at the club. As you get friendly with other musicians, they can recommend you, too.

Traditional Venues

Find venues where your music is performed live. Get exposure by doing open mics and freestyles wherever they're available. Create a bond between you and other artists. I can't emphasize that enough. What you don't know, somebody else will. Share your contacts. Be there for each other. Sometimes you can schmooze the promoter at a club that books larger acts and convince her to book you to open for one. Offer to do it for free and announce it to your following. If you believe in your music, a performance is the best way to show you're good. If the crowd likes you, you'll get a paid gig later.

Rock and blues has its own routine. When you speak to the booking person, he'll ask where you've played and how many people you can get to come. If you want to play there more than once, don't lie about numbers. Say you're not sure rather than alienate him by not having the good turnout promised. Be honest. It helps develop good relationships in the long run. If you honestly don't know if you can bring a crowd, ask the booking person if he'd put you on after an act with a large following. If he likes your music, he may work with you. Then you'll have a potential new following. Always thank the booking people profusely for helping you.

If you're playing in a town you've never been to, have a marketing strategy for trying to get PR, distributing flyers and posters, etc. (more in Chapter 19). Let the booking person know that you'll do what you can to get the word out. If she likes your music and your attitude, she may give you a shot. If you know bands in other cities, swap gigs. Make friends as you go so that you can help each other chart territories where the other has already been. A polite, professional attitude helps you get into new clubs.

Venues that book unknown acts often don't pay much. Most commonly, you'll get a percentage of what's taken in at the door. Some clubs pay as little as a flat fee of $50 to $100. Sometimes people play for tips. That's part of your dues for breaking into the industry. Policies and payments vary from city to city. Established clubs with a built-in following pay more, but they're harder to get booked into. Once you have experience, a following, press clippings, etc., it gets better.

No matter how little you're earning, a local club expects a turnout generated by your promotions. When you book into a club, you're supposed to do a mailing to everyone you know, giving them the details of your gig so they can attend. Send an announcement of your gigs to the press and to your targeted A & R people.

Pounding the pavement for gigs and hounding people to attend them isn't fun. It gets expensive, tiring, and frustrating, and seems like it's going nowhere. But each time you play, there's another chance someone might be there who can help you get to the next level. Take every performance seriously. Getting blasé hurts you as a musician. Never stop honing your performance. No matter how long it takes, it will make you more marketable in the long run. Brian Long, senior director of A & R at MCA Records, says, "My best advice for bands is get out and play, play, play. The more people you play in front of, the better the band you become."

Alternative Venues

Keep your eyes and ears open for events where you live. Call and ask if they need live entertainment. You may not get paid, but you have to do it to generate a buzz. The Roots created their own live exposure when they were trying to break into hip-hop in Philadelphia. According to group member ?uestlove:

> We thought that since America's never seen a group like us before and we're talented, that we'd make it. That was not the case at all. . . . There was a lack of outlets and venues for us to exercise our skills, so to speak. What we did was we started playing on the street corners. We figured we'd be our own PR machine, by any means necessary. That took a lot of sacrifice. We would play the corners every week to generate enough spending cash. . . . In our case, doing these shows every Saturday on South Street enabled us to get other gigs. People would approach us and say, "Do my bar-

becue." . . . We did that diligently until the right person, Jamaladeen Tacuma, saw us. He's a jazz bassist from Philly. He took us to Germany with him because he was doing jazz festivals and he wanted to take some rappers. We were representing American hip-hop over there without a record!

The Roots looked for every way to milk the opportunity they'd attracted from giving themselves exposure busking on a street corner. They had four months to prepare before they left on tour, so they saved up and recorded an independent release. This unsigned American group got encores in Europe, so they sent their CDs to record labels. When interest in The Roots was generated, ?uestlove says, "We got a good lawyer. He set up showcases for us to perform in." They had offers from many labels and signed with Geffen Records.

The Roots continue to capitalize on their ability to tour. ?uestlove notes that they live reasonably well from touring. He reflects, "We're doing well because we paid our dues. We're one of the few groups that doesn't even sell that much that can make a comfortable five-figure or high four-figure salary per show. Usually for a group like us, touring isn't even an option. It's such a rare thing." But it happens! Chapter 19 elaborates on opportunities for live performances.

● ● ●

Doing gigs is a thankless venture at first. But you have to accept what comes with the territory of trying to break in. Getting discouraged, angry, and frustrated won't get you anywhere but discouraged, angry, and frustrated. If you're not willing to go the distance and pay your dues, keep your day job. But if you hone your skills and create your performance foundation, you can use the tools in Chapter 19 to work toward the next level of live performances: making money.

14

TARGETING
the
COLLEGE MARKET

Myth:

The college market isn't lucrative enough to target.

• • •

When I started my record label, marketing a band through colleges was a tool used by smaller independent labels and unsigned acts. However, the majors have woken to the fact that the college market has tremendous buying power. Labels now have promotions people who focus on nothing but college radio. While colleges used to be easy to get support from, today there's more competition.

A majority of the college radio people I've spoken to, even those getting perks, are still idealistic enough to ultimately be true to the music. Students working in radio usually don't get paid, so ratings and money aren't their main motivators. College students are more interested in and excited by new bands, new sounds, and new trends than most other consumers. (Although younger people are also fervent about music, they don't always have the money that college students have to buy CDs and go to concerts.) College students are young enough to follow trends and support what's new in music, yet old enough to have sources of income to support the bands they love. The attention to the college market by the majors is a definite indication of how lucrative this market is.

THE POWER OF THE COLLEGE MARKET

The college market offers artists opportunities to reach large numbers of people within a relatively small area. The concentration found in most colleges of music-loving young adults who are open to the cutting edge is unequalled anywhere else. Students working at college radio stations, on college newspapers, and in student-activities departments are easier to reach than their counterparts in the commercial world. Yet they've got the power to reach as many people who might join your following, if they knew about you.

There are several avenues for getting a buzz going on your act at colleges: radio, gigs, and college publications. Depending on your genre, at least one of these outlets can be tapped to get you recognized in the college scene. Even if there aren't many reggae radio shows, for example, students may still want to see you perform or check out your music if they read about it in their school newspaper. Tap the resources. Most colleges with a diversified population have students who listen to all genres. Depending on the region, some music is more readily marketed on the college level.

Marketing music to colleges is hit or miss. Since you're dealing with students, it's extremely frustrating to work with their schedules—you call long distance to a music or student-activities director who is scheduled to be in during certain hours and find she's in the library, studying for midterms. Volunteers aren't as fastidious about their hours as paid staff in a more commercial environment. Once you reach them, though, the results may be rewarding. Patience is important when dealing with students who can open doors on the college level.

Working the college market is hard work. It involves locating schools and then finding the people at radio stations, venues, and other locations to call. Libraries have listings of colleges. If you get friendly with the people at one college, they might recommend you to other schools. ASK! DJs at one college often know DJs at another. Other bands may give you leads. One excellent source of information on the college market is CMJ.

CMJ

CMJ (College Music Journal) offers resources for those wanting to break into the college market. Among other things, they put out CD samplers and special publications, and sponsor a conference called CMJ Music Marathon & Musicfest in New York City every fall.

The conference is a good place to begin your education about the college music market. People show up from college radio stations all over the country. There are panels that focus on topics relevant to breaking into music on the college level. At night, attendees go to the many showcases presented in a wide variety of area clubs. Getting your act into one of the clubs can give you great exposure in front of a college-oriented audience.

Attending the event is an opportunity to be a part of one of the largest concentrations of college radio personnel assembled in one location. Bring a portable tape or disc player with a recording of your act so you can play it for each radio person you meet who expresses interest in your music. If you sense enthusiasm, offer the person a copy to play on her station. If the vibe isn't enthusiastic or she says she doesn't know if your material would get airplay, thank her and move on. Give your recording only to those who seem most likely to play it.

In addition to its annual conference, CMJ is well-known for its music publications. *CMJ New Music Report,* for instance, is a weekly tip sheet—available only by subscription—published for the alternative marketplace. It focuses on noncommercial radio-related information and contains airplay charts based on reports from college, non-commercial, and commercial radio stations, as well as from retail outlets all over the country. It also carries reviews of new album releases, so you can send in your new material for a possible write-up. The tip sheet is a great source of information concerning college radio. Musicians reading this publication see which regions have music being played that's most similar to their own. They keep up with the latest trends in college radio, thus becoming more aware of the most influential college radio stations.

You may eventually watch your own records chart in the *CMJ New Music Report.* Music and programming directors of other college stations will watch, too. A large number of them subscribe to this publication to follow what's new and good that they don't yet have. If DJs see a record charting at several schools, they're more inclined to play it. Knowing that others like an artist makes the record more appealing.

DJs (or anyone else, for that matter) listen with a different ear when they expect a record to be good.

CMJ also puts out a consumer magazine called *CMJ New Music Monthly*. It's slanted toward the person buying the music rather than for those playing or marketing it. The magazine carries reviews, charts, in-depth editorials, and feature stories.

COLLEGE RADIO

One of the best avenues for reaching the college music market is getting on their radio stations. Most college stations stay on the cutting edge of music. College DJs prefer to be groundbreakers for new music, airing what commercial stations don't play. Since most stations are funded by the school rather than advertisers, they can play what's new and fresh rather than what sponsors want them to play.

No matter what anyone says, less commercial rock and heavy metal get more airplay on college radio than do other genres. But hip-hop and other urban music get a lot more play than ever. The type of music played most frequently depends on the student population; different ethnic groups encourage their stations to play different varieties of music. Some stations even play demo tapes, which increases the variety played. Sometimes a station's music director may decide to give a certain genre extra exposure because it's something he likes, and the listeners may catch this enthusiasm.

When you want something played on commercial radio, you have to go through the programming director. A record must be on the station's *playlist* for DJs to play it. On college radio, DJs have freedom to play what they want on their shows. Reading the charts in CMJ indicates which music gets more airplay in different regions. Ask college stations for copies of their show schedules so you can see how many hours a week your genre is on the air.

Almost all genres of music are heard on at least some college radio stations. But in order to break an act, a song has to be played a lot. Airplay for a record in regular rotation on a commercial station is at least seven times a day, every day. Hearing a song over and over gets people interested in a band's music. While hearing it once or twice a week probably won't do much, it's still exposure. Just keep your expectations low.

For many reasons, some stations have more power and prestige—and larger audiences—than others. In smaller cities, there may be less competition from local commercial stations. The reach of college radio stations can range from being very powerful, covering a reasonably large area of listeners, to being able to be heard only on campus. New York University's radio station, for example, has a large following that goes way beyond its student population. Then there are colleges whose radio stations can be heard only inside the school itself. They may be played in the cafeteria and in other places on campus, so many listen whether they like it or not.

By simply speaking to a college station's music director or seeing its charts in CMJ, it's still possible that you might not be aware of the station's actual influence. I learned this when visiting my friend Leslie, who had a show on what was considered a prestigious college radio station in the Midwest. Leslie said there were few listeners because the school's power lines had been down for over a year and hadn't been fixed; only a few dorms had access to the station. Yet this school was sending its charts regularly into publications and was targeted as a powerful influence.

THE CLUB AND CONCERT CIRCUIT

Whether or not you have something that works for college radio, the college arena can still be lucrative, again depending on your genre of music and the region. College students go to hear live music more frequently than many other groups. They often have more money to spend on music than do high-school teens, and they'll come back to see bands they like.

There are many levels of venues on the college circuit. Probably the easiest to break into are local bars. Most of these cater to audiences that like rock, blues, and folk music, although this differs in various regions. Some bars have large stages and others offer just a small space to play. But the crowds, especially on weekends, can be large and enthusiastic.

Private colleges, especially those not located in major cities, bring in talent to perform on campus. The more isolated a college is, the more likely it is to bring in live music to entertain its student body. Such schools are concerned that if students get bored without a large city nearby, they may consider transferring to other schools that offer more social activities. Therefore these colleges book music, usually through a student-activities department.

If you're getting radio play on a college station, ask the DJ to hook you up with the student-activities department, if he has contacts there.

Even if he doesn't, use the name of someone at the station when you speak to the person in charge. Marilyn Dukes, associate director for student programs at the University of California, Santa Barbara, says the school books about forty to fifty live shows per year, with an assortment of acts. Students listen to all the submissions. They like a hook—a unique way of presenting the material would give a record the best chance of having a longer listen. She advises:

> Send a CD or tape and some press information, if you have it. Follow up with a phone call. People e-mail us, but a lot of those messages don't get followed up on as much as a phone call and the CD do. We get a lot of material. Call and find the right person to target it to. The way our board is set up, we have five or six people who book different types of things. When following up, strike that balance between making a personal connection and not being a pest.

Nathan Redus, event programmer at Metropolitan State College of Denver, says they do a lot of theme festivals at his school, which use a variety of music. They also have a gig series that's used mainly to showcase local music, but they consider nonlocal acts, too. How do you reach someone like him? Redus says, "We get people calling all the time. We tell them to send a demo, and if it fits into what we're looking for or planning on doing, we'll give them a call. Press kits are good, too, but it's the music that's most important." He advises sending well-produced demos. "The more production in what's sent, the better. It makes a person look more professional." Redus says that performers who can put an educational spin on their presentation have a better shot.

Call and get the name of a specific person to send your material to so you have someone to contact for a follow-up. Before sending material, ask someone who books acts if your genre of music would work for them. If you get someone friendly, ask if you can play music over the phone to give him an idea of what you do. Mailing many demos gets expensive, so don't waste money sending your stuff to a school that's unlikely to hire you. I'd send a package only to someone who showed at least some enthusiasm. Be aware that schools book way in advance.

College gigs can pay decent money. When I was in Boston I met Brad, a manager who regularly booked his bands at colleges in the New England area. He concentrated on smaller towns, booking several shows over one weekend at schools that weren't too far apart from each other. At first, Brad worked his butt off finding schools to get booked into. He investigated cheap motels, where the whole group shared a room to save money. He sometimes made a zillion calls to get one booking. But once Brad developed that all-important *relationship* with the people involved in student activities, he booked his bands into the same schools every year. He and his bands developed a regular circuit doing college gigs.

Brad says that a band wanting to break in on the college circuit must be prepared to work hard, give up comforts, and be available to travel a lot. He had a van that they traveled in together, along with their equipment. It was cramped. Sometimes they'd sleep in it. No matter how many people there were, they always shared one cheap motel room, bringing sleeping bags and blankets. Whenever possible, they'd crash with someone they knew. (Sometimes a school provides dorm rooms for the acts they book, but you can't count on that.) By keeping expenses to a minimum, however, the band had money in their pockets when they returned home. Brad's 20 percent share of the gigs made it worthwhile for him to keep booking bands.

Some groups work the smaller bars to get started. These venues don't usually pay much, but they can be good exposure. Many bands develop a large following at bars in college towns. It helps get the attention of the student-activities people and radio stations, and serves as a good opportunity to invite people with whom you're trying to develop relationships. If you sell CDs, tapes, and other merchandise, you can end up with some change in your pocket.

A little pre-planning gets you the maximum mileage out of the college circuit. When you book gigs in college venues, milk them for everything you can. Once you get the date, contact local publications to let them know about your act and to learn to whose attention a press release should be sent. College publications are often more informal than commercial ones, so you might get someone interested by just calling. If someone is willing to write a story about your act before the gig, it gets more people to show up at it. If you have anything to sell, mention it in the article.

Getting an interview on the college radio station or another local station helps bring people to your show, especially if your group has personality. Depending on your music, you can perform live on the air, always reminding people there's something for sale. Hook up with a local record store to sell your material, and promise to announce on radio or at your gig that your CD is on sale at that store; the store may like publicity. If there's time, talk to a store about making a personal appearance after a radio interview or gig. If you have nice 8″-x-10″ glossy photos and see photos of other bands on display, ask whether the store, club, or radio station would like an autographed picture of yours. I like to ask the bartenders, sales clerks, etc. at these places if they'd like their own autographed photos. I keep lots of photos of the band already signed "Thanks for your support" with a black marker. Then I ask whose name the autograph should be addressed to, which I write in myself.

NACA

Many colleges belong to NACA (National Association of Campus Activities; see Appendix 2). People interested in taking advantage of the college market can join as associate members. Membership is on either a national or regional basis; as a member, you get a national or regional directory—updated each year—of the member colleges. The directory includes the names, addresses, and phone numbers of different contact people involved in student activities, as well as information concerning what sort of music they book. (Associate members are also listed, so that colleges have your information, too.) Using the directory saves you the time and hassle of trying to track down on your own the specific people you have to speak with to book your act.

NACA also provides members with the resources for booking college tours. They get a subscription to the organization's magazine, containing articles of interest to associate members and information about new releases. NACA sponsors regional and national conferences as well. These conferences offer opportunities for artists to showcase their acts in front of a large number of people who book for their colleges. There are opportunities for artists to play their videotapes or audiotapes. While there are fees for all these services, it can still be cheaper than mass-mailing cassettes to dozens of schools. This way, you may be able to develop a relationship with some of the college personnel and get your questions answered in person.

If you want the college gigs, consider joining NACA. Singer/songwriter Lezlee did, and says, "I got a booth, which was expensive, but luckily got a showcase, which led to a bunch of decent-paying college gigs."

15

GETTING

the

RIGHT ATTITUDE

Myth:

Everyone in the music business has an attitude,

so I need one, too.

• • •

When I first got involved in the music industry, I had a hard time understanding the attitudes that prevailed. I noticed a discernible lack of respect for punctuality. "Everybody in the music industry is late," I was told. Instead of apologies, I got, "You know how it is." But I honestly didn't.

At first, I was considered a nobody, so certain people expected their asses to be kissed. Now that I've paid my dues, there are people who try to kiss mine, which is annoying and unnecessary. This business can change people. I see people who get a new title or a hit record and they forget where they came from. In what is sometimes a plastic world, the kissing up is phony. I've seen nice people turn into jerks I don't want to know anymore. They say, "That's the way this business is. If you can't beat 'em, join 'em." Is this counter-productive attitude really necessary?

I still don't buy into it. My spiritual outlook won't allow it! If you want to like yourself down the road, I highly advise maintaining a sense of integrity and respect as you work your music career.

DON'T JOIN 'EM. BEAT 'EM!

There are creeps in the music industry. It's a glamour-oriented business, so people are anxious to work in it. Competition is stiff and many people are willing to work for less in exchange for the perks and prestige of working for a record label. As a result, many let the prestige feed their egos, and we're expected to buy into it.

I've seen the industry change nice people. They feel it's the only way to survive and believe if they don't become cutthroat, their own throats may be cut. So they forget respect and manners, play on other people's needs, and do as they please, often as an affirmation of their perceived power. I've had people promise me the sun, moon, and stars, yet never return my calls. If you want to sell your soul for this business, go for it. But decency and respect go a longer way. The rewards of feeling good about you as a person are worth it!

Publicist Terrie Williams is president of the Terrie Williams Agency and author of the book *The Personal Touch: What You Really Need to Succeed in a Fast-Paced Business*. In her book, Williams emphasizes her refreshingly simple approach to dealing with people: by treating people with respect, being there for them, and showing integrity and compassion, it will come back to you multiplied. She says:

> *The fact of the matter is, everything that goes around comes around. It is the law of nature and you do not put your foot on anyone's back. You can't get away with doing wrong or evil, eventually there's no place for it. Nothing lasts forever. The way you treat people when you are on top is the way you'll be treated when the lights go down. It is imperative to treat everybody the same and never forget where you came from. You can lose all this tomorrow and then where would you be? How could I even think that because I've achieved a little bit of success I wouldn't take the time to talk to someone who's on their way up?*

This approach brought Williams great success and tremendous respect. Her positive attitude attracted Eddie Murphy as her first client. You don't have to screw people to advance in the music industry. Doing a good job and having the right product or talent wins out in the long run. When you have what it takes to succeed, you'll get the respect you deserve, without losing your values. Recording artist Pat Green advises:

> *You definitely can't be a prick. Nobody likes a prick. You have to be a nice person, or at least a person who's genuine and who cares, not only about your music but about somebody else's music. If you only focus on yourself, you get trapped and lost and it won't really happen.*

If you're not spiritual, I highly recommend developing faith in something besides money. It helps you hang in for the long haul. Faith helps you stay focused on finding that ONE person to help you. Without my faith I'd never have had the fortitude or balls to hang in for the length of time it took me to succeed. It keeps my balls strong. I'm neither religious nor trying to force anything on you, but know from personal experience that faith in a higher being nurtures faith in yourself and your path. We can use all the help we can get in the music industry!

WHAT GOES AROUND COMES AROUND

There are a lot of terrific people in the industry. I never sunk to the level of not being straight, friendly, and respectful with everyone, which was a large factor in my getting so far. People like me and want to help a decent person. I stand out among the not-so-nice people. Nice people attract other nice people. If you keep your standards high, you'll find each other. Over the years, I've gotten amazing support from people who said they helped me because they wanted to see a nice person win!

I teach classes called "Nice Girls/Guys on Top." Participants say they're tired of being nice, which is sad. We absolutely can be nice and choose whom to go out of our way for. Being nice doesn't mean groveling or getting taken advantage of. It does mean treating people with respect, no matter what you get back. Don't do to others what you don't want done to you. We must maintain these standards. If the nice people in the music industry get so fed up that they go in the other direction, this will be a sad place. There are many decent people out there. Be patient and they'll find you!

TO THINE OWN SELF BE TRUE

There are simple things that help you to be remembered as a decent person. Be aware of them as you create your music-business persona. People in my music-business classes always laugh when I advise remembering manners. *Please* and *thank you* go a long way in this business. People remember you for it. It's amazing how many people get so jaded that they forget basic courtesy. In comparison, people like and respect me because I'm polite and gracious to everyone. I always thank anyone who helps me, no matter how small the act. Assume everyone will be nice to you. If they're not, it's their problem, not yours. Nonetheless, keep your guard up. People say things they don't intend to follow through with all the time. That's just how it is.

Don't take promises seriously until actions prove their words. Keep expectations realistic to avoid setting yourself up for disappointment and resenting the ones making promises. If you don't take things seriously, you won't feel angry if they don't follow through; if their word is good, it's a pleasant surprise. People say things they don't mean to please you in the short run. Sometimes making promises causes insecure people to feel more powerful. Other times, people mean what they say at the moment, but forget it later. Temper your expectations. If someone promises to take your tape to an A & R person, don't get excited. You can't fragment yourself by running after people making promises. It's exhausting. Network until you find people who do follow through. Make sure you keep your own word. It'll give you a good reputation in the long run.

Don't be unsolicitous to those you think can't help you. If you meet others in the same position as you, be friendly and helpful. Don't be afraid to share information. Build a support system among peers instead of blowing them off for those in higher places. The struggling musician sitting next to you at a seminar may get signed tomorrow. Make friends with everyone. It increases your chances of contacts.

DO THE RIGHT THING

My own personal music-industry etiquette goes like this: Don't worry about those who aren't nice. Take care of yourself and go in the right direction for you. Laugh off the obnoxious club manager, the A & R guy who doesn't return calls, and the promoter who doesn't remember you after souping you up last week. It's just how it can be in this business. They'll get theirs in the end.

Rather than getting angry and frustrated when people don't return calls promptly, understand that there's a warped sense of etiquette in this business. It's common for industry people, even decent ones, not to return calls promptly, or at all. There are days I get no work done because the phone doesn't stop ringing, and I don't even work for a label. People legitimately get backed up, put your message aside to call later, and never get to it. It's not uncommon to have calls returned when you've long since given up. Just accept it.

I've learned that "Can I call you right back?" means, "I can't talk now and just want to get off the phone." I accept it. Don't bombard people with calls. If they want to talk to you they will. Before trying again, wait at least a few days the first time and a week or two after that. If they're backed up they don't need more pressure. I once left messages for five people at labels, all of whom know me. Four of them got back to me over two weeks later. The last took a month. She just said she was returning my call. I had to stifle myself from asking, "Do you feel no shame about calling after a month and acting like it was yesterday?" Instead, I thanked her for returning my call. People are very busy. Until you're a big success, you're not a priority.

Of course you should return calls promptly. Some will notice. Punctuality is another thing I highly recommend to make you stand out. Music people live by a different clock. People at record labels may keep you waiting hours for an appointment made weeks before. Things come up. Gigs are known for starting late. When my seminars begin, there may be three people in attendance. I always warn them the room will fill up. It does, with students arriving as much as an hour late. Disrespecting punctuality seems to be a music thing. That's a crock! I always remember the three people who were on time.

Be cheerful. Keep smiling. It will make you more pleasant to talk to. Many people are happy to see me because of my upbeat, friendly personality. Don't tell industry people your problems. Let everyone but your closest friends think you're doing well. When you see people who ask how your career is going, always give an enthusiastic "great!" No one will check. People are more attracted to those who they think are doing well and who have positive things to say. Be one of them and you'll attract more positive contacts and deals. The only attitude you should be showing is a confident belief in your talent.

NETWORKING

for

SUCCESS

Myth:

It doesn't matter how good my music is—

it's who I know that counts.

• • •

It's who you *can* know that counts, and you *can* meet the right people. Everyone can make the contacts necessary to get signed to a record label. If you learn to consistently be where industry people are, set specific goals, and learn how to ask for what you need, eventually you'll find the right people. I'll first remind you that no matter whom you know, a record deal is still contingent on your having enough talent *and* strong material to merit a deal. Make sure that end is in place before working your contacts.

When I entered the music industry, I knew no one. I was a school-teacher who no one took seriously. But I took myself seriously. I talked to *everyone*, letting them know my needs, and got help. As I asked for contacts and resources, my Rolodex got fuller and my world expanded. The more you ask for, the more you get.

LEARNING TO ASK

If you don't have contacts, you still have a mouth. Use it! It's your best resource. You need to meet people in order to make contacts. We often don't get what we want because we don't clearly articulate our needs. If we assume people will say "no," we don't ask. We stay in the box, passing up opportunities by second-guessing others.

You receive much more by getting over the fear of asking. I'd never be where I am if I hadn't accepted that the worst thing that happens is a "no" response, which I can handle. When I started my label, I asked for introductions and resources. If I didn't know how to do something, I asked for help. I'd get turned down but kept asking. Eventually someone helped me. Ask for more and expect more. A confident attitude gets taken more seriously. Ask as if you expect to get what you need. Don't sound apologetic. Raise your expectations. Only asking for a little won't get you a lot.

Six Degrees of Separation

Learn networking skills. I believe we're all no more than six degrees of separation away from people we need. We're all connected by someone. My networking proved this. I didn't get where I am by luck. My contacts weren't handed to me. I didn't know a soul in the music industry at first. But I talked to everyone. Each person led me to another. I worked every contact. Everyone is a potential foot in the door of someone who can help you.

There's always someone you know or can meet who knows someone who can get you further ahead. Your dentist may have a cousin at Universal. The man next to you at a seminar could be the lawyer of a famous artist. The woman in the coffee shop may have a sister who's married to a manager. You won't know if you don't speak up. Keep talking to everyone you can about what you're doing and you'll make contacts. Make sure to mention to everyone you meet what you're looking for. The more people to whom you convey your needs, the greater your chance of finding the one person who can open a door.

Use each contact as a stepping stone. Once you find one person, she can hook you up with someone else and so on. If you're shy, get over it! Hone your people skills. The more people like you, the more they'll go out of their way for you. Maintain a courteous, friendly attitude as you work the people you meet. Networking is the best tool for getting ahead and it doesn't cost a dime. It's the best way to begin relationships!

This industry is a small community. The key is putting yourself in the thick of it, which may mean visiting a larger city. When you feel discouraged, think about this: I was a teacher who knew NOBODY in the industry when I started, yet I've always been able to get to anyone I want. I may not get what I want from them, but I at least get their attention. It starts with a sincere smile, a positive attitude, and balls!

The Art of Networking

Networking is an art. First, know your needs. If you meet someone with good contacts, don't ask what he can do for you. That's a good way to blow the opportunity! Identify exactly what's needed for the next step in your career. A record deal is too broad. Determine what you need first and discuss it. He may have suggestions or offer more. But you'll sound more professional if you're definite in your objectives. Evaluate the overall picture of what you're trying to accomplish and focus more effectively. People prefer helping those who have their act together.

Develop short- and long-term goals. Target specific things you want when you network. List or outline what you need. Let each goal reached take you a step closer to the finish line. For example, figure out the best labels to approach and seek to find the best contact person at that label. You can call the label itself to learn the name of the A & R person who specializes in your genre of music. Next, your goal is to find someone who knows him or her to give you an introduction or another contact.

Again, don't be afraid to ask. If you meet someone who vaguely knows a person at a record label you're interested in, ask if you can use her name when you make the call. Often, just dropping a name gets you through. Sounding professional helps pull it off. If a label person says she likes your music but can't use it, ask for recommendations to other labels. She'll know who likes what. Ask to use her name, or, if you're really ballsy, ask her to make a call on your behalf. If she doesn't want to help, she may not like your material. But ask anyway! It can't hurt. The worst anyone can do is say no. All you need is someone to say yes.

When I went to London with my rap material, I met Martin, a promoter, who introduced me to a friend of his in A & R at Phonogram. When he turned me down for his label, I asked for names of others to call and for permission to drop his name. When I met others, I asked for more names. I always phoned afterward to thank them. From my one single promoter, I networked my way into almost every label in London. All you need is one person to work your way to a large number of contacts. If you make a good impression AND have the goods, people will help you.

FINDING YOUR INITIAL CONTACTS

One way to meet industry people is to join organizations. I've met wonderful people when attending panels and songwriter showcases. ASCAP, BMI, SESAC, the Songwriter's Hall of Fame, and NARAS have panels and showcases. Often they're free, and they're great for learning and networking. Many organizations have chapters in several cities. Call them or look online to check out their activities and locations.

Singer/songwriter Jo Davidson advises, "Go anywhere that people in the industry are speaking." Keep track of the *Billboard* calendar section for dates. When you go to an industry event, talk to everyone you meet. Be friendly, give out business cards, and get cards from others.

Conferences that specialize in your style of music are better suited for networking than large, general ones, as almost everyone you would meet is involved in your genre. I've made some of my best contacts in dance music and rap through sitting around the pool at the Winter Music Conference held in Miami. In the United States, SXSW, which takes place in March, is considered the best of the music conferences, with the most industry people in attendance.

Being at a music seminar offers great opportunities for meeting people. Participants wear name badges, so check out everyone. Talk to them. Don't be selective about finding someone "important." Talk to people at the exhibitions, at the showcases, and even in the bathroom. If you want to attract even more people, think of a good question or statement during a panel and ask it on the mic. Give your name and occupation. If possible, mention what you're looking for. If you sound good, people will come talk to you afterward. I've met great people that way.

Usually after a panel, the audience gang-rushes the speakers. It's hard to absorb anything they say. I've been a panelist, and often those people become a blur. Don't throw demos at a panelist, even if it's someone you badly want to reach. Be patient. When the crowd clears, introduce yourself in a professional manner and ask for a business card. Say you'll get in touch later. If you make a good impression, she might remember you when you call. Ask if it's okay to send a demo the next week. It's better to send material later and not risk its getting buried under all the tapes that are dumped on the person at the seminar. CDs are heavy and often don't make it back with the person.

For a professional connection, put out your hand when introducing yourself. Shake hands with a firm grip to make a good impression and show confidence. A limp handshake is wimpy. A solid grip gets noticed. Be professional in your approach so you get taken more seriously and stand out from those being pushy for attention; the individual may remember you better when receiving your demo.

Getting Down with the Music People

My best friends in the music business have been people who work in record shops. They're usually there because they love music. These folks are often DJs, producers, and engineers, and are up-to-date on everything in the music industry. People who work in record shops know what's selling and which label puts out which type of music. If you get friendly with them, they're great sources of information and can recommend producers, recording studios, and almost everything you need. Many know A & R people. If they believe in your act, they may help you. They can then brag about discovering you. I've gotten two record deals through someone who worked in a record store. He's now an A & R person at a major label. Things change quickly in this business.

Go to stores that sell your genre. Bring a demo and a friendly smile. Also bring a portable player. Introduce yourself to the DJ or salesperson that handles your genre. Explain that you're shopping your music and would appreciate suggestions, if they'd listen. Many will, especially if it's during a quiet time. People in stores are usually friendly. Many are trying to get their own careers off the ground. I don't know if I'd have succeeded without the help of my friends in stores. They gave me contacts, offered encouragement, and taught me about the industry. I'm grateful to them.

Club DJs are also helpful. Talk to those that play your genre. They'll be your toughest critics, but they know music. Many are producers and work with labels. Ask for their help! Hang out in the DJ booth. It gets annoying if they ignore you while they're spinning records, but you can meet good contacts there. Other people hanging out may help you, too. Often, even A & R people are there. Keep asking for help until someone gives you a name or recommendation.

If you can't get to a big music city, work the people where you live. Find a way to get friendly with people at your local radio station, the music writers for your local paper, club promoters nearby, etc. Somebody has to know somebody, or at least know somebody who knows somebody. Take it six degrees if you have to, but I doubt you will. IF you have the goods, somebody in your town can help you get to somebody further. Sometimes living outside of the music hub offers advantages since there is less competition. And when you do visit a big city, you'll have a better chance of getting appointments if you say you'll be in town for only a week. Lisa Zbitnew, president of BMG, Canada, advises:

> If you're really serious and committed to having a recording career, it's likely along the way you'll have an opportunity to meet local music people. Take the time to ask a lot of questions. Don't be afraid to ask for feedback. Don't take it all literally and assume that the experts, including people at record companies, have all the answers. You can always pull something from people involved in the music business.

Networking to the Max

Networking is selling or marketing yourself. You need to get people's interest in your talent or material. Publicist Terrie Williams recommends dropping a note to anyone who has helped you, such as an A & R person who met with you, a journalist who came to your gig, a promoter who gave you a contact that worked, etc. Williams has sent me friendly notes when I've done something for her and they always make me feel good.

At a large function, wear a jacket with pockets—keep your cards in one pocket and a pen in the other. Put other people's cards in the pocket with the pen. When you finish talking with someone, note on the back of the person's card who she is. If it's a good contact, note personal stuff you spoke about so you can bring it up when you speak with her again: if she had a cold, ask how she's feeling; if she loves the Yankees, wait until the team wins to call and comment on the game. It creates a personal connection between you. Work everyone you encounter. Use confidence, professionalism, perseverance, friendliness, and patience to find your way.

CREATING YOUR OWN SUPPORT SYSTEM

A creative support system keeps you going in lean times and kicks your butt when you're discouraged. Learn from and grow with other musicians. Once you've met like-minded people, see if they'd like to help each other more formally. Get together to discuss music and brainstorm. Recording artist Jo Davidson found this useful:

> *I started a group—Urban Muse. I wanted a sense of commu-*
> *nity in New York with artists. We meet every other week. We share*
> *ideas and play songs for each other. Sometimes we do group shows*
> *and double bills. It revolved around a discussion group, but we per-*
> *form together sometimes and draw from each other's fan bases.*

Some people create opportunities on a larger scale. Jazz singer Pamela Hart got a grant from the city of Austin and created her own venue, Women in Jazz. Since '95, they've done two concerts a year. This organization gave Hart the opportunity to network with others in her genre. She says, "People see me on womeninjazz.org. A local musician who I met networking through Women in Jazz is bringing me to Europe." Attorney Richard Dieguez created a huge networking group in New York City, called The Circle (currently accessible at www.rpdieguez. com), which others can learn from. For a small fee to cover costs, musicians come to monthly meetings. Dieguez keeps a well-stocked resource table, speaks about legal issues, and has an industry pro speak. Most importantly, everyone in attendance introduces themselves, so everyone knows who's there for possible networking. Encourage someone to start a networking group where you live.

Create your own support network. Many musicians would enjoy being part of something that benefits everyone. Give honest feedback about each other's songs, help each other solve problems, plan strategies to work together or do group gigs, and feel like there are people you can count on. Go to each other's gigs. Find people who are on somewhat the same level as you and who you respect as musicians.

VOLUNTEERING OR INTERNING

Get into the thick of the music industry by volunteering or doing an internship. Volunteer for an organization. Help out at industry events. By getting involved, you have more of a chance of meeting the ONE person who has a contact. Take that contact and build from it. Even if you start small, like getting active in a local songwriters' group, the people you meet can be indispensable.

If you have spare time and have access to a major music city, internships are valuable. Industry people recommend them as a way to learn about all aspects of the music business. While colleges often have formal internship programs, many individuals won't turn down an informal free helper who seems good. Talk to everyone you can about your desire to work for free. Interns do grunt work, but the contacts made can be priceless. If you have the goods, and a personality to work the people you meet, you can get several degrees of separation closer to a record deal. Everything helps. Being inside a company gives you proximity to good people.

Everyone runs to record labels as a source of internships. Try an internship at PR agencies, management firms, talent agencies, publishing companies—any biz that deals with music. Jeff Blue, a vice president of A & R at Warner Bros. Records, says:

> I use interns all the time. The guitar player in Linkin Park was my intern when I was a music publisher. I listened to his tape and signed him immediately after the first show they did. Nobody wanted to sign them [to an artist deal]. I stayed with them for four and a half years. When I went to Warner Bros. I signed them there.

FINDING A MENTOR

People may not want to help you, but they usually love giving advice. Asking for advice or opinions is less demanding than asking someone to get your demo to a label. People feel put off when you ask for favors; they're flattered when you want their opinion. It's nice having friends in the industry. Sometimes being able to sit down and talk to someone with experience gives you the encouragement and confidence to go on. Publicist Jane Blumenfeld believes:

> Most everybody in the music industry is open for advice. Even though they're not going to sign you or do anything for you, most anyone will be willing to talk with you. Call up or send a letter followed by a phone call, asking, "Would you mind if I stopped by your office for a few minutes just to meet you and talk with you? I'd love to hear your advice." Most people will give you a few minutes of their time. An entertainment lawyer would be a good candidate. Bring the person a cup of coffee or something. Establish a rapport with somebody who might talk to other people about you.

Going to an industry insider for advice can be the beginning of a relationship. If she likes you, who knows where it may lead? How do you approach possible mentors? Blumenfeld recommends sending a letter and following it up with a phone call. If you live outside of the city where the individuals work, fax them that you're going to be visiting, saying, "I wonder if I could stop by and speak with you for a few minutes. I understand you won't be interested in signing me, but I would love your advice." When singer/songwriter Carla Hall read about getting a mentor in the first edition of *The Real Deal*, she wanted one. Hall, who's gutsy and takes her music seriously, decided to go to the top, and explains:

> *My first choice was Ahmet Ertegun, CEO and founder of Atlantic Records. I researched his career in preparation for contacting him and learned he had been in the business forever, signing great artists such as The Rolling Stones and Bette Midler. In the meantime, I sent him and his assistant my music business newsletter, The Soulflower, as well as flyer notices. I had no idea if he would read them, but I figured it couldn't hurt. I finally sent him a personal letter asking him to mentor me, detailing why I'd chosen him, along with a bottle of vodka, his favorite drink. I didn't hear from him right away, but he surprised me by attending my next show. We spoke afterward, and he asked to set up a meeting the next week. I went to his office and we had a great conversation about the music business and its perils. Since then we've kept in touch. It's great having someone like him to brainstorm ideas with. The best part was going after something I wanted and realizing I could make it happen.*

Blumenfeld says a great way to find people most likely to give advice is to see who's teaching. Industry people teach or guest lecture at colleges, adult education programs, music seminars, etc. "Because they are already reaching out to help people, say to one, 'I know you were teaching at Columbia. I wondered if I could stop by and speak with you.'" They may not have time for everyone, but may make some for a resourceful person who asks politely. I regularly "adopt" as mentors people who I meet and like. By not making a pig of myself and limiting requests, I get help when needed. A friendly, respectful approach and appreciation for their time attracts mentors.

USING
Your Songwriting
TALENTS

Myth:

As an unsigned musician, there's nothing
I can do with my songwriting.

• • •

If you have songwriting talent, use it! Unknown songwriters can make a lot more money than unknown artists. Actually, they can make more money than signed artists. There's a much greater potential to earn money from songs than from record sales. Songwriting royalties are lucrative (more in Chapter 26). If you get your foot in the door, you can support yourself while pursuing a career as an artist.

Developing your songwriting skills can attract a record deal. If your song gets on a soundtrack, your chance of being noticed multiplies. Artists who write songs are in a better position to get a deal, according to Kenny MacPherson, senior vice president of creative at Warner/Chappell Music in Los Angeles. He says record labels prefer signing a complete package: singers who write their own material.

I asked Harriet Schock, a successful songwriting teacher and author of the inspirational book *Becoming Remarkable* (see Appendix 2), for wisdom about songwriting. Schock, who is also a recording artist and has had numerous songs covered by well-known artists, including the Grammy-nominated "Ain't No Way to Treat a Lady," says:

> *Assuming you have well-crafted songs that have something to say that will touch a lot of people, help that artist's CD, lift that moment in the movie, or launch someone's career . . . you have a world of options today. Provided that world doesn't get the idea that intellectual property belongs to everyone for free, you'll have a lot more ways of making money from songwriting than you ever did before. And when someone asks what you've written, you're going to have to say the most famous of those titles and film credits over and over, like a poem you know by heart. So make sure they're songs you can be proud of.*

MAKING SONGWRITING YOUR BUSINESS

Unsigned artists I spoke to who are making money from songwriting have a business attitude. If you pursue this career, don your business cap to figure out ways to market your songs. It's not easy, but it's possible. Be prepared to work as hard as with any other business. J. W. Johnson, director of writer-publisher relations at BMI in New York, says:

> *People that tend to be successful songwriters are the ones that understand this is a business. Most people work a forty-hour week or more. If you want to be successful as a songwriter, you have to get up every day, put in your eight to twelve hours, five days a week, and work extremely hard. Nobody is going to wave a magic wand over your head and say, "Hey, you're a songwriter." It's very competitive and extremely hard work. You can't sit on your bed and expect the world to come to you. You have to get out, mingle, and avail yourself of opportunities that are out there. There are a lot of resources that up-and-coming songwriters don't use.*

Create a songwriting business plan. You can't write songs and simply wish for them to get used. Sorry, the songwriting wish fairy doesn't make house calls! The good news is that resources for songwriters are plentiful. I've found more opportunities for songwriters to network and grow than for any other creative field. Songwriter organizations offer workshops, support, and great networking.

Learn what makes a song great and extremely marketable. Great *commercial* songs are worth money. But as I said in Chapter 9, some great songs aren't worth jack. J. W. Johnson relates, "There are people that are very good songwriters but are not in sync with the marketplace. It's frustrating because people can be very talented and good at what they do, but there's just no significant market for it." Study the market. Janet Fisher, a songwriter and the owner of Goodnight Kiss Publishing, in Hollywood, advises:

> *If you give them material that's too good to turn down, they may not turn it down. Do your homework. Investigate different avenues that might be good outlets for your songs. Listen to the radio. I cannot tell you how many songwriters do not listen to the radio. If you want to be a working, current songwriter, you have to know the working, current sounds that are being sold and in demand. You can't listen to the old music and be a songwriter for today's market. It doesn't make sense. Selling is the key word here!*

Singer/songwriter Michelle Lewis (signed to Giant Records), a staff writer with BMG Music for years, has written songs used in films and on television and covered by dozens of artists, including Shawn Colvin, Lauryn Hill, and the Dixie Chicks. She recommends, "If you go the songwriter route, know your market. Listen to the radio and don't be lazy about production values. Whoever listens to your song will want to picture it on the radio without much imagination, so make it that way."

Study songwriting markets. Gather information at songwriter workshops and panels. Target one avenue at a time, starting with the one you have most access to. Get advice from pros at organizations and from other songwriters. I must say that I've found songwriters to be the most generous and supportive group of pros I've had the pleasure of working with. Take advantage! Prepare for the long haul—until your skills are better or you meet the ONE person who can use your songs or introduce you to someone who can. Most songwriters pay years of dues before getting a break. Patience and perseverance are crucial. Rejection can wound your ego enough to quit if you don't believe in your music and have the balls to keep going. Keep thinking **WIN: W**rite your ass off! **I**mprove your skills! **N**etwork your ass off! If you do this and if you've got the goods, someone will recognize your songs. Tommy Williams, creative director of Curb/Magnatone, in Nashville, understands:

> *It's tough, but you have to edge your way in. If the music is strong enough, if it's that great, people will hear it. It takes time and patience. If the desire is in the person and they've got the fire in their belly, that will help get through a lot of down times. Even as a song plugger, I deal with rejection every day. Nashville is a crazy town and very subjective, too. Timing is big, and there's no way to know when the right time will be.*

CRAFT—CRAFT—CRAFT!

Step number one for making money from your songs: hone your craft. I'll repeat: never stop improving your skills! Never think you're such a great songwriter that you can't be better. Janet Fisher says, "If you're a songwriter, you have to write all the time and get better and better. Like an athlete, you have to train." There's a big market for good commercial songs. But you have to be THAT GOOD to have your songs used. Singer/songwriter Jo Davidson got an artist deal with Edel America after building a songwriting career. She advises:

> *People will hear it if you're a good songwriter. If you're not getting people interested, take a closer look and ask people to seriously give you their honest opinion of what you can do better. I've surrounded myself with people who would be really harsh and honest so that I could get farther quicker. You have to be willing to do that and be willing to hear what people have to say. If you're not a good writer, they're not going to be interested in you. That sounds cold but it's true.*

How do you hone your craft? Join every songwriters' group you can. Take workshops. Participate in events. Get your songs critiqued wherever you can and keep an open mind. There are regular critiquing events in the major cities. Join TAXI (see page 133). Davidson says that Los Angeles has the most opportunities for getting songs critiqued, but don't run there unless you're serious. There are chapters of major organizations in many cities. The NSAI (Nashville Songwriters Association International) has local chapters across the country. The SGA (Songwriters Guild of America) sponsors regular critiquing sessions in three cities. The best way to become a great songwriter is to learn from pros.

Above all, an innate ability to write songs is key. You can't manufacture a great song. Learn from the experts but stay true to your craft. While you need a commercial edge, you have to write with passion. Ed Razzano, the senior creative director of Spirit Music Group, in New York City, offers advice for making a living from songwriting:

> Write from your heart and from what you believe. If something becomes difficult to write, it may not be something you should be writing about. If something is truly somewhat channeled through you, that is your talent. If you only have a talent for ballads, the world needs ballads. It should be somewhat effortless. If it's not, reconsider your career path.

If you have songwriting talent and polish it like a shining star, you *will* get your songs taken seriously. If they become THAT GOOD, they *will* get recognized. The songwriting end of the music industry is about talent. As an unsigned artist, you might not get songs into big-budget films or covered by top stars. But if you're not worried about the glory and just want to make money, you can earn a living from it.

SIGNING WITH AN ESTABLISHED PUBLISHING COMPANY

Should you sign with an established music publishing company or market your songs yourself? If you're an artist/songwriter, getting signed to a music publishing deal is an option for getting a record deal. A publisher can get your material to labels. Tommy Williams says that for a publisher, "When a writer is an artist it can be a plus. If they get a deal, we'll have songs on their album."

Publishers have contacts to place songs in income-generating situations. They have relationships with A & R people, producers, managers, and music supervisors for film and TV, and are diligent in collecting royalties. They know who is looking for original songs. A publisher can guide you in developing your talent. They can also hook you up with writing collaborators. Some publishers pay for the recording of your songs. For all their work, most publishers take the full publisher's share of the songwriter's royalties. This is 50 percent of the total (more in Chapter 26). Some writers choose to publish themselves and keep it all. But if you don't want to do marketing, your long-term goal may be to hook up with a publisher. According to Kenny MacPherson:

Publishers do take a chunk of what might otherwise be your royalty. They usually control the use of your song so they can issue licenses. But a smaller piece of a much larger pie may still make you more money. Publishers can be more aggressive than you in getting your material in the position of earning royalties, protecting your copyright, and making sure your songs are licensed properly. If you're an artist, they can help you shop a deal with a label. Publishers used to just shop songs, but they'll now try to get a label interested in an act whose songs they represent. After all, if you make an album with your songs, the publisher stands to make money. So a publisher who believes in your songs may help you get where you want to be.

There are various levels of publishers. Some specialize in TV and film. Some do all types of marketing. Some will give you a single song deal, and others want exclusive rights to all your songs or a whole CD. Many publishers sign staff writers. Tommy Williams had six writers on staff when I interviewed him. He explains how he works with staff writers:

They are signed to us exclusively. They have a monthly draw, which allows them to write songs and keeps them from needing a day job so they can focus on their writing. Usually, when a writer has five songs I think are viable, I pick a studio and musicians and get the best demos we can. A normal contract is twelve complete copyrights in a twelve-month period. That means twelve 100 percent copyrights. If the writer cowrites with one other writer, we get twenty-four songs. We get 100 percent of the publishing. Writers get the writer's share.

If you choose to find a publisher, check their track records. Having a publishing deal assures nothing. There are no guarantees a publisher will do anything with your songs. *The Music Publisher Registry,* a directory of publishers (see Appendix 2), is a good resource, but word of mouth is the best way to find a publisher. Someone at your performing rights society may be able to recommend a publisher to you. Many publishers teach songwriting workshops at organizations and speak on panels. I have more suggestions for finding publishers later in this chapter.

WRITING FOR OTHER ARTISTS

You can make lots of money having songs on other people's albums. Networking helps you get to that point. Singer/songwriter Michelle Lewis recalls how, through someone in a singing group she'd been part of, she met a track writer who was getting a vast amount of work. He had a publishing deal but wasn't a songwriter. He loved Lewis's songs and had her write to some of his tracks. Four of them got cut. The producer signed her to a management contract and Lewis says, "I jumped through hoops, wrote with anyone I could, and took every stupid opportunity that came along. I signed with BMG as a staff songwriter in '93."

Ed Razzano notes that getting artists to cover your songs is not always about the song. "Songwriters need to realize that our not being able to place their song doesn't mean it sucks. It may be political. Or an A & R person may not be able to hear beyond the demo, which happens a lot." Rather than going after established artists, instead try to get to up-and-coming artists if you want your songs to be covered. Harriet Schock advises:

> I've always believed in the small fish theory: Rather than going after a cut on the most sought-after artist in the business, why not find the new what's-his-name, or someone who's not [now] on the charts but will be again. Go to open mics and shows in your own area. If you can't attract a local artist to do your material, what makes you think Faith Hill or Ricky Martin is going to cut it? Start local and spread out like ripples in a lake. Do the same thing with publishers.

Schock adds, "It seems a bit easier if you're also an artist. I've found that radio airplay helps me get songs covered from my own albums; it was the way I got 'Ain't No Way to Treat a Lady' covered in the '70s." Janet Fisher says, "Targeting is the hardest part of placing a song." She advises targeting whom each song would be perfect for. Look at previous albums, and for each artist see who published other songs he recorded, who produced them, who his manager and A & R person are, etc. Contact all of them. This isn't easy, folks! But there's money to be made from good songs!

PLACING SONGS IN TV AND FILM

There's a lot of opportunity to get songs placed in film and TV. Once you get your foot in the door and get credits, you can place songs regularly if they're good. Songwriter Barbara Jordan, whose publishing company, Heavy Hitters, makes over one thousand song placements per year in film and television productions, has also done independent music supervision for feature films and recalls:

> Many years ago, I wearied of writing formulaic songs for the limited number of singers who accept outside material. I felt "boxed in" by the needs of pop radio, and I didn't feel myself to be stretching creatively. So to keep myself awake, I explored the limitless stylistic possibilities involved in writing for film and television projects. I loved it because I was never bored! In the morning I'd be writing an angry grunge-rock song, midday a '40s-style jazz-crooner song, and in the evening a trippy electronica song. For the first time, I was able to support myself through songwriting.

While film may sound more glamorous than television, placing music in TV offers opportunity and money. J. W. Johnson says there's a growing market for unsigned artists:

> The reason the networks are interested in using unsigned artists for soundtracks is because it's one-stop shopping for them: The same person owns the master recording and the copyright to the song. It's cheaper and quicker. If you can get your foot in the door and establish a relationship, there's an open-ended demand for [music]. If you establish a relationship with a music supervisor or two, you can get enough work to make a living. It's a front-end and back-end deal. You're paid a sync fee up front, and then the performance royalties come from BMI and ASCAP.

If a TV show is syndicated or shown in other countries, you may collect royalties for years. Jennifer Smith, lead singer of Naked Blue, has placed songs in television many times and loves it. "It's free money; you've already made your record. For me, it has generated between $300 and $6,000 for a spot. It was probably the single most important move that we made in jump-starting our business."

Fees vary, depending on the project and the songwriter. Barbara Jordan says:

Synchronization and master-use fees (the up-front money paid for use of a song) for television are usually lower than fees for feature film uses, but recently I'd say that's changing—fees are evening out between film and television. It really depends on a lot of variables, including the budget of the particular movie or TV show, or what the show feels it wants to pay for music and how desperate the writers/publishers are to have their material used.

Recording artists Fisher were the only unsigned act on the soundtrack for the 1998 film *Great Expectations*. They agreed to no mechanical royalties (see Chapter 26 for more on royalties). Their song "Breakable" didn't make the film. But people who bought the soundtrack were drawn to Fisher's music. It increased their fan base. When Jo Davidson's manager passed a tape of her song "Mental Pollution" to a music supervisor, it ended up in a TV movie and the actress Shannon Doherty sang it on the program. That was exciting for Jo. So were the royalties!

How much opportunity is there in film & TV? Janet Fisher specializes in film and television. Being in Hollywood, she has relationships with directors, who call when they're doing a new production. She sees endless possibilities:

As many channels as there are on your satellite, as many production companies as are out there—all need music. In my opinion, with the high quality of recording most songwriters have at their disposal now, or at least affordable studios where you can get demos that sound like masters, you have a wonderful opportunity.

A nice thing about TV or film is the opportunity to write songs that aren't on the radio. Janet Fisher says, "There are better outlets and more creative uses for less mainstream stuff." Barbara Jordan agrees:

There isn't any one kind of music or song that TV or film productions ask for routinely. Certain shows stay with the style of music that appeals to their demographic. You'll hear a lot of alternative/rock/nouveau folk on the teen shows (many are clustered on the WB network) and a lot of rap/metal/hard rock on the grittier crime dramas. But each episode of a TV show is different and set in a different locale, so if one scene is shot in New Orleans, you can be sure someone on the show will ask for New Orleans-style jazz/blues. In other words, they need everything!

Harriet Schock says that she learned a lot from the Film Music Network (www.filmmusic.net or [888] 456-5020), which sponsors inexpensive panels geared to songwriting, and Film Music Magazine (www.filmmusicmag.com). They're a wealth of information. Schock says feature films have a lot of politics behind the music; she recommends going to film festivals to meet new directors:

> *The films are independent, but sometimes they are really excellent. Your song can be showcased well, and these filmmakers don't have every other publisher and songwriter trying to get into the same slot.*
>
> *In major film releases, the head of music at the studio wants the songs to help sell the movie, not just creatively. What's important to them is that the release of the record and possible airplay can help promote the film. So it's more like arranged marriages: The record company and the film company try to create a merger whereby the recording artist's release is enhanced by the movie promo and the film audiences are broadened by the exposure the song gets.*

GETTING YOUR FEET WET

Singer/songwriter Nina Mankin advises, "Join all the professional groups you can and any local music professional groups. Find out who the people are at those organizations. If they like you and your music, they can be tremendously helpful. Subscribe to trade magazines and tip sheets to keep up on what's going on in the industry."

Michelle Lewis says, "Go to songwriter circles and classes. I did it all in the beginning. There are loads of opportunities to network with people who might help you with your songwriting in major cities." Attend all events related to songwriting. Go to any pitch sessions you find so industry people hear your music. Barbara Jordan recommends:

> *Pitch your songs and see if anyone's interested. Even if they say they're not interested now, see if you can get a business card so you can stay in touch, and as your work develops you can send them new material. Building relationships is what it's all about.*

This worked for Deonne Kahler, a singer/songwriter with Bhoss:

> *We just completed our CD* Trust Me, *which we released on our own label. I went to a songwriters' conference to network, pass out free CDs, and see what was going on in the northern California*

music business. They were doing Demo Derbies [events in which songwriters play their demos]. I heard that one of the publishers was notoriously picky but had a great track record for placing songs in TV and movies, and I submitted a song for his considera-tion. There were about thirty of us. He listened to songs through the first chorus, then said either "Pass" or "It's good, but I can't use it." He came to our song and made odd faces. I thought I'd get a "pass." He listened to most of it and asked, "Is the writer here? The vocal is mixed too far back and the snare is too loud." I replied, "Thanks for the feedback." He said, "If you remix it, I'll take the song. Do you have anything else?" We remixed "1000 Years." He took another of our songs and placed both on many TV shows—Nash Bridges, MTV, *etc. I receive a royalty check every quarter for national and international airplay.*

If you don't live near a major songwriting city, plan to visit regularly. Go to events that seem the most lucrative. Barbara Jordan advises:

> *Go to as many highly regarded music industry events as pos-sible, even if it means traveling a long distance every now and then. Meet the panelists who speak on these topics, in addition to networking with everyone who attends the event. I'm always open to listening to new material, and when I speak on a panel, I make it known where and how I can be reached. I warn people that I might not be able to listen right away to the CDs and cassettes they give me, but that I will eventually listen to everything. If I'm interested, I will get back to them. Even if someone says they are not accepting unsolicited material at the moment, you can call them in a few months and ask whether they're open to receiving your material now.*

Tommy Williams agrees:

> *If people don't live [in Nashville], they need to come here on a regular basis. It's all about connections and getting to know peo-ple. In this town, there are people always trying to get time with record label people. I get approached by writers all the time. But time is a precious commodity. You have to slowly gain relation-ships with people. You need someone in town who will be your champion. Sometimes the best way is to come to town and try to get slots on writers' nights.*

Jo Davidson won a songwriting scholarship to UCLA. She went because they had panels with music industry people. Her belief in her songwriting ability gave her the drive to succeed. She went to the panels with a positive attitude.

> *I was determined that they were going to hear me, know me, and love me. I wasn't ready to make a record as an artist at that time. I thought I was, but I wasn't. What I was doing well was writing great songs. I had a pop R & B tune that had won a place in a Billboard contest. As part of the UCLA program, this song was played in a round where a guy came in to do a critique. He didn't believe I wrote that song and signed me to a publishing deal with Warner/Chappell. That's how I met my manager. It kicked everything off for me. Any time that industry people are doing critiques or any situation where you can get even a verse and a chorus in their ears is a good thing. A lot of it amounts to nothing, but sometimes it's amazing.*

When you meet pros, be professional. Use your networking skills wisely. Make a good impression so that they want to hear your material. Take advantage of any chance to get your music heard. Harriet Schock says the Internet offers exposure. She suggests:

> *Sign up for one of a myriad of online services that post songs. There are many sites other than MP3 that will upload your songs for showing to A & R people, publishers, music supervisors, et al., such as Soundartist.com. They are for the songwriter, not just for the artist or singer/songwriter. Sometimes sheer volume of exposure will lead to getting heard by the right person if the material is outstanding enough. You can create your own buzz.*

Singer/songwriter Ginger MacKenzie advises entering songwriting contests. There are loads of them. Often the prizes are cash. MacKenzie finds them fruitful. "I've won twenty awards by entering everything I'd written. It paid for my computer and everything for getting my website going. I still enter contests. Winning one is something you can put in your bio."

GETTING TO THE APPROPRIATE PEOPLE

It's hard to send your material to a publisher, A & R person, film supervisor, or any pro to place songs if they don't know you. That's why networking is critical. Call before you send anything. If you make a good impression, you may get permission to send your material. Barbara Jordan says she doesn't like receiving material from songwriters she doesn't know if they're not referred by someone, but adds:

> *Every now and then I'll get a call from a writer who I don't already know, who presents him/herself very professionally, and who asks me whether I'd be open to hearing some of their new material. This usually results in my saying, "Send the material, and if I like it, I'll get back to you. But you can feel free to follow up by e-mail if you haven't heard from me in over two months."*

Janet Fisher also notices how people approach her:

> *It impresses me very much when I get a letter from someone if they've taken the time to learn about our company and what our policies are. If they show they have invested a bit of time finding out what our company is about before they come tugging on my sleeve, it impresses me enough to give that letter and package a little priority over a letter just asking for my help.*

Do your homework first; the Internet makes it easier. Try every door. Recording artist Fisher says, "We sent demos to music supervisors for film. No film was too small." Many songwriters let indie films use songs for free; a credit may later open doors that pay. Try every avenue. Ed Razzano says you can learn about appropriate publishers through your performing rights organization. He advises, "Join ASCAP, BMI, or SESAC. They have creative staffs as well who can coach you in songwriting." J. W. Johnson agrees:

> *We're here to help writers. But they have to pick up the phone, call us, and be very organized. It's like any other business. If you're organized and present yourself in a positive way, you're going to get a good response. We'll say come on in and let's talk. Ultimately, you have to have the goods. We can really help people that have the goods. If a songwriter doesn't live in a city with an organization, they can still call or e-mail us and send us their material. Many towns have songwriting clubs. There are many things you can do to help yourself.*

"You have to have the goods." Did you get that yet? There's a market for the goods if you have them.

Most people I spoke to said sending press kits isn't necessary. The music is what speaks. What should you send? Ed Razzano says:

> *I love to hear the best demo you can do that you envision as the way the song should be. For some people, that's a piano and vocals, if you want to go for a balladeer like Celine Dion or Diana Ross. As far as tracks for the more current R & B world, you need to produce it as close as you envision it being. For film and TV it would be more of the performer/songwriter, so it would have to be finished.*

Barbara Jordan adds:

> *Most writers send widely varying promo packages along with their music. The packages I open quickest are the simple envelopes that have a CD (or tape) for listening with less than ten songs and a brief cover note explaining who they are and why they're sending me music. I really don't care at all what their photographs look like or how their press reads, and I'd rather not get the big folders with gobs of written information on how great everyone thinks they are. The music is all that matters. If it's something that I either need at the moment or expect I'll have a need for in the future, I'll put this artist on my "imminent call-back" list. I also recommend that artists not put only what they think is their best material on the CD—I almost always find that what I consider to be their strongest material (and most appropriate for my needs) is not what they consider to be their best material.*

Janet Fisher says that the needs for film and TV are specific:

> *What I want is the song and lyric sheets. For film and TV placement, you must be able to let us use your master. Ninety-eight percent of the music is done after the shoot. They call up and want it today. There isn't enough time to put out a call for it. For us, we want to hear exactly how the song sounds. If you send a CD, circle the song that's appropriate for what we're looking for. We're being asked for specific material from the industry. If the industry calls us for something, we put it on our free online newsletter. We make you aware of what our company needs right now on the Web. You can call and ask if we're looking for something.*

Publishers and music supervisors won't have time to search a CD for a song. Choose the one you think is the best for their needs. Indicate it on your CD. If you want to pursue films on your own, Harriet Schock recommends checking out the *Hollywood Reporter*, which comes out once a week and lists films in production. "You can read through them and go through the painstaking process of calling cold, asking who the music supervisor is and trying to get that person to accept a pitch. I would suggest doing this only if you have a song that seems perfect for that film."

If you can't meet anyone, Janet Fisher advises sending a letter or e-mail to publishers and music supervisors saying "_____ is what I do. My song's style is _____. My success has been _____. I would very much like to have a meeting or send you something." She says, "A blanket pitch like that should get you some responses that you can follow up with on a more personal level. Present it professionally." *The Music Publisher Registry* has the names of most publishers, and many have e-mail addresses. *The Film/TV Music Guide* has the same for music supervisors. If you go this route, be very specific when describing your music.

Another option is joining TAXI (www.taxi.com). According to Harriet Schock, "For years, TAXI has been helping people get their songs out there without taking any of the copyright." TAXI has relationships with high-level executives at top record labels, publishers, and others who need songs or recording artists. It offers opportunities to pitch songs for film, TV, artists, and more. It isn't cheap to join, but musicians I spoke to say it's worth it. As a member, you get listings of calls for songs, artists, and other needs and can submit a song to any or all for five dollars per song. This small fee tempers people from indiscriminately submitting to everything. Industry pros listen to all submissions and decide which ones are appropriate. If yours isn't chosen, you'll often get detailed, handwritten feedback from the industry pros who screen your material at TAXI—a good way to improve your skills. TAXI offers a number of resources to its members, including a free yearly convention, with many high-level pros in attendance.

TAXI's founder, Michael Laskow, says:

> *People in the industry have always turned away unsolicited material. During my years as an engineer and producer, I was amazed how much great material couldn't find its way to the desks of people who had the power to sign deals. All I did was cre-*

ate a way for the very best to make those connections. TAXI serves the industry side and the artists and writers very well. It's the classic win/win opportunity.

Jennifer Smith recalls, "We joined TAXI and have gotten a lot of songs in film and television. It's great money, which enabled us to shift gears with how we were doing business and do a bit of marketing and shows that we needed to do but couldn't afford to do before. It gave us more financial freedom psychologically." Do not join TAXI until you have great recordings of great songs. It's only helpful if you have THE GOODS.

COLLABORATING

Work with other songwriters and producers to expand your skills and contacts. You'll meet them at songwriter organizations and events. If you're a good writer, someone will want to write with you. Jo Davidson says:

It's important to cowrite. I write with people for different projects. There's no better way to expand your contacts than to cowrite with another established writer. Then you have twice the power to shop the song. It's good to hook up with writers who have access to their own studios to cut down on the cost of the demo. If you're a good writer and are out there, you'll meet other good writers.

Tommy Williams suggests you keep your options open to new talented people:

A lot of songwriters want to write with the established writers in town. Find cowriters who you really click with. You just never know when that magic will happen. If you keep writing with other writers until you find a good combination of cowriters, you may be the next writer that others want to [collaborate] with. If you love writing, just hang in there and something good will happen.

Michelle Lewis found collaborating a good tool and does it regularly. She advises:

Find a great track writer. I work with track people and producers to collaborate. Start at the bottom and write with everybody. Then, as you work your way up, you realize whom you hit it off with and whom your styles match the best.

GETTING STARTED ON A
SONGWRITING CAREER

This process can seem overwhelming. Songwriters moan, "I just want to write!" That's fine if you don't want to make money. The work you put in now lasts a lifetime. Focus first on making your music commercially great! Until then, nothing else matters. Work with other songwriters; develop a good relationship with your rep at ASCAP, BMI, or SESAC. Ask for honesty when they hear your songs. If they like them, ask for contacts. Stay in the songwriter loop of activities. A songwriting career is a ladder you climb one rung at a time. Watch lots of TV shows and movies to get a feel for the kind of music they use. Barbara Jordan says it's worth it:

> *As a publisher, most of the writers I represent are thrilled to be doing what they love to do and making good money at it, instead of "waiting for the record deal" or living "life after the record deal," wondering in the meantime how they're going to pay their mortgages without getting a nonmusical day job. My writers get to not only write the music they want to write, but also explore the musical genres they wouldn't ordinarily write—and get paid for their experiments!*

• • •

If you're serious about a songwriting career, I highly recommend reading Jason Blume's *6 Steps to Songwriting Success* (see Appendix 2). In his book, this extremely successful songwriter fills in all the gaps I had no room to detail in this chapter.

UTILIZING

Self-Promotion

TOOLS

Myth:

Until I get a deal, there's little
I can do to promote my music.

● ● ●

Artists who want to make money are turning to a DIY (do-it-yourself) approach by marketing their talent as a business for profit. The more you do yourself, the bigger the buzz created, the more money you make, and the better the chance of attracting a satisfying record deal. Recording artist Fisher says, "We decided to do the indie label and reached out to people. Every day we were controlling the day, good or bad." Try doing whatever you can to market your music yourself. As you find more ways to get your music out, you increase your chances of making money. I never said this would be easy! You have to work with whatever you've got and keep looking for more ways to increase your chance for success. In this chapter, I'll give you promotional tools for getting exposure for your music and getting your career rolling. Then put the tools to work with Chapter 19!

PRESSING UP YOUR OWN RECORDING

David Boyd, senior A & R director at Virgin Records UK, says, "If you're independently minded and can do it all, you can put out your music yourself. History is riddled with acts like Sonic Youth." Pressing up your own recording helps attract a record deal. A & R people pay attention to CDs that are put out independently; radio stations only play CDs; it's easier to get a review with a finished product; agents and clubs take a CD more seriously.

A self-pressed CD is an effective tool for marketing your music and making money. Manager Ron Stone believes:

> *In this day and age, I'm not sure that making the record deal is the right way. If you have the innate talent that everyone will want, the digital revolution allows you to make your own record, record it in your computer or in a studio, burn your own CDs, and put it out. Make your own record and start the process in the first go-round without a record company, manager, or attorney. Somebody will find you.*

Fisher says, "We started Rawfish Records and signed ourselves. Then we said, 'We're signed.'" Technology and lower prices makes putting out your own product more feasible. My "Start & Run Your Own Record Label" classes are filled, as people choose to do the DIY route. I recommend reading my book of the same name, *Start & Run Your Own Record Label.*

Think carefully about where potential sales might come from and how far you're prepared to work at it. You won't automatically advance your career or get signed because you release a CD. Wait until you're playing live, getting attention on the Internet, or have another plan for reaching your audience. Some DIY folks create their own inserts and burn CDRs at home; whether this is practical for you depends on how many you need and what your intentions are.

Some artists use a CD just for promotion, to send to radio stations for airplay, publications for reviews, club promoters for bookings, and managers and A & R people to get signed. But the best way to use them is to make money! Every time you sell a CD, someone else learns about your music. A fan may play it for friends, who'll buy it and come to live performances. A purchased copy may reach the ears of industry folks. So each CD that sells offers a chance for it to be promoted—two for the price of one!

Some stores will take your CD on consignment. Don't leave too many with any retailer. It's only worth it if people may ask for it. The more copies stores take, the more that can be returned later. Don't give so many on consignment that you've got to reorder—the first batch may never sell through. When leaving records on consignment, bring an invoice that the store can sign to show they were received. Handle sales as professionally as possible if you want to be taken seriously.

Playing live sells product. When you do a song that goes over well, announce that it's from your CD. Don't feel funny stating that it's for sale. It's expected. When people like an artist, they'll buy their recording. Most clubs don't care if you sell products during a gig. Have a friend on hand to sell it, and bring change. Price your product lower than what it sells for in stores.

If your music would work in clubs where live dance music is played, go to appropriate club DJs to get a buzz going. If a specific club is perfect for your music, find out which DJs are on when and what time they start. Give them an hour to set up and then visit before it gets busy. I always asked DJs to listen to my record and see if it could work for them. If you're friendly and confident, most will at least listen. DJs love good music; the bottom line is the quality of your product. This style of music usually does well with *in-store play*, which means the records that are played in a store. Get friendly with people who work in record stores. Ask them to play your music for customers.

If you do mailings, announce the release in your next flyer or e-mail announcement. Include a list of the stores that carry it or an address where fans can send money to order it (being sure to add in a fee for postage and handling; estimate the cost of a mailing bag and postage and round it off). For mail orders, wait until each individual's check clears before you send the package out. Give out info for ordering at your gigs, as not everyone comes with enough cash in hand to purchase a CD.

MERCHANDISING

Merchandising is a great source of income for musicians. Fans buy T-shirts, hats, stickers, koozies (can holders), etc. I've even seen panties for sale! Once you're touring, think about creating merchandise. Touring artists say it can be their biggest source of income. Cody Braun, a member of touring band Reckless Kelly, says:

We make as much in merch as we make at a gig. We have T-shirts, hats, long-sleeve shirts, koozies, stickers. You can get this stuff relatively cheap and make back 100 percent or more, so it's a good investment. Merchandise is one of these things that a lot of people don't get on until later in the game. By the time they do, somebody's got their finger in the pie. If you get it figured out early, you can make a lot of money.

Should you trademark your name? Attorney Joy R. Butler says, "While registering your band name with the U.S. Patent and Trademark Office will maximize your rights, registration is not required to develop rights in a name. In fact, all you need to do to develop trademark rights is to use the name in a commercial context." If you're thinking of marketing something with the name of your act, consider a trademark or make sure no one else is using your name. Think beyond today if you want to make money tomorrow. Don't wait until after you're successful. Butler advises:

Every band should conduct a trademark search to make sure its chosen name is available. If it doesn't, it risks suffering the fate of the country band Shenandoah, which was sued by three other groups using the same name. Shenandoah lost its recording contract and went through three years of litigation, during which time it was not allowed to perform under its name. Ultimately, Shenandoah bought the right to use its name and got back on track. However, the band lost a lot of its career momentum as a result of the trademark dispute.

Get someone to design a good logo for you. There are many manufacturers that create T-shirts, hats, etc., at a reasonable price, especially online. Get decent-quality shirts. Musicians say they pay about four dollars apiece for T-shirts and sell them for up to fifteen dollars. Artists that are doing well with merch say it's best to set up a merch table at gigs and have a friend or crewmember man it. Hip-hop artist MC Overlord says:

If I could recommend one good promotion, I'd say make things available to fans that they're going to have around that has your name on it. Anything that has your name on it is important. People love T-shirts. They eat them up. T-shirts have saved my behind on the road—I'm paying band members. Merchandising is key.

ESTABLISHING AN INTERNET PRESENCE

The Internet allows us to connect to people. While the big potential for selling music electronically is in the future, the Internet is very effective as a promotional tool. It offers endless possibilities for networking, booking gigs, getting exposure, and, in general, creating a buzz. And, it's beginning to offer opportunities for getting a record deal. The Internet is also a great way to communicate with people around the world in a quick, inexpensive way. Fisher, who got signed to Farmclub.com/ Interscope because of their exposure on the Internet, says, "The Internet is a fantastic place to get info and have a meeting place for people who love your music." Michael Caplan, senior vice president of A & R at Epic Records, says:

> In another few years, the Internet will be everything. Now there are 50,000 records in stores. How do you direct somebody's attention there? Eventually, there will be 50,000 records on the Internet. You still have to figure out how to direct somebody to click on yours and pay for it.

If you're not familiar with the Internet yet, get someone to give you a tour. A great tutorial site is www.webteacher.org. And it's free! According to David Wimble, editor of *The Indie Bible* (see Appendix 2), a directory that lists thousands of websites that are helpful to independent musicians:

> There are an endless number of sites that offer a free service for your band. These resources are varied, but are all worth visiting. Take advantage of as many sites as you can. Some will allow you to have your own page on their site, including sound files and a link to your regular website. Others offer less, but exposure nonetheless. The more places you place information about your band, the more places the search engines will detect its name.

Setting Up a Website

If you're serious about a career in music, get a website. It's a place where people can learn about your music and you as an artist. You can post tour dates, samples of your music, upcoming releases, and other relevant news. A website needn't be fancy but should be well organized and have good content. Pianist David Nevue used the business savvy he developed marketing his own music when he wrote his book *How to Promote Your Music Successfully on the Internet* (see Appendix 2). He advises:

Know your customer. The question to ask yourself is, What are people who like your style of music searching for on the Internet? Figure that out and design a website geared toward that topic. Once you are bringing targeted traffic to this "topical" website, then you can introduce them to your music. The result is a much higher sell-through rate. As a pianist, people who like George Winston's music tend to love mine as well. So I try to target fans of George Winston. Most piano music lovers haven't heard of David Nevue, but they have heard of George Winston or Jim Brickman. I use that to my advantage to attract new listeners. Also, the word "free" has a lot of pull on the Internet. Find a way to use it!

If you want traffic for your site, maintain it well. Update it to give people an incentive to return. David Wimble says, "You can create the biggest buzz in the world, but if it your site looks lame, people will stay for five seconds. Offer visitors additional information, helpful links, contests, chat rooms—anything to make them want to come back or tell a friend about your site." Include relevant info, updated photos and stories from touring, current news, clips of songs, interesting links, and a bulletin board. Cody Braun says the Reckless Kelly site is worth the investment:

We get thousands of hits from all over the world and we've never been out of the U.S. Any link helps if it's relevant to your music. Our website address is at the merch table at gigs. Fans check it twice a day. We have a chat room where people talk about the band. They check our tour schedule and new merchandise. We spend quite a bit of money every month for someone to update it and keep it interesting. It's well worth it. The more times people return, the more likely they'll buy something. That helps pay for the guy who keeps it interesting.

Should you have a full song or just a snippet on your site? A whole song allows people to have it for free. Many musicians say doing so helps to create a fan base and entices listeners to want more. David Wimble reasons, "Give visitors a reason to buy your music. I like the idea of having one song available for visitors. They can listen to it, and if they like it, they may choose to purchase a copy of your CD." Others don't like the idea of giving a whole song away for free. It's your decision.

How do you draw folks to your site? First, list it with search engines. Read the instructions for doing so and choose your keywords carefully. They're critical tools for driving people to your site. Exchange links at music-related sites. Get your name out. The pop rock duo Red to Violet, based in Holland, is a perfect example of how the Internet can promote music. Because of their Web exposure, they're getting airplay on over two hundred radio stations in the U.S., as well as video play on TV, all while never leaving Holland! Member Onno Lakeman says:

> *I do my best to keep our website as up-to-date as possible. It's the center of our Web activities. Whenever there's news about Red to Violet, I mail our webmaster and he adds it ASAP. I come up with new ideas for the site constantly. On the site, there's audio, video, pictures, radio and TV sound bites of Red to Violet, competitions, and links to other music sites. The Web offers many links to more opportunities.*

How can you sell products from your site? Include a mailing address so folks can send a check. There are services that allow you to have a customer use a charge card, taking a percentage for themselves and sometimes charging fees. These companies come and go fast, so spend time researching them when you're ready. As of this printing, one I like is www.ccnow.com. Or work out an arrangement with a site that sells music, such as CD Baby (www.cdbaby.com) or amazon.com.

Most artists say they don't sell much online yet. But Terri Hendrix swears by it:

> *Without the Internet, we couldn't have [sold so much merchandise]. It's crucial—beyond anything I could have imagined. If the business shuts down for a few months I can live off of Internet sales. If you put CDs in stores, you get returns. If you have an online store, you can make more money.*

CREATING AN ELECTRONIC PRESS KIT

Before developing an online presence, create a very good electronic press kit on your site. This is a priceless marketing tool that can include photos, a bio, and quotes from anyone who wrote about you. Provide links to reviews and articles. List upcoming gigs. An updated news section is good. Have samples of your music and options listing where people can buy it. You can have an assortment of photos that can be downloaded on your site, in color, too. Don't just throw stuff together. Make it look attractive. A poorly designed site can turn people off. Brad First, manager/booker of Antone's, in Austin, Texas, says, "If it's a stinko website, that colors our perception of the band. I like to be able to download an MP3. I notice the details."

There are two major advantages to having an electronic press kit. First, it saves you money, which we all love. Reproducing photos, making copies of written material, and buying folders, envelopes, and stamps all cost a chunk of change. If your material is on your site, many people will take your photo and other info from it. A thousand people can get your press kit and it doesn't cost a dime extra.

The second advantage is that many industry pros would prefer going to an artist's site for photos, the bio, and other info, to getting a package. Brad First says, "I deal more electronically. There's more room for promo packages. We throw tons of stuff away because we have no room to keep it if we haven't heard from the band or booked them in six months." Many journalists say they'd rather get material electronically. It's easier to store than paper materials, and they can check it out themselves at their convenience. It allows for greater variety of material, since a website can hold more than a folder. Also, people like instant gratification: if someone is interested in you, he can go right to your site and not wait for a package in the mail.

Once you have a nice presentation on your site, work it! It does you no good if no one sees it.

PROMOTING ELECTRONICALLY

There are thousands of online publications with the potential to review your music, and radio stations that might play it. Research to find the best ones—though any exposure is good. David Wimble's book is a good starting place, as it contains thousands of sites. Musicians say getting reviewed doesn't necessarily translate into sales, but it gets your name out. Include reviews in your press kit and on a quote sheet. Inquire first to make sure your music is appropriate for review before submitting it. Use reviews at smaller sites to get to bigger ones. In order to get online radio play, contact DJs of shows that you feel are appropriate for your music. Develop relationships using a personal approach. Only send music if there's enthusiasm. If your music is good, you'll get support online. Onno Lakeman says:

The indie music scene is doing well. It takes time and effort to get the name of the band known. But there are a lot of promotional opportunities out there for every indie musician. You can do it yourself if you recognize an opportunity when you see one. After having filled in the contact info on many music sites, it's easier for others to find us, too. All contacts are made through the Web. At times I make telephone calls, but most of the time promotion is done by e-mail. In the beginning, I went overboard investigating all the music possibilities on the Web, often for fourteen hours a day. Now I promote six days a week—from early morning to noon. Red to Violet is getting more and more known as a new colorful name in rock 'n' roll. Will this result in large CD sales? High radio airplay and TV broadcasts in any area create a demand sooner or later.

Many sites will make your music available to listeners. Find them by surfing and asking other musicians. Some people swear by MP3.com, though in general I've gotten mixed reactions when mentioning it to various artists and others in the music business. Singer/songwriter Ginger MacKenzie says, "I went number one worldwide last year on MP3.com. My manager developed a good relationship with them and the head liked my song, so he promoted it. Once it's on the chart they keep loading it. My website has had over 300,000 hits." But Michael Caplan says, "Many bands come to me and say they got 5,000 hits on MP3.com for free. But they only sell two CDs." Sales impress, not hits! David Nevue finds MP3.com valuable:

> *For me personally, MP3.com has been an incredible networking tool. I've licensed music for a documentary, signed a record deal (in Korea), been offered a studio gig, and been approached by a sheet-music publisher—all from contacts made through MP3.com. Aside from that, I've created an MP3.com "pianist" community, and it's been a great place to get advice and bounce ideas off of others in my genre. Collectively, a community of twenty like-minded musicians has a lot more experience to draw on than a musician trying to do it all on their own.*

MP3.com put Fisher over the top. The buzz had started prior to their initial inclusion on the site, but when their page was featured, the buzz became strong enough to enable them to get a record deal. The visuals on their page had a strong influence. Fisher emphasizes the importance of your image on MP3.com:

> *The first thing anyone sees on your artist page is the picture. This is where so many artists totally blow it. A lame or copycat image of you instantly says, "I'm not ready." Capitalize on the strong points. If you have a band that isn't that good-looking, don't worry about it. Come up with fantastic artwork. The public won't really care and labels will think you have a realistic view of yourself.*

E-COMMUNICATING WITH YOUR MUSIC COMMUNITY

Use the Internet for communication that has no equivalent in the real world! It doesn't cost anything to communicate with anyone in any part of the world. E-mail everyone with one click, at no cost. Recording artist Pat Green says:

> *The website is our biggest tool as far as people finding out how to come to our shows. You want to dump some money somewhere—there it is. I used to send out up to 7,000 cards to fans with our monthly tour dates, every month for three years. The mailing list was what started it all. The website makes it so much easier today to get a consistent fan base—send them an e-mail.*

Create an electronic mailing list. Send regular newsletters or updates. Answer e-mails. Most people don't do hard-copy mailings anymore. You can get the e-mail addresses of most writers and even A & R people through The *A & R Registry* (see Appendix 2). Organize your fans into different groups. Manager Michael Norton says:

> *We don't use one master list for e-mails. If [we did], they'd get an e-mail from us three times a week. Then it's nothing special. People can get too many e-mails and delete them before reading them after a while. I'm keen on having region-specific e-mail lists. That way, people get an occasional e-mail from us about a special CD we put out or a gig in their market. We play three or four times a week, and [sending a message to everyone prior to each show would generate] too much e-mail.*

UTILIZING SELF-PROMOTION TOOLS

145

Create a virtual street team. Get fans involved on the Internet on your behalf. Go to chat rooms to find similar acts and make friends. Include your site address on everything you give out. Invite people at your gigs to visit. Fisher says, "We created relationships online and kept them tight. When we need help, we get it. We've created a little family." Ask fans to spread the word about you online. IF you've got the goods and treat fans right, they will. Some may help with your site, create a fan site, and tell friends in other cities when you're gigging. Onno Lakeman says:

> As I am currently based in Holland, I've found my contacts in the U.S. through the Web. Contacting people this way works. The tone of the e-mail is important—be enthusiastic but not pushy. I've found out that an e-mail is almost like a natural contact of voice to voice. I stay in contact by sending a monthly newsletter about Red to Violet and informing people in between newsletters when something special comes up. This interaction adds a personal touch and it's fun. I deal with humans and they deal with a human being, too.

GETTING TO RECORD LABELS ELECTRONICALLY

Some A & R people use the Internet to check out new artists. If one hears about you, he may see if you're on MP3.com or if you have a website. You're more likely to hear from A & R people if your site has good press material and sound samples. According to Michael Caplan, at Epic Records, "When I talk to a band who calls me, the first thing I'll ask is if they have a website. I also have people send me MP3s or video clips." Unless the buzz is so great that they have no choice, most A & R people won't call you if they want more. But they may check you out online. Of course, this varies with music genres and A & R people.

The Internet makes it easy for A & R people to learn more about you and your music without dealing with you. No offense, but it's less of a hassle to go to your site or listen to your music without your even knowing it. Brian Long, senior director of A & R at MCA Records, loves to check out new artists online. He says:

> The Internet is an extremely useful tool from an A & R perspective. When I hear about a band, I try to find their URL. I like to check out what they're like because I can see them. I can usually

stream audio, see where they're playing, and get a vibe on what their background is from their bio.

A & R people watch which acts stand out in the sea of music being promoted electronically. Some A & R people will go to your site if you e-mail them. But you better have your material in excellent order before seeking them out. I asked Brian Long whether he would go to the site of an act that sent him an e-mail with a URL attached. He answered, "I do it all the time." Michael Caplan adds, "I'll be online and someone will instant-message me saying 'Click my site.' I will."

MARKETING REGIONALLY

The best opportunities for networking, attending educational events, getting critiqued by pros, and pitching songs are in Los Angeles, New York, and Nashville. At the same time, probably the worst opportunities for getting paid performances and publicity and developing a fan base are in Los Angeles, New York, and Nashville. There's a trade-off for everything. Living in New York, I thought of playing out as either bringing in your own fans or playing to an empty room. Even with tremendous talent, it's hard to initially get to all the folks who might love you. Fisher adds, "L.A. is the worst place to be a musician. You have to pay to play. Clubs aren't friendly to musicians. We kept getting asked who our following was and where our music would fit in." There's a glut of talented musicians in these cities because so many come to take advantage of the networking opportunities. It's harder to surface as an artist and get the attention available in other places.

Musicians from smaller towns ask if they should move to one of the top-three music cities. It's good to visit when there's a pitch session or seminar that can help you. But I believe that it's easier to break an act that has the goods in smaller markets. I talked with writers, club owners, radio stations, college people, etc. in smaller markets, and the attitude was more open, friendly, and receptive to new music. These people are part of the music business, too. They may not have as much clout as people in big cities, but they can help you develop your career. When you can generate press in ten papers, get played on local and college radio stations, perform to audiences who join your fan base, and sell lots of merchandise, you can roll from there.

I think that working your career outside of the big three is better than going to event after event in Los Angeles, New York, or Nashville and the rest of the time bitching that you aren't getting one of those competitive slots for press, can't play more than twice a month, and don't get a response from radio and industry people, whose eyes you hear rolling when you call. In New York, musicians know that if they play more than twice a month they burn out their fans. I'm told that Los Angeles and Nashville are no better. Industry people are more jaded in these places because of so many musicians kissing up for attention. So don't pack your bags yet!

Wherever you live, start there. Be the star of your town! Milk what you can out of being a hometown talent. Then polish your balls and try the next town. Find ways to visit a music city to attend events that benefit you. IF you're THAT good, you'll have a better shot at creating a bigger buzz where you are than you would being part of the pack trying to get attention in bigger places. Being in New York, Los Angeles, or Nashville can bruise your confidence. Build it first where people are more willing to appreciate your music.

Outside the Big Three: Austin, Texas

I heard a lot about Austin, Texas, and went there to see why so many musicians swear by it as "the live music capital of the world." It's an amazing city. Whether young or old, most people I met were aware of the city's talented musicians and took pride in supporting them—because they love music! What a novel idea for this New Yorker. The state of Texas supports its musicians and I applaud them for it. Other states could learn from the Texas Music Office; its website (www.governor.state.tx.us/music) offers loads of resources for musicians, as well as listings of radio stations, newspapers, and much more throughout the state. According to its director, Casey J. Monahan:

> Our model expands on the traditional grants-to-artist method by serving as a kind of chamber of commerce to people in the music industry. We make more than 14,000 referrals every year. We try to help the bands help themselves.

Austin supports music. Wendy Morgan is director of music marketing for the Austin Convention and Visitors Bureau and knows the musicians. She advises them and places them into corporate and other well-paying gigs. Rock artist George Devore says, "I don't fit formulas that record companies have. Record labels don't know what to do with me— whether to send me to Los Angeles, Nashville, or New York. So I'm in

Austin, where I can be what I want to be." IF you've got the goods, the opportunities for live play are endless. As a New Yorker, I couldn't believe that in Austin a musician can play out every night, every week. Brad First says:

> It's the attitude of the whole city. There's an opportunity of lots and lots of places to play. If you are willing to book yourself into a lot of the tiny cubbyholes and not expect much money, you can cultivate your stage show and a following. You'll eventually get to the point of playing the "A" rooms in town—those that are dedicated to bands that do original music and have an in-house production that's high quality. There's always been a strong music vibe in Austin and in Texas. Lots of good music has, does, and will continue to come out of Houston, Dallas, Austin, and San Antonio.

I admit that Austin doesn't have the networking, educational, and pitching opportunities of the big three. But they have SXSW, one of the best music conferences, which people attend from all over the world. Jazz artist Pamela Hart says, "Austin has been the best nurturing ground I could have found. There are great musicians here that are willing to share. It's sort of a small town with access to everything." Finding a supportive community is helpful. John T. Kunz, owner of Waterloo Records, says, "We've got a very supportive triad of what it takes—good radio and press for local music, good venues, and good retail for supporting local music." Okay, I admit I'm in awe of Austin. It's so refreshing to find that kind of supportive vibe for music in a city.

19

TAKING YOUR
Music to the
NEXT LEVEL

Myth:

Until I get a deal, there's little I can
do to promote my music.

• • •

Are you still skeptical about why you should do all the work? Too many poor artists have label deals. The info below can enable you to create something that a record label can build on. Booking agent Tom Baggott says:

> *If you don't have a top-twenty hit, a label cannot "instamatic" you a fan base. You need to develop one by touring and playing, fan by fan, mile by mile. Develop your fan base before the deal so fans will buy your record. If there's no fan base to buy it and the label's promotion doesn't work, you won't go anywhere. I consider grassroots development to be the key to the career. Labels*

in general are looking for artists who have something going on for themselves. They'd rather build on a fan base.

Get proactive! This chapter includes specific things you can do to get exposure for your music and make money—ammunition and guidance for taking control of your career to attract a good record deal. I interviewed musicians who've done it. Some have label deals. Some are on their way to one. Others are happy on their own. I'm including large chunks of what they said to give you a feel for how various artists got their careers going. Each has a career, record deal or not. Learn from their experiences and get inspired to do what's necessary for your own career! Hip-hop artist MC Overlord says:

> *Developing my career made me more marketable and mature about what to expect. Expectations get distorted when you don't have experience. Too often artists lose sight of the real focus—the art—in search of the record deal. Keep it simple and enjoy the journey.*

PREPARING TO TOUR

Broken record time: If you want to tour, you have to get VERY GOOD. Practice by doing as many gigs as possible. Touring artists say you can't worry about money at the beginning. If you can't develop a following where you live, ask why. If you're good, people will eventually come see you. Or, try another town. Cities like New York and Los Angeles are discouraging. Rock artist George Devore says:

> *Play anywhere, anyhow, anytime, anyplace. The only way to get good is to play a lot. I moved to Austin with two hundred dollars and half a credit card. I played my ass off every night I could, anywhere I could. I played for whatever money—it didn't matter. People were coming out to see me. It built from there. I started my label and put my own records out. I've been earning my living from my music for three years.*

Devore would love a record deal but only a good one. He tours constantly, sells tons of merchandise, and did an endorsement for Miller Light. He got this far working his butt off—and being good. Jazz singer Pamela Hart says, "I volunteered for gigs every chance I got—mostly political receptions and events at universities—entertainment for their parties. I did weddings. When I started getting recognition, I began charging for private events." Be prepared to sacrifice if you want to make money as a musician. Cody Braun, member of roots/rock band Reckless Kelly, says they earned their success:

> We played any gig we could get, any time—for tips or nothing. We played seven to eight gigs a week. Then we quit our jobs and focused on music. We all lived together—had two cars between the five of us. We did whatever we could do to make it through, month to month. It got the band together and brought the sound around. It's the best thing you can do to get better. We lucked out when a friend recommended us to a good local agent. He's been working with us for over four years. We were willing to go on the road. We'd go out for a month playing everywhere we could. The first year he booked us, we played over 250 shows on the road. It was insane. We barely made enough to pay our bills and traveled in a Suburban. It got easier when we got a van.

Braun says that because many artists tour only on weekends, Reckless Kelly was more marketable to an agent. They're willing to go as far as and for as long as necessary to perform. He smiled as he explained how much it makes a difference for them to have more comfortable transportation and not sleep together, now that they're earning more money. For them, that's a level of success. While they would like a label deal and have received offers, they haven't accepted one yet. It has to be the right one.

Reckless Kelly is a great example of how balls take you far. If you don't consider this balls, tour with five guys in a small vehicle for months and play for peanuts. It's a tough existence. You can do it only when you believe in your music.

Schrodinger's Cat sings in harmony, dances, and does their organic pop music accompanied only by the sounds and rhythms created by pounding their chests, stomping on acoustic boxes, and making vocal effects. Are you surprised they don't fit record label molds? Member Lester Chiu says, "We created a new style so people don't know what to do with us. We have to tell them." They're showing the industry by making a fortune touring (including two tours in Japan), selling CDs and merchandise, and doing corporate gigs. They got their start jamming in college; as crowds grew, they convinced skeptical club owners to give them a slot. Their attention to business took them far. Chiu advises:

To make it in this industry, you have to have your business down. If you don't have your business down, you're dead at the gate. Make sure you know where your revenue streams are and how you can generate more revenue, who your market is, who will be your loyal fans. Know how to market yourself.

Sometimes you have to pare down in order to tour. Some artists say that all money made on the road goes to their musicians. It's cheaper to feed and maintain one or two people than a band, so singers cut their band. Singer/songwriter Nina Mankin says:

I started writing with another writer/performer and we really liked singing together. We started playing each other's songs and this turned into a duo. It was always way too expensive for me to tour with any band I'd had, but the duo was easy. I never lose money, which is more than I can say about playing with a band.

BOOKING GIGS

Buy *The Musician's Atlas* (see Appendix 2). It lists resources for tour-ing—radio stations, clubs, local publications, college radio and booking offices, music conferences, and much more   broken down by city. It's the best place to begin your touring plan.

Breaking out of your hometown is doable. I interviewed enough artists to believe that. Warning: You may not make money at first (or second or third). Folk singer Terri Hendrix says, "When you go to a marketplace the first time, you're lucky to break even. But you have to go back—that's when you make money." George Devore says, "I lose money on the road but you have to do it. It's getting better and will continue to get better. I put on a show that's worth the money they paid, so I believe they'll be back." Word spreads if you don't quit. Tom Baggott advises:

Don't have delusions about making serious money. At the ini-tial stage of artist development, you have to build a foundation. It doesn't necessarily mean losing money, but it always means spend-ing it. Look on a map and draw an imaginary circle within a three-hundred-mile radius all around you. Focus on all the major, secondary, and tertiary markets in that circumference. Wherever you go, you have to go back. Give every venue or market a few shots. No matter how bad the show was, you have to go back. Don't stretch yourself out too far. Artists have to pinch pennies and work their butts off to develop a regional fan base. If an artist has a strong demo, an understanding of their market, and persistence in attempting to contact a talent buyer or promoter, is polite, follows up on phone calls, and accepts a cheap opening gig, he can start to establish a relationship with that venue/talent buyer. That gig can lead to opening up for a larger band and essentially beginning to develop an audience.

Another example of balls is MC Overlord, who began by sitting in with pop rock bands. When he gained an audience of his own, those clubs invited him to perform. He does hip-hop but found a way in through rock clubs! Friends helped him press up a CD, and he says, "I was very conscious about promoting myself—appearing live whenever I had the opportunity. People invited me to open for them." He put together a live band, which set him apart from many hip-hop acts. He copied the tour itinerary contacts of a friend in a touring band. Then he called them. He recalls:

> *I let each contact know I'd opened up for that artist. That's how I got on the road in other states. They didn't book me for much. But they loved it and brought us back. Most clubs had a built-in audience. It was mostly rock clubs. I didn't care. If they had a stage and P.A., I said, "Let's go do this." They were so used to the same music and loved it. I was rapping to a band. We were something out of the norm. I played with talented people and knew I was one, too. I gave them a good show and used my resources to get seen and not fall victim to being stereotyped. When a lot of other rap artists in this town couldn't get into the rock-only clubs, I made my way in.*

Singer/songwriter Sara Hickman recommends doing what she did when she was just beginning. She got into any venue she wanted. "I figure out my favorite place to play in a town and figure out how to play in it, even if it's opening for another act. Find a place. Go talk to the owner/manager and figure out a way to perform in that club." Hickman did this many times. Persistence pays off! Call talent buyers and send packages. Every club is different; some want the material electronically. Give them what they want, if possible. Brad First, promoter/booker at Antone's, says:

I want a demo, bio, and some clippings, and let me know you've been playing somewhere else, with contacts I can call to ask. Follow-up is always good. I don't mind a weekly call, as long as the band knows it might be as long as six to eight weeks before I get them a show. They need perseverance and patience. If they send a package, it will probably take three months to get booked.

Be patient! Approach talent buyers months before you plan to tour. Being polite and professional begins relationships. Tom Baggott says, "Deals come and go, but relationships are what will keep you working. Be nice to people, be honest." Amen, Tom! It gets you far in this biz. Take risks if you want to succeed. Touring musician Lucky was a local talent in New Jersey and wanted to break out of that scene. He cleverly created a facade by having balls in how he presented himself:

I started touring in upstate New York and into Canada. First, I signed up for mailing lists for other bands. When I got mailings, I'd call those clubs and try to book myself. I didn't have a following and started as an opening act. I passed myself off on a higher level than I was. I had a lot of press from local places where I lived. I always worded my interviews in ways that looked a little more like national press. I acted like a big shot and it worked. I got articles written the way I wanted them to appear. That got me a good press kit to book myself into clubs in areas I hadn't toured.

Create a company, however informal it is. Use it when you book. Call as a rep from your company. Tom Baggott says, "I don't take artists who represent themselves that seriously. They can form a company and say they're representing that company. That's not lying. It's creating another organization to represent the business of the band." It gives you a higher level of professionalism. Be resourceful. Once you've gotten experience, press, and confidence, try to get guarantees (a minimum amount that you'll be paid) from the venues. Singer/songwriter Lezlee says, "I've learned that when venues have to pay a guarantee, they generally spend money on promotion, which leads to larger audiences."

I asked Lucky for advice on booking a tour:

Here's how to do a little mini tour. I researched radio stations throughout the country. Do it on the Internet. I targeted a geographic area and four radio stations that played my kind of music. I made up a package and got it to them. I kept calling them as my representative. I got them to listen to my record and told them I was on tour and would be coming by their way. I asked if they'd interview me and recommend some of the better clubs in town. They gave me what I wanted, with contacts, and then set up interviews. I set up a tour before I had a tour, but then all the pieces came together. While I was there I'd research what was an hour further.

"I think, therefore I am." Descartes was right—when you act the role you want, you can become it. Lucky did it well. By sounding like he was a somebody, radio stations took him seriously enough to interview him and give him contacts to clubs. He told clubs they'd been recommended by the radio station where he was going to get interviewed for his tour. Clubs booked him. So Lucky got his tour by approaching people like he already had one. You're all somebody, so act like it. Recording artist Shawn Mullins adds:

I went through struggles of figuring out what not to do, but eventually I'd call as another person—use another name and call radio stations representing me as a company. I'd tell them about the show that was in town and ask them if they would be interested. You start by sending the CD; they never listen to it. You have to call back a billion times.

Sometimes when an act is on tour they use local artists to open for them. *Pollstar* (see Appendix 2) lists most significant tours. Check out their website to see if any appropriate acts are coming to your region. Contact everyone involved in the tour to convince them to let you open for the act in that leg of their tour. Manager Michael Norton relates:

Even though it's hard to get onto big tours, the first step is finding out about them. I used to think that once it's in Pollstar *the tour is in place. But often, the support act is not sorted out until three to four weeks before. Sometimes they're scrambling for an opening act if they can't get their choice. I approach the manager, label, promoter, and agent of the act that's touring, all at one time. It's a matter of persistence.*

Manager Lois Chisolm adds:

If you hear an act is coming to town in advance, find out who the promoter or manager is and try to get yourself on as support. I went to a concert at Six Flags and there were several unknown artists performing first. They weren't announced or on the posters, but they were there. Find out who is lining up entertainment. Call them. Beg. Stand in front of their doors and do whatever you have to do to get them to listen to your CD. Tell them that you're worth a listen. You have to show them you're different.

If you have the goods, you might get the gig. After a talent agent saw rock band 50 Mission Crush perform, they pursued him, resulting in their opening for Sugar Ray at Sea World in San Antonio. Buoyed by the response, they made cold calls and now perform at highly attended events, including an appearance at the qualifying rounds of the Indy 500, in the footsteps of Smashmouth, and at a state fair opening for Lifehouse. They built up a good press kit through regional touring and worked it. I know musicians who opened for big names by being persistent. Call. Be professional, confident, and enthusiastic. Don't make money a big issue at first. If you have lots of stuff to sell and do a great show, you'll go home smiling.

SUPPORTING YOUR TOUR

If you want a successful tour, support it. Ask the promoter for suggestions. I already spoke of tour support using publicity. Here I want to elaborate on how to have the best chance for a successful tour.

Do grassroots development in the markets you're playing. This means contacting the press, along with college and commercial radio stations that support your format, and doing whatever else you can do. Tom Baggott tells his clients, "I can book you anywhere you belong but cannot put asses in seats." Put asses in seats by promoting the tour well! Shawn Mullins says grassroots promotion works:

> *It's funny, because major labels are now working indie style all the time now by looking at the independents. They use street teams and the kind of promotion that's more organic: word of mouth. The urban guys have been doing that for years with their independent records.*

Many artists make fliers and posters. They give them to the clubs and, if possible, use street teams (see page 159) to get them out. This kind of promotion brings people down to the shows.

Contact as many radio and TV stations as you can. Radio stations in smaller cities will play your CD if they like it. *The Musician's Atlas* lists loads of stations that play indie music. Tom Baggott suggests, "Have a page of snippets from the press with the supporting clips attached, so people don't have to wade through everything." The more places you contact, the more chance you have of getting good exposure. That's how Schrodinger's Cat can get 350 people at a gig in a town where they've never been. Lester Chiu says:

> *We have our own label, Lodge Music. So we call as Lodge Music and say we have a group coming to town and would like to send a press kit. We tell them about interviews on stations with similar formats. We research what the best markets for those things are and hit the TV and radio stations, find all the papers in town, send press releases, and really work it. We go to commercial and NPR stations.*

Lucky recommends, "Start small and pick an area. Once you get local radio stations to commit, call local newspapers and say you're coming to town. Speaking as your representative, ask to set up an interview with the leader of the band. I always get nice press before the gig in the entertainment section." As your rep, call local papers and say something like, "XXX will be in town for her tour on May 1st. Would you like me to arrange for you to interview her before she arrives?" Let them think you're offering them something good instead of asking for press like it's a favor. The greater the facade you create, the more they'll want you.

Push to get press; it's ammo for gigs. If the press doesn't respond at first, keep at them when you return, with a friendly attitude. Don't let annoyance interfere with developing a good relationship. If you keep asking and have THE GOODS, they'll come around. Maintain relationships with everyone you can at radio and the press. Cody Braun says:

> *We get back to places as much as possible. If you find radio stations that play your songs, keep in touch with them. If you're in their town, go by the station. At this level, there are stations that will play your stuff. We sent ours to a lot of AAA and college stations. Whenever we went on tour, we'd try to stop into every radio station that was playing our stuff and meet the people who are into it. Radio, even on smaller levels, is so helpful. It's tough to*

do business and play music. But we're doing everything we possibly can to keep our band going.

Nina Mankin recommends connecting with local songwriter organizations in town. Ask if they'll announce that you're coming to town, at least via e-mail. Post your gigs online on every site possible. My website (www.daylle.com) has links to sites related to touring; lots of them will list your tour.

CREATING A STREET TEAM

Create street teams where you play. If you have no fans, develop some! When you perform, ask for volunteers to be part of your team. Put the call on your website. Get people in each market. Offer a few free tickets in exchange for handing out fliers, putting up posters, and contacting local radio stations, college papers, and other places that might promote your event. When you make fans feel like they're part of your crusade, they'll work their asses off for you. THANK THEM! Make them feel important—they are! Pop singer/songwriter Ginger MacKenzie has gathered fans on the Internet to spread the word about her music across the globe:

> *I hear from people from all over the world. I have a global street team. I sent fans in different cities five CDs each to pass to their friends in exchange for putting up posters or putting out cards in shops—a little buzz thing. I noticed that whenever I do that, I get orders from wherever it is. I can see where the orders come from.*

Hip-hop artist Nook puts street teams to good use. He explains, "All the guys I work with for the label put together a street team. Each one has quotas. I help them with their careers in exchange for helping me." Nook has weekly business meetings and takes them seriously. When Jerry Jeff Walker started his own label, he went out with his guitar and played. No one had created a mailing list while he was signed, so he built a fan club and sent out newsletters three to four times a year, announcing his dates and, eventually, new releases. Jerry Jeff developed a great rapport with his fans. His wife, Susan Walker, says:

> *I made Jerry Jeff pay attention to his fans—meet them, shake their hands, and sign autographs. He knows who his fans are, and that's been really important. When I want to go into a*

market, I contact fans who live there and ask them to find us a place to play. And they do. I have 50,000 people who worked for me at no charge. I call what we did the Mao Tse-tung theory of the music business—we were going to get the little people and cause a revolution. We cater to our fans.

Shawn Mullins went a step further:

I built a family all over the country—a road family—with places to stay. I traveled around for eight to ten years, and there were spots all over the country with an extended family. It just happened through playing enough. People would put me up and we'd become friends. I like going out after a club and talking and hanging out with people. It's difficult now, because once you have some popularity, the dynamic that occurs is pretty weird. I still want to be laid back and they want an autograph. It wasn't like that in those years. I miss that.

SEEKING OUT ALTERNATIVE VENUES

There are many alternative venues. Keep your eyes open or create your own venue. Pamela Hart says, "When I bring in national artists for Women in Jazz, I put myself as the opening act. I opened for Nancy Wilson last June. People were able to see I was ready, and I got a lot of respect." When Nook was seventeen, he saw a lack of opportunity for urban artists in Austin. Instead of just complaining, as many do, he worked with the city to coordinate the Jump on It summer concert series. Through this venue he got exposure and made contacts that led to radio play, gigs, and CD sales in other states. Nook began by playing everywhere he could, often for free. By doing so, word got out that he was good. Now he gets paid. Nook says:

I play it all, from churches to schools to nightclubs to event centers to you name it. We always ask for radio promotion and flyers. That's important, too, for an artist coming up. If you do a show and the promoter is putting out 10,000 flyers with your name on it, that's better than getting $100 to perform.

There are opportunities to perform in schools. It can be good exposure, especially if you can get publicity from it. Organizations offer opportunities, too. Lois Chisolm advises:

Go to a school. Talk to the kids about being an artist and throw your rap into it. Get exposure by any means necessary! Go to volunteer organizations that deal with kids, like boys' and girls' clubs. Organizations look for something the kids can do. If you figure out a way to tie your music into something that's interesting to kids, you get exposure, too. If it's a nonprofit, you may get funding. When it comes to getting exposure, you've got to think outside the box. People are always thinking of clubs, but everyone else is going there. Why not go to other places?

Chisolm says cruise ships offer good money for people doing jazz, blues, pop, and standards. She recommends going to European lines, such as Hapag-Lloyd, Seetours, and Reederei. Find ships online and call the entertainment directors. The gigs average three to twelve weeks. Jeri Goldstein, author of *How to Be Your Own Booking Agent* (see Appendix 2), advises:

Look at offbeat performance venues, like shopping malls and grand openings for local businesses in your community. Ask yourself, "Who are you?" "Who is your audience?" "What are you focusing on in your career track?" Many artists are not what record labels look for, but more have the potential for a bigger, better career outside of that mainstream. For artists with a real concern for a full-time career as opposed to a three- to five-year life span in the industry, it's important that they really focus on how they really want to live their lives, because there's money out there.

Goldstein advises finding a niche market that allows you a unique, non-competitive avenue. She says there are many conferences out there for a variety of professions and interests. "I recommend that artists think about things they really care about, affiliations that they have, and interests in their life or careers. Those things pay money. Narrow your focus to expand your audience." Goldstein used an example of a nurse who got gigs at nursing conferences. Conferences usually have decent budgets for entertainment. If you get to know meeting planners and find a way that you or your music might tie into an event, you might find your niche in a lucrative career. Then you can try getting club dates while you're at the conference. If you tie into organizations, there may be alternative outlets for selling your CDs.

Fairs and Festivals

There are thousands of fairs and festivals across the country. Some pay well, but all offer opportunities to perform in front of large crowds and sell CDs and other merchandise. Playing these events attracts new fans, who otherwise wouldn't know you, and gets you to cities with clubs and colleges you can contact for future bookings. People from that region may come to see you at other venues. Playing in festivals gets you exposure through their advertising. According to Jennifer Smith, of rootsy pop/rock band Naked Blue:

> We started doing city-sponsored events, festivals, and anywhere else where there would be a few hundred or few thousand people who had never seen us play. We'd beat the club circuit to death and got twenty to a hundred people each time. But outdoor events are a great way to have a built-in audience and sell merchandise and CDs. The money can be really good or just enough. We've sold as many as one thousand CDs at an event. It's much more financially feasible than at clubs, if your music's appropriate. They tend to be family oriented. Playing in these events has helped build audiences in areas where we're unknown. Then we go back later and book club dates.

How do you begin? Choose a region and research what events are planned for a specific weekend. Many are listed at Festival Network's website (www.festivalnet.com); though it charges to access the information, musicians say it's a highly detailed source. Search other sites as well. Jennifer Smith says the Web is her biggest resource. And every city paper publishes an events calendar. She advises, "If you're just starting out, go to the three closest cities and widen in a concentric circle. Just in the Baltimore/Washington area, there's probably about five hundred events every summer." Check to see which events are going on when so you can book for the following year. Some have deadlines for applying, so get an application as soon as you can. Once you begin doing festivals, you'll meet other acts and can learn from them.

A "one-sheet" is helpful for booking festivals. This is a synopsis of your press kit on one sheet of paper. It should open with a description of your music and what makes you special. Festivals may use your opening paragraph to promote the show, so make it shine! Include a list of recent gigs, press quotes, contact information anything that highlights your act. Think of it as a press kit condensed onto one page. Send it with a photo and a CD or video. Your cover letter should explain which event you're sending the package for.

Festivals are a great place to give out the postcards I mentioned in Chapter 1, as people might order your stuff later or visit your site. Terri Hendrix says, "The more festivals you play, the more you'll get hired. We played the Newport Folk Festival; it broke us on the East Coast. Some festivals are radio sponsored, so you get promotion."

Bookstores

Bookstores are becoming great alternative venues. I've seen a surprisingly wide range of music in them. They bring musicians in to attract people who'll buy spend money. Most stores will sell your records and let you sell merchandise on your own, which can be lucrative if you put on a terrific show. Tom Walker, of power acoustic band Friday's Child, recalls how they were doing club touring, when a friend who was working at Borders asked if they'd do an in-store appearance:

> He said he'd pay us a little money and sell our CDs. So we set up a facade. I believe you should set up a stage wherever you are. We sold seventy-five units in an hour. Then we had a listening post in the store, which normally costs money. We got referred into another store and they referred us to another. Everywhere we went, we blew units out of the store. Café and store sales spike when we play. We get upwards of two to three hundred people to see us. We play in stores up and down the East Coast and in the Midwest. We make from $200 for the whole band to $100 a man. But there's also CD sales. We sell hats and T-shirts and keep that money. Otherwise, we couldn't afford to do it. Even at roughly four bucks a unit to make, they sell at fifteen dollars. People love them.

Walker says they get gigs out of town by playing Borders. They invite club promoters to see them and work the radio stations for airplay. Walker doesn't call it playing a bookstore. He says, "When we do Borders, we market it as a CD signing and in-store performance." They set up their own stage and P.A. system and use the appearance as a form of showcase so others can see them perform to an enthusiastic crowd. I couldn't imagine how they could play their instruments in a bookstore, as they have a particularly energetic performance style. Walker explains:

To play in Borders, you don't have to play loud to hit hard. People turn the amps up. We use stick bundles instead of sticks. Dave [the drummer] can reel into his drums. People make a mistake with unplugged. They tap everything so the stuff that's supposed to have balls doesn't. We use lighter equipment—a tiny drum set. Rick [the bass player] and I turn our amps almost off and then really lay into it. It sounds like the radio. It punches but doesn't knock the windows out.

If you want to play a bookstore, contact the community relations coordinator (CRC). Call the store for a name. Be prepared to get the person psyched when you speak. Start with local stores so your friends can come. It's free admission, so people show up. Ask for a letter from the CRC afterward. Use that person as a reference to get into other stores. Be prepared to kick ass in the store. It's the sort of gig that shoppers will gravitate to if you attract them. Pass around your mailing list and push anything you can sell. Bookstores are an opportunity to reach new audiences. If you win them over, your fan base increases. Plus, in a bookstore, you never know who might see you and offer another opportunity. Industry folks shop in bookstores, too!

Frat Parties

Fraternity parties are great venues. The budget for entertainment often comes through the school, so there's money. You need to supply good music to party to, and you may have to do a few covers to get the students started. Attendees are there to have fun and that's what you need to give them. Pat Green got well known through this route and says, "We played mostly colleges. A lot of students recommended us. We'd try and get into frats. We'd play a frat three or four times and then get into a bar and all the frat kids would show up. And then it would get popular to the non frats." Tom Walker adds:

If you get into a nationwide fraternity, you can get more gigs. If you do a regular college gig, you've got a 50 percent shot at getting an audience if they don't promote it right. You do a frat party and everybody in the fraternity has to go to the party. You can make good money and sell discs. Part of the rider is expense money.

Walker recommends that when you're doing a gig, ask if anyone in the audience is a member of a frat, as it's easier to get a gig at a frat party if someone recommends you. If you know anyone who was a member of a frat, even years ago, ask him to contact someone at his old house on your behalf. When you play at a national fraternity, they can recommend you to their chapters in other cities. Once you get in the frat door, you may find it lucrative to keep doing these gigs.

House Concerts

Held in people's homes, house concerts are becoming a profitable alternative venue for acoustic acts or others that aren't too loud. These gigs are intimate and friendly. Attendees make a reservation and pay a fee or make a donation to cover the costs of food and the artist. There's a whole circuit of house concerts throughout the country, and many artists prefer them because they get a good financial guarantee and sell lots of products. Some are listed at www.houseconcerts.com. Sara Hickman performs at larger house concerts and says:

> House concerts are huge. They're fun because they're no smoking, the people want to be there, you can usually stay at their house, they treat you well, and you can sell tons of product. They average one to two hundred people. There's a whole house concert network—start asking around. Other performers talk about them. They pay well. They generally charge between ten and fifteen dollars a head. You may sell all the stuff you bring. I would build a following through house concerts in your town. If there's not one, start your own—invite all your friends and neighbors and get them to talk about you, and do another one two months later.

TOURING EUROPE

I've gotten different takes about touring Europe. Some say it's great money, but more say they make just enough to make it worth the trip or to have a European vacation. The key to making money for most artists is merchandise. Nina Mankin says, "Foreign audiences pay more for CDs. If I know I can sell at least fifteen CDs, it's almost worth doing a gig just to know I'm leaving my music behind me." Another perk is that some expenses are paid for. They may not pay airfare, but they'll feed you and often put you up. It's more civilized than touring in the U.S., and everyone I spoke to who has toured Europe says they get spoiled. Lucky comments, "Everything is music oriented. The culture of people wanting to do nothing but listen to music is awesome." Lezlee loves it:

> *The attitude among audiences and the venues are different. If they don't know who you are, they take the time to get to know you. Venues spend weeks before your show promoting it, which means potential audience members walk around seeing your poster and reading about you in the paper. I never worried that no one would know about the show. The audience's attention spans are longer. Unlike playing in the U.S., I was the only act that evening, and expected to play at least two one-hour sets. Audiences were attentive throughout the performances. Dinner, drinks, and accommodations were always included. The owners of the venues usually ate with us and wanted to know us. In some cases, they opened their homes to us.*

European audiences love music. How refreshing! George Devore adds, "Americans kind of consume a fresh carcass and move on. Once you have a fan in Europe, they're your fan until you're dead. They'll always come see you and buy your records." If you want to get to Europe, take a trip and meet people. Find out which clubs are appropriate and visit them. Try to meet booking agents, although it's hard; you may have to book your own tour the first time. Holland and Belgium are the most receptive to indie music. Peter Slagt, who has run Non-U-Agency in Holland for ten years (but which, sadly, is closing) advises:

> *Invest in a tour. The first might be a big financial loss, but good contacts may result in a second tour and maybe more. That's what happened with a lot of our artists. Some tour with us for many years. Make sure on your first tour you have a mailing list to keep your fans informed about a second tour and releases. If the band is special, the audience will come back, which is a bit of a guarantee for bigger clubs.*

When you approach an agent, Slagt recommends, "Be enthusiastic; be good; send a good demo CDR or CD, plus good-looking promo material such as a bio, photo, and reviews. Don't give up after a 'no.' Some artists whom I first said no to kept trying with new demos, which resulted in a tour." Slagt cares whether the artist is good and has an album, even if it's DIY. He warns that many bookers only want bands with a record or distribution deal or who are on the brink of that. Lucky was able to get on a European tour. He says:

> *I got associated with a songwriter who'd worked with a Dutch agency, and he pushed me to them. They finally brought me over as part of a three-band tour. We did thirty shows in thirty-six days. It was hard, but it worked. Since then I've been associated with his agency. We get treated like kings. Most club dates come with dinner, hotel, and breakfast. I'm touring a couple of times a year now—Germany, Switzerland, Belgium, Holland, the U.K. It's a completely different scene, which has changed the whole way I approach music. The clubs in Europe are large, filled with really enthusiastic people that don't have to know you to come see you.*

Lucky says he'd go out after gigs and find other clubs he could play in. Then he'd give his agent the names of those clubs to book him into. He says having an agent makes it easier, but agents are limited in the clubs they book, so he did their legwork.

How do you find agents? Lois Chisolm recommends calling them. They all speak English. She says they can be very accessible and are often more approachable than their American counterparts. There are publications that list agents. A U.K. resource is the White Book, available online. It lists the leading businesses in every sector of the music industry, including agents. Chisolm recommends the German version, Branchenhandbuch, also available online at www.mmbranchenhandbuch.de. She advises finding names and calling. Send a regular or an electronic package if they ask for one. Networking helps with finding names. That's how Lezlee did it:

> *I was friends with a musician who convinced a German band to let his band go on tour with them in Germany. He offered to set up a tour for me in Europe and thought I would break even. I paid him a fee, which covered phone and mailing expenses. He arranged for a German drummer and bassist to accompany me, and booked sixteen shows in twenty-one days, all over Germany. I broke even the first time, between merchandise and performance fees. Most clubs paid a fee plus gave us room and board for the night. They plastered posters of me all over town, arranged for articles in local papers with photos, and were very hospitable. The audiences were great. I grew tenfold as a performing artist and*

felt it was worth the investment. This would never happen in the U.S. My friend booked another tour a year later, which drew twice as many people, especially in towns I had played before. My second tour expanded into the Netherlands and the Czech Republic, and I actually made money from this tour. But I had to be a sharp businesswoman.

When you get one agent, try to get others. Lois Chisolm says, "Agents have partners in others countries. Once you get an agent, you can ask who their partner agents are." She advises asking agents if they have an artist coming over whom you can open for. Manager Michael Norton, who has also worked in Europe as a booking agent, agrees. He suggests:

> *First figure out what acts are going to Europe that are like your music. It's pretty logical.* Pollstar *shows who's going over. Find out who is [on] the team they have set up over there and not just what clubs they're playing. The clubs want to buy the shows from local agents for their own protection. If there's an independent artist that's like yours, find out who's releasing their music over there. If they're having success, approach someone on their local team. Do searches on the Internet. Most agents want to know if you have a label over there. If you contact an agent, they may tell you about a local label that might work with you. They're very helpful people.*

Club dates don't always pay a lot. Lucky says, "We make from $400 to $800 a night, but you can play every night if you want. Product is unbelievable. I'll sell upwards of fifty CDs and forty T-shirts a night. Unless I have a big hit, I make a lot more money than I would if I were signed." Lucky earns a full-time living touring mainly Europe. Pascal Zander of Z music, a booking agency in Belgium and Luxembourg, says bands should know that being from the U.S. won't open doors for concerts. In the past, he says, it was a draw, but nowadays the public doesn't come to gigs as easily. Getting booked isn't the problem; you may not make enough money. Z music won't pay for a band to come from the U.S., as it is too expensive. But they can get the artists on a tour. He adds:

> *Indie music has a real potential in Belgium. But bands have to know that if they want to come and play here, they should be prepared to do a "door" deal and not expect more. I'm talking about bands which are not distributed over here. When you have a good distribution deal with good promotion, the situation is different.*

Peter Slagt advises, "Try hard to get your album distributed because interest will be higher if your record is available." Michael Norton says, "I would not take an artist to Europe without a record label, small or large. You have to have a local partner over there, even if it's just a mom-and-pop label. You need someone who's there locally, who understands the language and the media, and is working the music, preferably one who is manufacturing the record there." If you have a serious intention of touring Europe, try to get a licensing or distribution deal with a local company. One good source for finding foreign labels and distributors is the worldwide distribution and licensing directory included in ALL ACCESS®, a CD-ROM that contains over 10,000 music industry contacts, and much more (see Appendix 2). Smaller labels are receptive to working with an artist who is willing to come over and support the release. You tour and they sell CDs. They'll give you tour support, which makes agents more likely to work with you. If you go the DIY route, Nina Mankin advises:

> Bring enough CDs with you. There's nothing more frustrating than a line of people wanting to buy a product you just ran out of. Space in your suitcase for CDs is more important than for clothes. You can make a lot of money on a gig just by moving your product—and you continue to have impact after you leave.

Unless you're well known, festivals are the bigger moneymakers. Europeans had seen Mankin play in the U.S. and asked her to come to their festivals. Mankin says, "[I played] established festivals where my airfare and hotel were taken care of, I was paid generously, and treated with real hospitality." Manager Lois Chisolm advises calling the mayor's office in individual European cities to find out about local festivals. She has lived in Europe and says people that deal with music speak English. Chisolm found many cities receptive to artists who ask to play their festivals. Search the Internet for festivals in Europe or for city contact numbers. With inexpensive long-distance rates available through companies on the Internet, it may be worth a try.

Another option in Europe is to get in touch with anyone you know in the military who is stationed in a foreign country to see if they can help you get booked. American music is best appreciated in areas where a lot of Americans are living. Lois Chisolm says, "A lot of hip-hop is centered around military communities. If you know someone in one, it's a place to stay and you can get started there. Talk to the local NCO and Officer's club, even if you call cold."

Since Europeans have a passion for live music, the possibilities for touring are endless, if you get creative. Don't be afraid to ask anyone you meet for a gig or contact. The more musicians you get to know, the more resources you'll gather. Lezlee feels the European approach to live music makes more business sense:

> *Everyone wins. The venue pays a performance fee and accommodations, but it forces them to pay for promotion. Then more people show up, pay to get in, and pay for drinks and food, so the venue is happy. The audience is happy—since they've paid for a ticket, it raises the value of the show. They are also more likely to buy a CD if they've paid for a ticket; it's psychology. The artist is happy because their needs are taken care of and they have a better show.*

GETTING INTO PROMOTIONAL CAMPAIGNS

There's money to be made from getting into advertising and promotional campaigns. Agencies use a lot of music, and it's possible to reach them with yours! Promotions agencies are easier than ad agencies for unsigned artists to reach; they often do local campaigns in malls and other public places that feature live music. Madison Bedard, a promotions manager who's worked on both the agency and client side, says:

> *Figure out what company is marketing a product to people who would be interested in your music. Once you figure out what company, you need to find the agency who is creating their ads and doing marketing for them. Research! Look in trade publications—they talk about the business and may mention who's working on what account.*

Bedard recommends that if you watch commercials and see something you can fit into, research to find out who does their ads. Local grassroots programs come out of smaller promotions agencies. Find out which agency handles a company you want to approach by searching the Internet, using resource directories at the library, or calling the company and asking. Bedard advises, "Call the person who's managing the account or send a package. Have a cover letter ready. Show that you know their products and campaigns. Tell something about yourself and send a CD.

Then call back." She says that sometimes the person may pass your package along to someone else if you make a good impression.

Check advertising and promotions trade publications. The best one that covers promotions agencies is called *Promo*. By reading such publications, you may learn which companies are looking to use music. Bedard adds, "If you see in *Promo* that someone is looking to sponsor a tour with artists and [you] think your music can fit in, quickly send them a package. Include a note stating, 'Feel free to share my music with someone else at your firm.'"

Getting into an advertisement or promotional campaign is possible! Schrodinger's Cat saw an ad on the Internet for a contest sponsored by Kit Kat. They entered and won an appearance in a Kit Kat commercial. Be vigilant to anything that might be suitable for your music!

HANGING IN THERE

I hope you see more options for yourself after reading this chapter. If record labels aren't responding to you yet, keep working! Terri Hendrix says, "When you get turned down, you can sit on your couch and wait for someone to knock on your door or you can do it yourself." Please don't give up if things don't go as you'd like them to. Nook advises, "You have to have a vision. That's the first step. Write it down and look at it every day." Focus on where you're going, not on what didn't work. Jennifer Smith suggests:

> *Keep plugging away in whatever way you can. Be prepared for discouragement because it can get very discouraging. We shifted gears. We stopped trying to force ourselves onto people who weren't that excited and instead went out and tried to develop great relationships with the people who were excited about our music. Always make sure that you're enjoying what you're doing. You may get through ten years without getting that brass ring, so you want to figure out how to make the business of it enjoyable. Then it won't seem like a waste of time.*

PART
FIVE

REACHING
THE
RECORD
LABELS

20

DIFFERENTIATING
the Advantages of
MAJOR *and* INDIE
LABELS

Myth:

It's always better to sign with major labels because
they have more money and power behind them.

● ● ●

In my classes, I find that most of the students want a deal with a major label. Major labels have higher profiles and spend more money than the independents, making them seem more appealing to sign with. But despite their lower profiles and smaller budgets, independent labels are responsible for breaking some of the biggest acts on the music scene today. Consider signing to an indie. Don't limit your possibilities when shopping a deal.

WEIGHING THE PROS AND CONS

Both major and independent labels have advantages and disadvantages. If you're in the enviable position of having a choice of which label to sign with, there are many factors to take into account. The biggest is probably what style of music you're looking to get a deal for. Certain genres, especially very commercial ones that need a lot of radio and video promotion, might favor the majors. Music that's more specialized, a little off of the mainstream, or still too new to be widely accepted has more potential on an indie.

I usually recommend signing with a strong indie label over a major, if you have a choice. The people working at indies have more creativity, vision, and courage in terms of trying to break music that's innovative. Majors have been picking up indie labels like crazy because these labels have tremendous success at recognizing and breaking new talent. Karin Berg, formerly a senior vice president of A & R at Warner Bros. Records, says, "If I were starting in the music business today, I would probably work at an independent label because I feel that everyone at independent labels is dedicated to breaking new music."

Independents work very differently from major labels, often to your advantage. I saw an example of this when I released my third single. When the record took off, I got calls from major labels about picking it up. Because the record was doing well, I wanted the deal to be quick. However, three or four months was the shortest period of time any major could offer me for getting the deal together. Everyone felt badly knowing that although the single was doing well, it would probably die in the red tape. As a result, I accepted a deal with a strong indie and the single was out in two weeks. This is a good example of the difference between major and independent labels.

Most strong independent labels are tied in with a major label for distribution, or they have good independent distribution. Indies usually specialize in a specific genre of music and consequently know more about the nuances of marketing it. You won't get quite as lost at an indie. Of course, being signed with a major gives you more prestige, as well as more potential exposure in promoting your music. Booking agents may take you more seriously as well. I've put together a table to help you understand some of the differences. I admit I'm biased, but I know many others agree with me. If you're lucky enough to have a choice, think about the following:

Major Labels	Independent Labels
Major labels are larger. They have bigger staffs working the projects. They can be less personal.	Indies are smaller but can be more personal. You can get to know the staff more easily.
Majors have more money behind them. They spend the most on promotion. They have higher budgets for videos.	Indies don't have as much money, but there's usually much less waste. They spend wisely and more creatively.
Majors are distributed by major distributors.	Many strong indies are distributed by the same major distributors.
Majors don't specialize in a particular genre of music, so their marketing focus is not in one particular direction. This is especially true of new styles of music. They do have specific divisions for some genres.	Indies usually specialize in specific genres, so they become extremely knowledgeable about marketing and focus their connections in one direction. They get a reputation for doing certain genres.
Majors have a sink-or-swim policy with most new releases. When they release artists' recordings, they wait to see which ones head for the top without much help. They let the others sink.	Many indies work each act as if it were their last. With fewer acts to market, they can give each more attention. They can't afford losses like majors so they promote what they release.
Many people on top at the majors have been there for many years and may not know quite as much about trends. They may rely on staff to make musical judgments.	Indies tend to have younger people working for them, who are more into current trends in music. These labels are often founded by people who love the music they put out.
There's more turnover in the middle level staff (promoters, sales reps, etc.) at major labels, so it's harder to develop a rapport. There are more acts vying for attention.	The people who founded the label may be its staff. Often, they bring in friends, who are more loyal to the company. The staffs are small and tend to stick around longer.
Major labels have more clout in getting radio and video play and other sorts of promotion.	Indies have a harder time getting commercial radio play and other forms of promotion, but they do work hard.

DECIDING ON WHICH PATH TO CHOOSE

One consideration in deciding whether to pursue a major or indie label is your style of music. Artists with more commercial appeal may need the big money and contacts of a major label. This is especially true of music such as pop and commercial rock, which need high-budget videos and heavy radio promotion. On the other hand, alternative styles of music may be more attractive to a specific audience, which looks to indies for their music. According to Wendy Goldstein, vice president of A & R at MCA Records, "A lot of bands don't want to be signed with major labels because they've heard such nightmares from their friends about what happens. A lot want to go to smaller labels." Happy Walters, CEO of Immortal Records, feels:

> If it's a pop kind of band, you're better off with a major. But if it's a Korn or Limp Bizkit, a lot of times it's best to be on an independent label that's distributed by a major and have the best of both worlds. We have the distribution and the muscle when we need it. The bands get the attention and handholding when they're starting and need it most. . . . Indie labels take more time.

On the surface, the big budgets of the major labels may seem enticing. But ultimately, much of the money spent comes out of your royalties (see Chapter 25). And if your record sales don't quickly make back the money spent, you may be history just as quickly. Therefore, an A & R person at a major is concerned about being able to break an artist on her first or second album, before the artist goes into too much debt. Indie labels don't spend nearly as much money, so they have more leeway in terms of giving the artist an opportunity to develop. Ricky Schultz, president of Zebra Records, says:

> It helps if people can be realistic about assessing where they are. Not unlike the sports world, you've got independent labels of all sizes and varieties that serve as a farm system for talent. An artist may have what it takes three to five years from now to be an important and viable artist on the biggest label in the world. But today, they may be at a developmental point.

You may be able to develop your career at an indie and eventually build it enough to move on to a major. But be careful! Those inviting major-label budgets can be what ends an artist's career on a major label. As Karin Berg explains:

Very seldom is an artist dropped because the company doesn't believe that the artist is a good artist. Very often artists are dropped because their sales are not increasing and the record company cannot afford to keep increasing its debt. With each record release, as the debt becomes huger, the artist must sell more, to the point that they must be platinum to recoup. It's very difficult for a major to offer an inexpensively produced record to radio and expect it to get played. That's not to say that we don't want to do it. But there's different expectations once you're on a major, not just from the major but from radio and from the "marketplace." I still think it's possible for majors to break acts, but in order to do that there has to be a big campaign and almost total financial commitment on every level. Which is not to say that majors are unwilling to do that, but if you do that with every release, somebody's not going to make some money. That can only last for so long. Right now, there are a number of start-up labels, and they are generally given about five years to recoup. A major that is already in the business and has been in the business for a long time doesn't have that luxury.

How do you decide whether to go for a major or independent label deal? You may not have a choice. If you target labels, focus on both indies and majors that seem best for your music. Since there are advantages and disadvantages in going with either choice, my recommendation is to make decisions based on the individual label. Be open-minded about labels, giving yourself the most possibilities for your music.

FINDING THE
All-Important
A & R PERSON

Myth:

An A & R person is not that important

in getting a record deal.

• • •

It's amazing how many people whisper that they feel stupid asking because they know they should know the answer, but "What exactly does A & R mean?" Most people know that an A & R person is the one they want to get demos to at a label, but many don't know why. Even more have no idea what A & R stands for. And because it seems so obvious, they're too embarrassed to ask.

A & R stands for *Artists and Repertoire*. An A & R person finds the *Artists* and develops their *Repertoire* of material. This individual listens for new talent and decides or recommends whether to sign an artist to the label. Once you get signed, the A & R person oversees your development. An effective one finds songs and producers, if needed. In general, an A & R person supervises the development of the artist from inception of ideas to a completed product.

UNDERSTANDING WHY A & R PEOPLE ARE SO IMPORTANT

An A & R person is your in-house manager. Michael Caplan, senior vice president of A & R at Epic Records, says, "Some artists need a lot of A & R input—from selection of songs, producers, imaging. There are some groups that come really realized and it's just a matter of guiding them through the recording a little bit." According to Brian Long, senior director of A & R at MCA Records:

> The role of an A & R person is to seek talent and then work with the artist in making the album. They coordinate the team that will actually execute the production and mixing of the record. The A & R person is the primary conduit between the artist and the label, in terms of introducing that artist to the label and walking them through all the departments and different facets of a record label. It's a multi-dimensional job.

And according to Jeff Fenster, senior vice president of A & R at Island/ Def Jam Records, the A & R person "is hopefully closest to the artist's vision, and will help motivate the entire company to get behind the artist." Fenster adds that an A & R person deals with the artist's manager and keeps in contact with the label's publicity, marketing, promotion, art, and video departments. A & R people used to be more involved in the production of an album, but with the growing use of independent producers, the role has changed. An A & R person may exercise the right to tell you to use certain people for specific areas of your production, however, and has the final say on the finished product.

BUILDING RELATIONSHIPS WITH A & R PEOPLE

Most A & R people I've spoken to emphasize the importance of developing a good relationship when working with an A & R person. It makes the process of production and artist development go smoothly. According to Wendy Goldstein, a vice president of A & R at MCA Records, "A & R is all about relationships. I've been more effective on certain projects over others because of my relationship with that particular artist. The role of an A & R person is sort of like the role of an agent to an actor. It's a personal relationship, built on trust and mutual respect."

A good relationship helps get you more label support. When an A & R person and the artist don't respect each other's judgment, it creates a tugging of wills, leading to disharmony, which obviously isn't good for the project. Learn to listen objectively. You don't have to follow every piece of advice the A & R person offers, but working with your label is a team effort. Jeff Blue, a vice president of A & R at Warner Bros. Records, notes:

> *A band needs the ability to communicate. You find that out when artists are open to suggestions and improving themselves. Nothing's perfect, and so many of the buzz bands fail because they refuse to take directions from labels and those they should take directions from.*

FIGURING OUT WHAT LABELS ARE LOOKING FOR

It would be much easier if there was a formula for what the labels will sign. But then creativity could go down the tubes. I've talked to top A & R people at many labels and they all have their unique criteria. One way to call attention to yourself as an act is to create a *buzz* about your music. If yours gets good enough, labels will hear it. A & R people keep their ears to the streets. Many have scouts, while some go hear bands themselves. Happy Walters, CEO of Immortal Records, had a good ear when he signed Korn:

> *Korn was mixing a hard type of music with hip-hop. We heard about them. No one was checking them out seriously. At the time, I had hip-hop bands—Cyprus Hill, Wu Tang Clan, House of Pain. Korn knew they'd probably be better served on a label like Immortal because they needed to have guidance and patience. I signed them in '94. Nobody was checking them out. Now bands are influenced by Korn.*

Jeff Fenster emphasizes that he likes to see an artist who's willing to work to get his or her music exposure. Having drive will impress an A & R person, as long as you have the talent and material to back it up. Jeff Blue is one of those special A & R people who believe in artist development. He signed Macy Gray because he saw her potential:

> *Macy was given to me as a fluke. I got an old demo tape that she did. Nobody was managing her at the time. She was dropped*

by Atlantic Records and her publisher. Someone was shopping something and I asked what else they had. She gave me the demo tape of Macy Gray. I loved the voice and immediately recognized that she needed some different beats and structuring the music more around her voice instead of having the voice structured around the music. It was just undeniable.

A & R people have contacts all over. I've gotten deals because someone working in a store called an A & R person to recommend a record I'd released. Many artists get signed by putting out their own CDs. Rose Noone, vice president of A & R for Epic Records, is always on the look out for good bands. She reveals:

We look down the CMJ charts. We read local papers from all over the country looking for bands. We make phone calls to people we know in different cities and ask, "What's happening? What's going on? What bands should I look into?" If you create a buzz and create some action about you or your band in your area, town, or territory, you're bound to be heard of. If the music stands up, people will come and see you. It's word of mouth. You have to give someone a reason to talk about your band. Sometimes it doesn't necessarily take creating a whole buzz, but I think it's healthy for a band to build a foundation, even before you get into the process of shopping to a label.

Rose Noone was involved in signing singer Tracy Bonham. She recalls, "We heard about her through a publicist friend in Boston who called us up and said 'I saw this artist last night who's phenomenal.' She sent a tape down and it was fantastic. We went up to see her and she was great. We wanted to sign her right there and then." A & R people say that a great live performance, combined with great material, is what they look for the most. Brian Long signed the Chemical Brothers in the U.S. "There was nothing visual about them, but they had one of the most incredible connections to their audience. And their tracks were great. I figured they could connect with both a rock and dance audience, and they did."

FINDING THE RIGHT A & R PERSON

Ideally, we should be concerned with finding the right A & R person to work with. Not all are good at what they do. You can't lose heart if an A & R person doesn't recognize your talent. Remember, all you need is one who does. Ricky Schultz, president of Zebra Records, advises not letting rejection stop you:

> *It's important that artists understand that music and art is a highly subjective and personal arena. There are some terrific A & R people out there, some good A & R people, and some people doing A & R that frankly probably shouldn't be. So if somebody really thinks they have the stuff to be out there and having success, they shouldn't be too flustered by at least a modest amount of rejections.*

Most large labels have A & R people who specialize in different types of music. It's good to try to find out who focuses on your genre. If you're not sure, call the A & R department at the label and ask. An excellent way to get names is to use the *A & R Registry*. It's a fantastic directory that lists every A & R person at every label, by genre (more info in Appendix 2).

● ● ●

A & R people can be the key to your successful music career. They are instrumental in getting you signed to a deal. They can also lead you in a direction that will help you get the most out of your record deal. Since each A & R person is different, you've got to try every way possible to get their attention. There's no one way, however, or, as Rose Noone says, "There are no rules." Remember it takes only one A & R person to recognize your talent!

GETTING

to

RECORD LABELS

Myth:

You can't go to a record label
if you don't know anyone.

• • •

Labels don't like dealing with an artist directly. They prefer speaking with your formal representative. An A & R person speaks more candidly about your material to someone else. No matter how much you think you can speak for yourself, as the artist it's always better to have someone representing you who has good contacts and your best interests at heart. In this chapter, I'll give you suggestions for finding the right person to get your music through the door and give you options for doing it yourself. There are lots of ways to get in the door. The best way, as I've been encouraging, is to develop your career to such an extent that labels find you. As your story grows, keep A & R people informed by sending them mailings. The more familiar they become with your name, the more likely you'll be to get a response when you approach them by whatever means.

SENDING UNSOLICITED MATERIAL

Most A & R people don't want what's known as unsolicited material, which means they didn't ask for it. If they don't know you, your demo may go directly into a box to be discarded. According to Wendy Goldstein at MCA Records, "For the most part, the general stock statement when you call up any major label is, 'We do not accept any unsolicited material.'"

The most common reason given in the past for A & R people being reluctant to listen to unsolicited tapes was a threat of lawsuits: by listening to such material, they could risk later being accused of stealing a piece. A singer/songwriter can submit a tape of original material, not get signed, hear a similarity between one of her songs and one released on the label, and sue the label for copyright infringement. Having a policy of not listening to unsolicited demos avoids this problem.

But nowadays, there's a different reason for accepting only solicited tapes: A & R people say there's too much bad product coming in. Technology makes it easy for anyone to make a demo. It takes time to go through hundreds of them, looking for the pearls. Ricky Schultz, president of Zebra Records, explains, "A & R people don't take unsolicited material because they get tired of going through stuff that's not even remotely in the ballpark." I don't blame them. They'd rather get material from someone whom they know. Lawyers, producers, other signed musicians, etc. are more likely to hand them material that's worth listening to. If you get lucky and an A & R person agrees to hear your material, ask how to address it so he receives it. You may have to write something special on the envelope or send it to someone else's attention.

THE REAL DEAL ABOUT SHOPPING FOR A RECORD DEAL

When I wrote the first edition of this book, the dynamics of getting a record deal were different than they are today. In the '90s, A & R people took CDs more seriously because people paid big bucks to professionally press them. Nowadays, they're burned right off computers. Anyone can record something and make a CD. Because there's a glut of material being created with new technology, most A & R people no longer deal with all the material they receive. They've become pickier about what they listen to. Most A & R people I spoke to (interviews are in Chapter 23) say they want material given to them only by a profes-

sional. Bruce Lundvall, president of the jazz and classics division of
Capitol Records, says:

> *It should be solicited. If I go to any industry function with
> unsigned new artists, I end up with a satchel of CDs and tapes
> and can't get to them all. I can't give anything a serious listen
> when I have so many to listen to. It's better if someone I respect
> gets something to me that they're excited about.*

Here's the real deal: If you have THE GOODS, someone will recognize
it. It may sound unobtainable but it happens. It's true! Getting your
music heard by as many people as possible increases your chances. Ginger
MacKenzie says, "I showcased in L.A. a few times and met a publisher
who heard me. I got a publishing deal with Warner/Chappell." The
more you build your career, the better your chances that the ONE contact who can open doors will find you. Network as much as possible.
A & R people have feelers out across the country. They read reviews and
notice artists that create a buzz. Put your energy into making enough noise
to get someone's attention instead of moaning about not getting a break.

Labels are looking to sign new artists. They want to find the artists
with THE GOODS. Various professionals enjoy being the one to discover someone who gets signed. So people want to find you. The more
visibility you have, the more possibilities there are for you! Get out—
be seen and heard. Play at showcases and pitches. Join TAXI (see page
133). Get all over the Internet. Send e-press kits to A & R people, producers, lawyers, and anyone else you can. It doesn't cost anything. You
can search for folks online.

Get your demo to pros who can give it to someone at a label. Look at
CDs of artists who do music similar to yours to see who produced them.
Call them or send a demo with a professional-sounding note. When you
go to industry events and meet established producers or lawyers, ask if
they'd be willing to listen to your music. If they like it, they may pass it
along. If someone thinks you're worthy of a deal, they may help because
you may use their services later. A word of advice: NEVER force your
demo on anyone. Ask if they're willing to listen to it. If they don't give
you a definitive yes, don't waste it. There are people who will listen.
They're the ones most likely to help you. Having a polite and professional approach gets you taken more seriously.

Some independent producers whom you hire for a project will use
their contacts to shop the material, without signing a production agree-

ment (see page 188). They'll make money if you get signed. So you may hire a producer who has contacts to work on your album. Some producers will give it to people they know at labels because they believe in the project and want to help. Some may charge a fee. It depends on the producer.

SHOPPING DEMOS

You have options if you want to actually shop for a deal. But be careful! There are attorneys who shop demos for a fee. They promise to get your tapes to many labels in exchange for a large fee, paid in advance. I've been told that sometimes these attorneys simultaneously shop material from other artists. This doesn't offer much chance of getting signed. Since they get their money from you no matter what, there's little incentive for them to push for a deal.

Record labels are wary of attorneys who make shopping deals a business. Attorney Wallace Collins recalls that an A & R person once asked him if he knew a certain attorney. When he asked why, the A & R person said he was getting a tape a week from this attorney and assumed he was taking fees. The A & R person related that he couldn't take an attorney like that seriously because it would be unlikely that anyone could have one act a week that's so good it would be worth shopping on speculation.

Find an attorney who believes in your music enough to be paid only if he gets you a deal. It's hard for someone to get you a deal if he doesn't feel good about your music. Part of the pitch to an A & R person is enthusiasm. If an attorney believes in your music enough to shop it on a contingency basis, obviously he'll work harder. Some attorneys may ask for their expenses (mailing out packages, etc.) to be reimbursed, which isn't unfair. Some ask for a small fee for their time.

Attorney Larry Rudolph believes that using an attorney is "an excellent way to shop and get deals. However, there are many lawyers who try to take advantage of young, aspiring artists." He recommends avoiding attorneys who charge fees. Rudolph shops a very limited number of acts per year. "If I shop a deal it means I believe in them." Getting someone who believes in your material to represent you is the best way to go.

Wallace Collins agrees. He rarely, if ever, shops for a deal, believing an artist instead needs a lawyer who can negotiate contracts and advise them in legal matters. "An artist is better off having a manager shop his tape or doing it himself." Collins says he wouldn't have gone into the practice of law if he had wanted to act as an agent. "You should choose a lawyer based on his ability to be a good legal advisor."

While an attorney looks to secure you a good contract, if she is getting a percentage of your advance, her priorities may be skewed in that direction. Although most lawyers are ethical, some put their own needs first. You must be careful. A manager, on the other hand, is concerned about your career, and is therefore more focused on getting you signed to the right label, with appropriate promotional budgets. If you use a manager to shop, you'll still have an attorney negotiating your contract, hence two people watching out for you.

According to attorneys I've interviewed, the most typical arrangement is to give the attorney a percentage of your first album proceeds. Sometimes, the amount is taken only from the advance and sometimes it's from royalties as well. Some attorneys want a percentage of all future albums. That's too much! There are attorneys who'll try to take a piece of everything you earn, including money earned from songwriting. Stan Soocher, Esq., the editor of *Entertainment Law & Finance*, says that "the real issue is what financial compensation the attorney should receive rather than whether the attorney should have a copyright ownership interest in the musician's songs or sound recordings. Musicians should be wary of the latter."

In most cases, an attorney offers a written agreement if he gets a percentage of your deal. Read this carefully, as signing an agreement with the attorney who's supposed to represent you is a conflict of interest. Don't assume you're being offered a fair deal. Most lawyers will be straight with you, but there are always a few who have other priorities. Have another attorney look over the agreement to be on the safe side. Soocher advises you to be aware that "an attorney who is giving a musician a contract to sign has an obligation to tell that musician to seek independent counsel to review the agreement. What many attorneys will do is to place a clause in the agreement with the musician, stating that the musician has been advised to seek legal counsel." If they don't advise you, it's a way to get out of the contract later.

If your music attorney doesn't shop deals at all, ask if you can write a letter and refer to him as your contact person or, better yet, have him send it on his stationery. If there's interest, your attorney can then negotiate the deal at an hourly rate. Wallace Collins says that this is the method he prefers to use. "But check with your attorney before using his name." There's a difference between representing you and shopping a deal. Representation is ideally what an attorney should do. But since the music business isn't ideal, we sometimes have to do whatever gets us to the deal we want.

GETTING A PRODUCTION DEAL

Sometimes artists don't have enough resources to make a good-quality demo. Consequently, they hook up with a production company that believes in them enough to get their material recorded and out to record labels. If you sign with a production company, they usually get a percentage of your deal—often as much as 50 percent. A production deal might be limited to your first album or extend to the length of your recording contract.

A good production deal is with a legitimate producer who gets your material recorded and then has contacts to shop it. According to Wallace Collins, a lot of people call themselves production companies, even when they don't produce. These companies act more as management does in going to a label to shop a deal. But they often take a lot more of your earnings than a manager would. In many deals, the production company signs an agreement with the artist that's similar to a deal with a small record label, splitting everything fifty-fifty. The monies paid by the record label commonly go to the production company. They're supposed to take their half of the money, paying the artist her share.

Collins warns, "More problems in this business arise based on production type contracts, because all the money goes to the production company as a middleman, and it's human nature that people will calculate the money in the most favorable way to themselves." There are many ways to interpret how the money is recouped and dispersed. Sometimes a production company takes all expenses out of the artist's share. By the time everything is paid for, the artist is left with little money while the production company has a nice profit. Collins recommends that you have the record label pay you your share directly. Many labels prefer this because you as the artist are happier if money is coming in. Collins says it's not in your best interest to have just any production company running your business. That doesn't mean production companies rip people off. Rather, the producer may be a good person but have no business sense. You shouldn't suffer for that ignorance, though.

Attorney Micheline Levine says that when representing an artist, she prefers a direct deal with a record company because the artist gets more. But if an artist has no other way to get to a label and finds a producer/production company with talent and good contacts, it's an option. If you sign a production agreement, Levine recommends:

> Try to get as much as possible a value of the deal as you would have received had you gone directly to a label. Try to get the major deal points as close to a direct deal as you possibly can. Try as much as you can not to give up any portion of publishing, and certainly avoid sharing merchandising whatsoever, which are two points that production companies frequently attempt to secure. Educate yourself. Find out what a new artist deal looks like when dealing directly with a record company (in terms of major deal points), so you can see how far off you are. Frequently [a production company] does a fifty-fifty deal—they make a production agreement saying whatever they get, you'll get half. When I make a production deal, I say [the artist] will get half but not less than that.

Both Levine and Collins assure me there are many legitimate production companies that do well for their artists. In choosing one, make sure it's a company with a track record, lots of label contacts, and, if they are going to be handling your money, a good sense of how to do business. Whether to take a production deal or not depends on what you need and the quality of what's offered. No matter how much you need access to a studio, it's important that you have faith in the producer's ability, both musically and business-wise. Just because a producer has a studio doesn't mean you should sign a production deal with her—especially if you're giving away half your money for it! Have an attorney review the agreement. Collins says that problems with production companies are a universal concern. A lot of artists wind up taking their production companies to court.

In Chapter 6, I spelled out the role of a producer and the importance of finding a good one. For a production deal, working with someone who knows how to produce well and has a good feel for your music becomes even more critical. When you hire a producer, you can replace her if you're not satisfied. In a production deal, you're tied to her. Producers usually own your recordings, and possibly a piece of your career. So the person you sign with had better be good.

REPRESENTING YOURSELF

If you're not able to meet pros or get heard by them, you *can* shop yourself. Michael Caplan, at Epic Records, says, "Unsolicited is hard but possible." If you believe in your music, find the open door. If you know you have THE GOODS, go after a deal however you can. I still advise focusing more on your career. But if you believe you have the foundation to build from on a larger label, don't let anything stop you. I'm showing you reality so you'll be prepared. But people do get through doors on their own when their beliefs motivate them to be persistent and patient. Toughen your balls for this one!

Since it's considered unprofessional to represent yourself, some musicians create the facade of a manager. Artists say they do something similar to what I did when starting my label: use fictitious names to sign letters when your own tag won't do. When my label first opened, I was also the artist and didn't want people to think they were calling me to talk about myself. To create the aura of a real business, I signed letters with different names to represent the PR person, president, promoter, etc. Nobody knew the difference.

Some artists contact A & R people as the act's manager, knowing that it makes label people more comfortable to think they're dealing with the artist's representative. Once there's a deal on the horizon, the label can talk with a lawyer and the manager can disappear. This isn't a recommended route, but it's an option that works for some. Many industry people say that an artist may have to take inventive measures to get signed. Wallace Collins agrees. "You gotta do what you gotta do. If you cannot get in through the front door, try the back door. If that fails, look for an open window. You must use every trick in the book to get your music heard."

As I suggested earlier, set up a company for your music. When you press up a CD, open a business. It may not knock doors down, but calling from XYZ Music sounds better than just using your own name. Even if your business is informal and it's just you, no one has to know. Speaking with authority and presenting a professional front gets people to take you more seriously than if they see you as just another musician clawing for a deal.

PREPARING TO SHOP YOUR OWN DEAL

Whether you're the artist, manager, producer, or representative of your company, there are ways to make your pitch have the best shot at getting results. Don't just do a random mailing. Shopping a deal directly takes preparation. Consider it the preproduction of a record deal. Patience plays a major role in determining whether you're thoroughly prepared to take the first step. Naturally, you need an appropriate package to present. It would be absurd to get someone interested and then rush to pull it together. Patience keeps you from running to labels before your demo is done to your total satisfaction, your bio is written in a professional manner, and you have press clippings, a following, and effective photos. In other words, wait until you can put your best foot forward.

Take on the persona of an industry person. A professional facade helps get through doors. Earlier, I recommended immersing yourself in your music as you develop it. By the same principle, you'll be more effective if you immerse yourself in the culture of the music industry when approaching labels. Besides learning the business end of music, it's also helpful to learn about the people running this crazy industry. Remember, the music business is basically a small world. If you understand that world and its protocol, language, relationships, etc., you have the best chance of becoming part of it.

GETTING EDUCATED ABOUT THE PEOPLE IN THE MUSIC INDUSTRY

Educate yourself about the people who work within the industry. While it's not crucial to know who works where, it helps. Getting to know the names of industry people is a useful asset when you're networking. For instance, if you're involved in a conversation, you may at least sound as though you know whom others are talking about when they mention people you've read about. If they think you know them, you're more likely to bond. If you know of a person, you can talk about him in more familiar terms.

Get familiar with names of key players at labels you'd like to reach. You'll recognize them if they come up in a conversation. For example, if two promoters you're chatting with mention someone you want to know, ask for an introduction. Had you not known the name, the opportunity would have gone by. If you're at a party and a person you've read about is mentioned, act as though you know her and ask for her number. If you meet someone from a label, it helps to recognize her name. "Are you the Lauren Daniels doing artist relations at Atlantic? I've been meaning to get in touch with you." Again, if the name doesn't ring a bell, the opportunity is wasted. You never know whom you might bump into at a club or party, or in your dentist's office.

Learning the Industry Walk

The more knowledge you have, the more ammunition you have and the more you'll sound authoritative. The more knowledge you have, the more you'll come across as a professional and the more confidence you'll feel when speaking with industry people. It's almost the parallel of name-dropping. You drop names you're familiar with even though you don't know the people personally. The music industry is a business of schmoozing. People chat and interact and gossip and observe. If you want to fit in, you need knowledge of the people, politics, and interactions of those with whom you're mixing. As attorney Larry Rudolph emphasizes:

> Get educated. If you're gonna be in this game, you have to know how to walk the walk and talk the talk. If you do get to the position where you are finally standing in front of the person who may be your ticket to getting where you want to get, and they start to talk to you about some industry something, if you have no idea what the heck they're talking about they may not take you seriously. Learn what's going on. Read Billboard. Find out who's who and what's what.

Before getting inside the industry, observe from the sidelines. At my first music seminars, I people-watched like crazy to see the interaction between professionals. I listened in on conversations. I went wherever groups of industry people might be to get a feel for how they talked to each other and bonded. Then I'd practice speaking that way with people I already knew. It's an art you can learn.

Finding Out Who's Who

How do you learn about industry people? Read a lot. Study trade (meaning industry business-related) publications. Chris Schwartz, CEO of Ruffnation Records, recommends:

> You should read any and every trade publication you can get your hands on, i.e., Billboard, R & R, etc. It is important to know who the players, labels, artists, producers, etc. are. Also, it helps to

have a historical knowledge of the music industry. Until very recently, this information was only available in books about the film industry. However, there are numbers of books about the record business available at the public libraries. Remember: Knowledge is power!

Obviously, *Billboard* is a great place to begin your quest. Read all the articles that relate to what you're doing, as well as to what you're interested in doing. Be up on who's doing what. You may learn who's looking for new artists. Become familiar with names of CEOs of smaller labels that may have good distribution. Read as many trades as possible.

It's helpful to learn everything you can about industry people. For example, if you read an article about an A & R person whom you may someday want to approach, you might learn something you can use to get your foot in the door. If she has an interesting hobby, watch for articles on that topic that you can send to her along with your pitch. Keep files on A & R people or others at labels where you might want to shop a deal. I keep track of specific people on index cards and write down pertinent information as I learn it.

I know of a blues musician who read about an A & R person who signed rock but was a major blues fan. Based on this knowledge, the artist tried to convince the A & R person to come down to one of her gigs. After sending reviews and numerous invites to blues clubs, the musician got the A & R person to show up for a gig. He loved the artist and introduced her to a friend who signed blues.

Read *Billboard*'s "Executive Turntable" column. It talks about people who just got hired or promoted. Often, people new to a company are more accessible. Sometimes they're looking for new material. If there's someone in particular who might be helpful, drop him a note congratulating him on his new position. Don't pitch anything, though. Later, if you approach him again, he may think he knows you!

Getting Names and Numbers

There are many listings of record labels and industry-related people. One excellent directory is the *A & R Registry*, put out by SRS Publishing and compiled by a terrific guy named Ritch Esra. It lists the A & R staff for all major and independent labels in New York, Los Angeles, Nashville, and London, with their direct-dial numbers and the names of their assistants. The directory is updated every eight weeks; people change jobs so often in this industry that listings get stale quickly. Esra works on this full-time to insure information is accurate. Esra also publishes *Music Publisher Directory* and *Film/TV Music Guide.*

Another good resource is published by Pollstar, a company that, as I mentioned earlier, puts out a nice assortment of Contact Directories. One is *Record Company Rosters,* with a listing of executive contacts for almost every major and independent label in the business. More info on all the directories is in Appendix 2.

GETTING IN THE DOOR TO A & R PEOPLE

I want to do an exercise using imagery so you can better understand the various factors affecting A & R people each day. If you can picture what they deal with on a regular basis, you might better comprehend why it may be impossible for them to be accessible to people they don't know. The following isn't necessarily a day in the life of an A & R person, but it's a typical scenario.

> All day you deal with tons of phone calls from managers, producers, lawyers, mothers of signed acts, and wannabe signed acts. You have contracts to go through. You're still unsuccessfully looking for three songs for an album. One of your biggest acts isn't selling and you're getting pressure. Then there are a zillion other things going on with some of the acts you've signed. Added to this, you were out late the night before, checking out an act you might sign, so you're tired. Your secretary walks in with the latest mail and puts it next to the mail you haven't had time to review for days. There's a pile of packages containing tapes and press kits. You don't recognize the return addresses on any. Your phone is ringing off the hook.

What mail would you give your attention to in these circumstances? Whose phone calls would you take? Be honest! A & R people are under pressure. If you were one, you too might have little choice about prioritizing your time. As much as A & R people might like to spend time just listening to tapes of potential talent, the system doesn't allow for it. The idea of A & R people who ask their secretaries to hold calls so they can listen to demos or return calls of people they don't know is only in fairy tales. Chances are the unsolicited demos are never listened to.

Finding the Right Approach

There's hope. I painted the above picture so you know what you're up against. Perhaps your idealism has been bruised but your approach to the labels is more realistic. When you try to get in touch with A & R peo ple, show respect for the fact that they're very busy. Your approach should be professional. But be on the lookout for any cracks in the door that you can push your way through.

There's no one way to reach A & R people—each person is different. Some are more into music and may respond to a creative overture. Some respond to an extremely business-like approach. Many won't respond no matter what you do. Sometimes you can learn about them by asking around. Finding one who responds to your approach is a matter of trial and error.

The easiest A & R people to get the attention of are those at indie labels. They're more approachable because their ears are more attuned to the street. Most indies attained success by being open to what's new and fresh. They're also more open to hearing demos, aware of treasures to be found. Based on those I've interviewed, A & R people doing urban music are the most open-minded to demos. They know how much of the music on the charts comes from young people who don't have the money or contacts to get to labels through traditional routes. These A & R people also seem more likely to see beyond the poor quality of a demo and recognize talent. A more specialized label has staff that's usually younger and more knowledgeable about their genre. They may remember what it's like to try to get heard, so their doors may not be shut as tightly.

Reaching A & R by Mail

It's best to make your initial contact with an A & R person with just a letter. Forget sending a demo cold, unless you know the person accepts unsolicited recordings. I told you earlier to send mailings to key publi cations and targeted A & R people as your career develops. Keep these people in the loop. If you're playing a gig, make sure they always know about it. When you're ready to shop your demo, they may be familiar with your name after seeing your mailings.

A well-written letter can get the attention of an A & R person. Develop your own stationery on a computer, with the letterhead of your company at the top. Write a professional-sounding, concise letter introducing your act and explaining something about your music.

Describe your music in a sentence or two. Mention where you've performed, any gigs that are coming up, who has written about you, and anything else that shows you're a marketable artist. End the letter by saying that you'd be happy to send more information about the act. Keep what you say as brief and professional as possible. If something in the letter catches the A & R person's interest, she may request a demo or come to see you play. This letter is a sales pitch, so include a great synopsis of the foundation you hopefully have been building. It may entice her to ask for a package.

About a week after you send your letter, make a follow-up call. When asked what your business is, say that you're calling to see if your letter was received. If the A & R person is interested, you'll eventually get through. If there's no response in a reasonable amount of time, there's probably a reason. I don't call more than three or four times without getting encouragement on the other end of the line.

Some people use creative approaches to get an A & R person's attention. I heard of someone who sent a boom box with his tape in it. The A & R person did listen. People send demos inside gifts as well as in creative presentations (e.g., in a bouquet of balloons, in the hand of a stripper, etc.). I've never heard of someone getting signed that way, but some A & R people might listen out of curiosity. The bottom line is still having a good product. A & R person Ricky Schultz agrees:

> One day I was taking a lunch break. We opened the mail. A guitar player from Chicago had sent a letter written on a lead sheet. Nobody had done that before. While we ate our lunch, we popped his cassette in. His first track blew us away. I was on the phone with him in fifteen minutes, which led to his being signed to a major label. So it just goes to show you never know.

GETTING THROUGH ON THE PHONE

When you call an A & R person, have a specific agenda in mind. Just in case you actually get through, be prepared to quickly explain why you're calling. Is it to follow up on a letter or to invite him to a gig? Is it to ask him if he's interested in hearing your demo or for a few minutes of time in person? Whatever your agenda, be prepared to spell it out in thirty words or less. Acknowledge that you appreciate the person's talking with you and promise not to keep him on the phone long. State your case and thank him for his time. If he's interested, he'll tell you.

The Power of Secretaries, Receptionists, and Administrative Assistants

You call an A & R person. His secretary tells you he's busy and will call you back. After waiting a few days, you try again. Same scenario. "She's on the other line," "He's in a meeting," "She just stepped out," "He's in the middle of something," "She'll have to call you back." This can go on for months. Assistants know all the excuses. Is it useless to call? Can you get past the person on the other end of the line?

Instead of trying to get past the people who answer the phone, attempt to get friendly with them. The people who answer phones can be the key to opening those tightly locked doors. Remember—they're inside. Who better can you ask about the A & R person's schedule, artist needs, attitude, personal preferences, and other information? The people who answer phones are the ones who guard the door you need to get through. They're the gatekeepers for A & R people. Developing a friendly relationship can get you to their superiors. By the way, a number of A & R people started in that position and worked their way up, so the one who answers the phone today may be the one you're trying to reach in a few months!

I always have a short, friendly chitchat with whomever answers the phone, no matter whom I'm calling. To me, it's basic courtesy to treat everyone as a somebody. Getting on familiar terms can give you license to ask them for advice later. What's the best time to catch the A & R person? How do I get him to come to my gig? Will *you* come to my gig? Yes. Invite the people who work for an A & R person to your gigs. Put them on the guest list. Treat them like honored guests. These people love music and might come. Thank them for coming. If your performance blows them away, they'll go back and talk about you inside the doors. How do you get on familiar terms with the people up front? If you have the *A & R Registry,* look up the name of the person's assistant. Or call the label and ask for the name of the assistant. Call back later, armed with a name. Use it when you call. After asking for the A & R person and being told to leave your phone number, ask, "Is this Lori?" She might think she knows you or that you know her on a professional level, and she'll take you more seriously.

Whenever I call anyone, from an A & R person to a plumber, I ask the person who answers the phone for his name. Then I say, "Thanks so much, Michael. I'd appreciate your giving BH my message." Again, it's courtesy (though not that common). People treat those who answer the phones as nonentities. They aren't! Treat them with respect. Be friendly. I have wonderful relationships with the assistants of business-people I deal with. When I call back later in the week, I'll ask if I'm speaking with Michael. If it's Jonny, I talk to him in a familiar manner, saying I'd spoken to Michael a few days ago. Is Michael there? If not, perhaps Jonny can help me get through to BH. Friendly, friendly, friendly. If Michael answers, I remind him who I am and ask him how he's been. Then I say I didn't get a return call. What would he advise? Sometimes it works, sometimes it doesn't. But it has worked for me more than it has bombed.

Getting Past the Gatekeepers

Something that works for me a large percentage of the time is calling with so much confidence, professionalism, and a positive attitude that the person assumes she knows me. People have few listening skills these days—if I call and say my name immediately, the person on the other end of the line will usually ask for it later, as if I'd never said it in the first place. If you say your name in a crisp, positive manner, she may assume you're a colleague. When I cold-call people and am asked who I am, I say my name in an extremely firm, confident voice, like they should know me. I'd estimate that over 25 percent of the time, I get put through to the person without being asked my business. My whole approach says that I expect my call to be taken seriously. Depending on who it is I'm calling, I may ask for the person by first name only to give the impression that I know him.

The best time to try reaching industry people directly is after hours. That's when their phone guards go home and they may answer them-selves. This applies to all ends of the industry. When I want to reach someone directly, I try every evening after 6:00 or 7:00. Industry people work late. I've been told by many people that late in the day may be the only time to get them on the phone. Of course it's a crapshoot to call every day in the hopes of catching the person, but it's worth a shot. Sometimes I can get from the person's assistant a clue as to the best day to call late.

Here's another approach. Ask the person who answers the A & R person's phone if you can send him a demo for his opinion as to whether it would work on his label. Don't ask him to pass it to his boss should he like it. People like giving advice. Asking for their opinions is less forward than asking for real help. It also strokes their egos, which most people love. At that moment, ask for nothing more than their opinions. Treat them as experts. Trust me, if they like your demo, they won't miss the opportunity to get it into the right hands so they can later brag they discovered you. Coveting the assistants to A & R people is your best shot at getting there on your own.

23

A & R FORUM:
Interviews with the Labels

I asked a good assortment of people at various record labels for their input on the three questions below. Following the name of the label that each person works for, I've indicated the distributor (in parentheses) and the genre that he or she specializes in (in italics).

QUESTION 1: WHAT ARE YOU LOOKING FOR IN A NEW ARTIST?

Bruce Lundvall, president of jazz and classics, Capitol Records (Blue Note Records and Angel Records) (EMD), *jazz and classical*: There's only one word from my point of view—originality. I want someone that has their own musical voice. I don't care if it's an instrumentalist or a vocalist—a distinctive musical voice that's not a copy or imitation of someone else. Hopefully the artist is a composer as well, but it's not essential. There are many wonderful interpreters who don't write. If an artist has a fresh and completely unique sound, I'd sign them without even thinking about marketing considerations or whether we are going to sell a lot of records. I want a roster of meaningful, real, serious artists. This applies to both vocalists and instrumentalist in both jazz, classical music, etc.

Merlin Bobb, executive vice president of A & R, Elektra Records (WEA), *all genres*: Most of the new artists I meet are through demo tapes. Initially, I'm looking for a unique singer or rapper who can represent a new vocal style, a style that I know is strong enough to compete in this market and who has qualities which set him or her apart from the crowd. The artist's lyric and music are very important and need to reflect his or her vocal style, with clever lyrics, strong melodies, and infectious hooks. If I meet that artist, he or she should have a strong, outgoing personality and image, as well as the ability to perform well and express their creative ideas.

Jeff Blue, vice president of A & R, Warner Bros. Records (WEA), *all genres*: The first thing would probably be the ability to write songs. What's most important to me is believability—that you believe what the artist is saying to be true—that they're not manufacturing themselves to be in a certain genre. Then, I want to know if that artist can deliver to the listener—are they delivering it in true form or does it seem like they're just singing someone else's songs? And last, is that artist a star?

Happy Walters, CEO, Immortal Records (EMD), *urban/alternative*: I sign three or four bands a year. When I signed Korn, they were doing something that no one had done. At a time when heavy metal was not cool, they were doing a heavier thing with a hip-hop feel to it. When I signed Incubus, they had the hard music but were also great songwriters, had a great voice, and were very earthy, kind of like Grateful Dead in a certain way. It's gotta be something that stands out. It can't be just hearing a hit song and deciding to put it out. When those things hit, they come and go very quickly. The goal in my company is to have something that lasts a long time, that you could build a career out of. They have to play live amazingly well. If a band isn't together, I wouldn't touch them.

Hosh Gureli, vice president of A & R, J Records (BMG), *all genres*: The one thing that is very enticing for us is when an artist comes with at least two to three songs that they have either written themselves or they have gotten from a songwriter or production team attached to them. For us, and I'm speaking for me working at Arista for eight years and now with Clive [Davis] at J Records, it's a nice carrot if we feel that we have something already going with the artist, that given the appropriate funds, we can get production that's commensurate with the lyric and the melody and the hit aspect of it. Then we would use our power to go to top songwriters and get additional material that would hopefully provide a hit album. The best scenario is to find an artist that's self-contained—that can sing, write, and do it all. Those artists are very few and far between, but there are some.

Danny Kee, director of A & R, Warner Bros. Records, Nashville (WEA), *country*: I look for artists who are unique and different. Developing an original is always better than trying to clone or chase something already successful. In this business, we all react based on our gut and level of personal enthusiasm. We all listen for something "great"—music that is compelling, interesting, and makes you want to hear it again and again.

Michael Caplan, senior vice president of A & R, Epic Records (SONY), *all genres*: Charisma, what I call the ephemeral "it."

Brian Long, senior director of A & R, MCA Records, *all genres*: First thing I'm looking for is great songs. And a more organic artist that composes their own music and writes lyrics from some muse they tap into, as opposed to the prefabricated pop sort of model. I'm looking for an artist with artistic vision, who's saying something lyrically and can perform—has that energy that when they get onstage, they make a certain connection with their audience.

Jim Guerinot, president, Time Bomb Recordings (BMG), *rock/alternative*: We focus on and specialize in artists that tour. That's the primary criteria. I believe that you can have great songwriters and great records, but if the performance element is absent, you're selling songs, not artists. Ultimately, to have a good label, you want to have it artist driven, not song driven. I think that's a real general criteria for determining the artistry.

Monte Conner, senior vice president of A & R, Roadrunner Records (IND), *rock, hard rock, heavy metal*: Besides the obvious (great songwriting, great vocals, and a star personality in the band), I look for any possible kind of selling point, anything to set the band apart from the rest of the pack, whether it is something as major as the singer having an incredibly unique voice or the band having a groundbreaking songwriting style, to something as simple as the guitar player plays in a wheelchair, the bassist has two heads, or that the band is from Siberia or some exotic location, etc.—literally any angle to make the media take notice and want to pay attention to the band. Of course, angle alone won't sell it, but these days, a band needs that something extra to give the media a reason to take notice. There are so many new bands competing for attention that the obvious attributes are often not enough, sad as that may be.

Aldo Marin, vice president of Cutting Records (IND), *urban/rock/pop/dance*: I always look for something original, whether it be in the sound of their voice, the style of their music, the way they write, or a certain look. If you have all the above, let's talk.

Bruce Iglauer, president, Alligator Records (IND), *blues*: As we're a blues label, we look for something specific—a great feel for our genre; something fresh to say in the blues that is still true to the tradition, preferably including original songs; excellent vocal and instrumental skills; good stage presence (our artists sell themselves live—we can't get enough radio play to work with artists who don't tour); hopefully, a booking agent; hopefully, a manager; a band that they can lead and is organized professionally; a reasonable lack of substance problems; some idea of what business they're in.

Andrew Shack, senior vice president of A & R, Priority Records (EMD), *urban/dance*: Individuality—that is the one thing that attracts me to new artists. I'm looking for innovators, not followers. I try to stay away from trends, as someone who is eclectic and "weird" today may be the star of tomorrow.

Tara Griggs-Magee, vice president/general manager, Verity Records (BMG), *gospel*: The first thing that I look for, besides the natural talent to sing/write/perform, is that the potential artist has a "serious" passion and mission for ministry. Gospel music should be more than someone being able to sing. Most important is the artist's understanding of the "responsibility" that comes with being in professional music ministry. I am not one to give a potential artist a platform to reach so many people if their personal life does not mirror what they sing about. I take this area very seriously. I also love self contained artists. Great artists that can write moving hit songs are the lifeblood of our industry. I look for originality in artistry and avoid those who are simply "cloning" their favorite gospel star.

Ricky Schultz, president, Zebra Records (WEA), *contemporary jazz and quality adult*: Greatness. Something unique that will allow the artist to stand out or distinguish him or her from the other talent out there.

Angel Carrasco, senior vice president of A & R, Sony Latin American (SONY): I'm looking for uniqueness. They have to be different and have their own personality. I want a freshness that I haven't seen. They have to have the voice and the love for the music.

Bo Crane, president/owner, Pandisc Music Corp. and Street Beats Records (IND), *urban/dance:* Originality in sound and/or performance.

Lisa Zbitnew, president, BMG Canada (BMG), *all genres*: We're obviously looking for great talent and great songs; something that is distinct in the marketplace; an act with long-term opportunities—one that's strong now and will be four years from now. It's more than just the musical talent and songs. It's their ability to interpret songs and represents an overall vision of who and what they are. We're looking at the overall package. We want an artist who can deliver on record what they can deliver live; who can deliver in an interview. An artist must come in with an understanding of the commitment of what it's going to take to work with the record company to build a career. We look for artists who we feel can be competitive on the global landscape as well.

David Boyd, senior A & R director, Virgin Records U.K., director of Hut Recordings (development label), *all genres*: I'm looking for good songs primarily. Also passion, hunger, drive, and self-belief.

Chris Sharp, vice president of A & R, 4AD U.K. (IND), *alternative*: Obviously, we want to hear inspirational music. Preferably, it will be breaking some kind of new artistic ground, too—both for the label and for music generally. As we try to think about building artists' careers for the long-term, over five albums or even more, we're looking for evidence of a talent capable of that kind of sustained creativity. And we're less interested in current trends than in music which transcends them. Of course, lots of things that we like don't fit this rather idealistic bill straight away, and we know that new artists often need time and investment before they do their best work. So most of the time we're just looking for a spark in something which indicates that whoever it is might be capable of reaching those rarified heights.

QUESTION 2: HOW CAN AN UNSIGNED ARTIST BEST GET YOUR ATTENTION?

Bruce Lundvall: The best way in jazz and classical is to have a manager or attorney that people know. Even better is to have a musician/artist that's already on the label present your work. But I still go out a few nights a week to look at talent, particularly if an artist says I have to check someone out.

Merlin Bobb: By being persistent as well as professional and respectful when you call the company to get your product heard. Submit only your best, even if it's one song. Don't compare yourself to another artist. Be able to express what your music and style is.

Jeff Blue: Through an attorney, a manager, or just by meeting me.

Happy Walters: We accept unsolicited material and listen to everything we get. It's helpful for an unsigned artist to get to a lawyer or manager that people respect. It makes it easier. Playing around the area you're from and building a regional following is invaluable. Slipknot did the hard kind of world of rock music in Iowa. Korn did it in California. Dave Matthews did it on the East Coast. If you do that, it definitely gets the attention of people.

Hosh Gureli: Send in something that showcases you in the best possible way. No matter what any A & R person will tell you, the bottom line is if you can hear the closest thing to a finished record, that showcases someone's voice in the best possible way, that will grab someone's attention. It's so cheap today to make a good demo. It's a lot easier today to make a great demo than it used to be. We require it to be solicited through an attorney or publisher. There have been certain persistent artists. One found me—on the Internet—that was not a pest, who was respectful and persistent. It does take a bit of chutzpah and being relentless. I appreciate someone who's really trying to make it and will give the benefit of the doubt and will maybe listen to something that's not solicited—if the person is coming off in a genuinely excited manner that's not overdoing it.

Danny Kee: Local following is a good place to start. A lot of good experience performing live many times develops a buzz. If there's a buzz, eventually someone in the industry will hear about it. I get the best leads from people in the industry that I know and work with on a regular basis. If you can make that happen in New York City, Los Angeles, or Nashville, all the better.

Michael Caplan: If they're a rock or hippie band, they should play live. If they're a pop group, they need to get me a tape and drive me crazy. I advise all people that are just starting out to try really hard. Don't leave any stone unturned.

Brian Long: They can get my attention through demo tape submissions, word of mouth, articles and reviews in print publications—I read a lot. The best is word of mouth. I do take unsolicited demos.

Jim Guerinot: The best thing an unsigned artist can do is to not look to me or anyone else but start doing it. All the artists I manage started out doing it themselves. They set up a tour, made their own recordings, and put [them] out themselves. By the time that they come into working with other people as a part of the process, they have a greater understanding and give themselves a greater chance of success. Social Distortion put out their own record. Soundgarden, The Who, No Doubt had a very hands-on approach to doing things, and as they grew and had bigger partners in the form of record companies, they had experience, had already done something and created an environment for success. It's nice to see that a band can draw one thousand people. It means people like them and there's something to this group before you've even gotten involved.

Monte Conner: Any great A & R person has a strong network of contacts, like lawyers, club owners, booking agents, journalists, radio DJs, studio owners, producers, pressing plants, and even fellow employees of your label, etc. And some of these people are in every town no matter how small. All of them have some sort of a connection to the record industry in New York or L.A. If a band is really starting to happen locally and make waves, one of these people will hear about it and tell someone from a record label. This is how all A & R people find bands. We don't wake up in the morning and a lightbulb goes off in our heads and all of a sudden we know about a great new band. [Someone] will call and tip us off.

Aldo Marin: The only way a new artist can grab my attention is if they can write, sing in key, and/or sing with feeling. So if I can detect some talent in any of these fields, we have a potential meeting on our hands.

Bruce Iglauer: Get in front of the public, even on open-mic nights. Write your own songs and insist on performing them. Make a good demo, with three or four songs—decent sounding, concise, as original as possible. Put together some kind of press kit. Remember, this is a job like any other. The work you put into it leads to rewards. No work, no rewards.

Andrew Shack: Live shows and touring are the best way to get my attention. If I see a packed house with fans that are responding, then you know there is potential for success. In the end it's about the fans. Of course, any exposure, whether by touring or collaborating with an established artist, always works.

Tara Griggs-Magee: Great singers come a dime a dozen in the church community. [I look for] an artist that has worked very hard on their own to build a following at the grassroots level. It is a great situation for a record company when an artist (especially in gospel) has paid some dues at the grassroots level, because a work ethic builds real character in the artist, which positions the artist for longevity. I want to know at some level that there is a "natural buzz" on a potential unsigned artist. My goal would be to build upon that base.

Ricky Schultz: We maintain a fluid policy as far as submission. Generally, we tend to favor submissions that have been solicited by people who are known to us or who are credible sources. From time to time, we have been known to accept unsolicited material, and I've made signings right out of the mailbox. Presently that's not the case. When I was running the jazz division at MCA or at Warner Bros. and people would get through to me, one thing I would ask them first was, "You're soliciting me to consider signing you to my roster. Are you familiar with my roster? Have you done your homework?" If you've got a roster of truly world-class artists, somebody has to be realistic. Doing the homework is always good because if you ever get the opportunity to speak to somebody, know what their world is. And their world will largely be defined by their roster.

Angel Carrasco: The recording is first. I usually listen to an artist before I see them. If the tape does something to me, I go to the next step—to meet them.

Bo Crane: Sending a CDR or being submitted or recommended by someone already in the industry.

Lisa Zbitnew: Because there's such a massive number of tapes, it's generally required that something come solicited. An artist should build relationships in the industry—with local promoters, radio programmers, people that are part of the system. If these people come to us, that's sort of the starting point to get to A & R. After that point, presentation becomes important.

David Boyd: Any way possible—through phoning every day for a year or sending music or getting friendly with an existing manager or getting friendly with one of the bands. There's lot of different ways to get through the net. Sending the cassette in blind isn't happening. We get three hundred tapes a week here and nothing ever comes of it. Putting the music down on cassette or CDR is the first move. But what you do with it after that is where they get lost. I was a musician. I had a band and we actually started our own label rather than doing the rounds.

Chris Sharp: Like most labels, we get tons of demos—maybe twenty or thirty every day. And while we do listen to all of them, it's hard to think of too many that have led to an actual signing without other factors being involved. There's nothing less enticing than a lazily designed CDR with some hyperbolic press release telling us that four lads from Bradford are about to change the world with their unique rock-based sound. So many demos just scream "mediocre!" The things that make us prick up our ears are evidence that the artist is putting a bit of thought and originality into developing their career.

At the very least, we like to see that they know a bit about our label's history and the kind of things that we've released over the years, and have an idea of how their music relates to that. And we tend to get more excited if the artist has gotten it together to release their own single or has been doing a bit of networking, getting in touch with other like-minded people, generating a bit of word-of-mouth about what they're up to. We're in touch with record shops around the world, club promoters, people who run little vinyl-only labels, and anything that's above average will make waves amongst those people with their ears to the ground—and that's what we're looking for! In addition to imagination and initiative, we'll spend a bit more time on something with an interesting presentation, a striking sleeve, or a well-designed flyer. These things are a good sign that the artist in question really cares about what they are doing and has some kind of a vision.

QUESTION 3: WHAT'S YOUR BEST PIECE OF ADVICE FOR AN UNSIGNED ARTIST?

Bruce Lundvall: You have to have a great deal of patience and you have to be prepared to be rejected. Every artist has to know that. It doesn't always happen right away. Sometimes the best things happen when you have more experience. A good example is Rachelle Ferrell. She had been out there working as a background singer, teaching voice for quite some time. She had nine albums on a small label. I heard her perform and told her she had a gorgeous voice but was hiding behind the instrumentation. I said to her, "The first bit of advice I can give you is to get rid of your band." I suggested she get into an acoustic situation so we could hear her gorgeous voice and her lyrics. When we made that record, her career shot completely up. There's a lot of dues-paying that needs to go on. Get as much experience as possible. Some people have that magic early on. John Coltrane didn't become successful until he was in his forties.

Merlin Bobb: Stay true to your own style. Don't believe you need to imitate another popular artist to gain recognition. This industry is built on the "next best thing," and the only way to achieve that recognition is to create from within.

Jeff Blue: They have a responsibility to listen to what's out there and be forward thinkers. That means studying the marketplace. Unfortunately a lot of artists' material is very dated. It's absolutely not going to fit into the marketplace. You should always look for a niche that isn't being taken care of, and you want to be contemporary. You've got to watch MTV, read the trades, be knowledgeable about what's going on in your business, because this is a business.

Happy Walters: Don't give up. Build something slowly. Put something out and try to get a local buzz. If a radio station in your town plays it and it does okay, that will help.

Hosh Gureli: Don't think that you know everything. Do more listening than talking. Take everything that you've gathered from people you respect and you see are successful. It's not a fluke that executives who have been around for a while are still around. This is a very big-money business. So listen to what is said and put it all together, without sacrificing your artistry. You should never sell yourself short but just factor it all in.

Danny Kee: An artist should know who they are and have something to say. New artists should do one thing and do it well, not try to be all things to all people. Figure out what is unique and different about you and capitalize on that. Having definite ideas about direction and song material is mandatory. A big mistake is to say to a label, "Just tell me what to do and I'll do it." No one told Mick Jagger what to do. His artistry came from within himself. The music should be an honest and genuine extension of who the artist is and what they have to offer. If not, it comes off as manufactured and insincere. The public will usually pick up on that. Hence the "one-hit wonder."

Michael Caplan: Don't take no for an answer.

Brian Long: Make something happen on your own. Don't expect people to come to you, even when you put out a CD. Make your own noise. Create your own energy around it. Get out and play.

Jim Guerinot: Don't give up. This business is survival of the fittest. Read, read, read. I read everything I could get my hands on. Everything.

Monte Conner: Don't wait for a label to discover you—be proactive and create such a local or regional buzz that the labels find out about you via one of the channels [I've] mentioned. For example, if you are a local band that draws two thousand kids to your shows, that is a going to impress the hell out of a club owner, who may mention your band to [someone] doing scouting for a record label. Or it may blow away the local journalist, who mentions it to his publicist contact at a record label. Or a record label doing retail research may notice that your CDs sold six hundred copies in three local stores. They figure that if something is doing that well locally, than it can explode nationally with a record label behind it. Thousands of bands have gotten signed in similar scenarios.

Aldo Marin: Work on a great demo. Ask your friends and family to tell you the truth. If it's no good, keep working on it till it's right. First impression means a lot to an A & R person because their time is limited. As they are looking for new talent, they are also developing new talent. So if someone is interested in you, be patient and let them get to you so they can spend some time developing you. Also don't forget your look— simple or elaborate, make it shine.

Bruce Iglauer: I still listen to demos and go to gigs. But the persistent artists get the attention—if they're good.

Andrew Shack: Never give up!

Tara Griggs-Magee: Be committed to your music ministry, even if you can't get a record deal right now. I truly believe that if you have a "real ministry" it is not determined by having a record deal or not. Be prepared to work very hard in the beginning! Most gospel artists are not made overnight, and it takes a strong work ethic to make it. Before getting your record deal, sing everywhere that anyone will care to hear you (church, community functions, conferences, etc.) to start building the grassroots following. If you have what it takes, everyone will start buzzing about how amazing you are, and, believe me, we will hear about it.

Ricky Schultz: Believe in yourself and be tenacious. Realize that some of the biggest single successes in our business have been achieved by artists who at one time were just like you—artists who collected rejection slips.

Angel Carrasco: Prepare yourself. Study music. Take lessons in voice and dance. Learn the business. Read the trades. It is your career, like being an architect or doctor. You should know as much as you can about the business so you can understand it and work within the system better.

Bo Crane: Be consistently persistent and don't be discouraged by turndowns. All of us in the industry have at least one story where we rejected Prince, Madonna, Eminem—you fill in the blank. Music, as in all art forms, is very subjective. There are no artistic absolutes. Accept all criticism with a grain of salt and do not let it deter you. Keep writing, recording, and performing and eventually you will be discovered.

Lisa Zbitnew: Things don't happen quickly. You have to be patient while you're waiting for the big opportunity and stay focused on developing your craft. Learn. People have to come into the record company knowing what we do. Read trade magazines. Get a sense of what is out there. Understand what the expectations are to step into this with a better understanding of what's important. Ask lots of questions.

David Boyd: Be true to yourself. Realize who you are and where you come from. Don't try to emulate anybody else. Keep making music and being inspired. Draw from the past and make music for the future in the time that you're here.

Chris Sharp: Think seriously about doing it yourself. If you're any good, bigger record labels will take an interest in you eventually.

PART SIX

GETTING A GOOD DEAL

24

Contract Commitment:
LESS CAN BE MORE

Myth:
The longer the period of my contract is, the better.

● ● ●

The *term* of a contract is the length of time you're tied to the record label. Most recording contracts require a commitment of exclusivity for a specific period. This means that during that time you can record only for them, unless your label gives you permission to record for someone else. Sometimes a label will allow an artist to do a special project with an artist on another label. Usually, all members of the band that sign the contract are obligated to record exclusively for that label. Someone who leaves the band can't just go out and record for someone else; a release is first needed from the label.

Most often, you can still work on other aspects of your music with some freedom. If you're also a producer, you'll be able to produce and develop other acts on your own time. You can also write songs for other people. Of course, none of this can interfere with your primary obligation to your record label. But as long as what you're doing isn't a conflict of interest, you can work on independent projects.

TERM OF COMMITMENT: FROM NUMBER OF YEARS TO NUMBER OF ALBUMS

When I started my record label, the industry was signing recording artists for a specific number of years. A typical deal started at one year, with the option to renew the contract four times, which amounted to a five-year commitment. These days, the term is established by the number of albums you're committed to record instead of the number of years.

Record labels prefer a commitment of albums because they then know up front how many albums they'll have the option to record, no matter what the circumstances. The term of a record deal is for a specific number of albums to be completed. Until an artist records the number of albums called for in her recording agreement, she's still bound to that record label. Therefore, the commitment of a successful recording artist could end up going beyond the old five-year limitation.

Specifying one or two albums a year doesn't always pan out. Some bands take a long time recording. Other bands have taken two years or more to create an album. Some albums have a multitude of hit singles, so a follow-up album isn't called for as quickly. An act may go on long tours that keep them out of the studio. If the tour is successful and the current album is still selling well, the label will wait longer for the next album. If the terms were for a limited number of years rather than albums, the label would feel more pressure to record more quickly.

LESS IS ALWAYS MORE WHEN YOU'RE THE ARTIST

For an artist signing a record label deal, the shorter the term of the contract the better. I know this might not make sense to you at first. Mentally it feels great to have a larger commitment to the label. It makes you feel more secure in the beginning. You might assume the label will do more with you if they've signed you to more albums.

Unfortunately, it doesn't work that way. While it sounds good to get a deal with more albums, the fact is that if you're not doing well, the label won't pick up the album options anyway. No matter how many albums are in your contract, they can ignore you if they choose.

Record labels have it sweet. They never have to record any albums if they choose not to, no matter how many are in the terms of your contract. That's right. No matter how many albums are agreed to, the label doesn't ever have to pick up their options to record them. They don't even have to release one album. They can put you in the studio, give you a nice recording budget, get the finished album, and let it collect dust on a shelf no matter how many albums are in your agreement. If they don't choose to exercise their options for your act, you, of course, will eventually try to break your contract. But that wastes a lot of time.

Why wouldn't you want a long-term contract? If your agreement is for a lesser number of albums, the label will still want you for more albums when that contract expires, if you're doing well. So a short contract won't hurt you if you're successful. And if the label isn't supporting your act, you're better off out of your contract. Then you're free to pursue your career with another label, one that might support you. Sadly, I meet recording artists regularly who are signed to labels, yet their records don't get into most stores. What's the point of staying on a label that doesn't market your music? The status of having a deal wears thin when nobody has heard of you.

If you're doing well, you'll want to be out of your contract as soon as possible. A new act doesn't usually get a great deal. So if your records are selling well, you won't be able to get out of your contract fast enough to suit you. If you're becoming more popular and the label is making money from your recordings, you can probably negotiate a much better contract the next time around or, alternatively, sign with another label, once you've met your recording commitment. If you do well, the label may renegotiate your recording agreement before the terms are over, just to keep you happy. But the best arrangements are negotiated when your agreement runs out. That's why you're better off signing the shortest deal possible. A short-term contract is a win-win situation for the artist. If the record label does nothing with your act, you can get out of your contract more quickly and move on. If your act is doing well, the label will want to renew your contract when the term is up. Then the ball is in your court for getting a more favorable deal. Or you may get interest from another record label; then they can bid on you. Either way, you win.

MORE IS ALWAYS MORE WHEN YOU'RE THE RECORD LABEL

The record label, meanwhile, is always trying to get the longest terms possible. Why? It can't hurt to have all those albums locked up, knowing they never have to be produced if the act isn't working. If you're not doing well, they'll ignore you, despite a long agreement. But just in case you become a hot act, the record label has the option on more albums. They're content knowing that if circumstances keep you out of the studio for a long period of time, you'll still have to produce the stipulated number of albums before the recording agreement is up.

So contracts these days can last way past the five years they used to tie you up for. It's reassuring for labels to have you until you fulfill the required number of albums. But for you as the artist, a shorter term gives you more freedom to advance financially, or at least not to be stuck too long on a label that may not do right by you. Attorney Micheline Levine says that the average number of albums that record labels want a new artist to sign for is six to eight, with seven to eight being most common. "When [the labels] are putting the investment in, they want more because they want longevity."

Whatever the term offered, don't rush into signing a recording agreement. When a label wants to put out your music, you need to look beyond the initial excitement of having what may seem like your dream coming true. Discuss the terms with a good lawyer. Accept that being tied to a record label for a long period of time may not help your career. Be patient and prudent in deciding whether or not to take the deal. If your lawyer says the terms are for too many albums, respect the advice. A label that's serious about developing your career will compromise at least a little.

25

Record Royalties:
WHAT THE ARTIST
Actually Gets

Myth:
If my record sells, I'll be rich from the royalties.

• • •

You'd think that an artist whose record goes gold would be rolling in royalties. Royalties are what artists earn from the sale of their albums. While receiving large royalties is possible, an artist's receiving practically no royalties is a stronger possibility. According to ?uestlove, of The Roots, "The biggest misconception is that you can make money through selling records. We definitely milked the other area of our talent—our live show has kept us on the road, working."

Many artists never see any royalties, due to a number of factors that will be discussed in this chapter. According to Susan Walker, who markets Jerry Jeff Walker's albums on their own label:

> *Even without distribution, we sold enough to pay for the record and probably make more than our royalty checks would have been from MCA. The royalty checks are frightening. When*

Randy Travis was selling five or six million albums, Jerry Jeff and I figured we made more money than him, selling thirty thousand CDs.

There are provisions of royalty agreements that you must understand. While these are discussed here, under no circumstances should you negotiate a deal on your own. Let a music/entertainment attorney do it for you. I've provided this information only to give you a working knowledge of contract provisions so you can discuss them with your attorney and have some understanding. Don't discuss any part of it with the label, even informally. Everything should go though your attorney.

THE RECORDING CONTRACT

There's no such animal as a standard recording contract. Although record labels try to get as much as they can, nothing is set in stone. Certain provisions of a recording contract are considered "customary." Record labels want deductions from your royalties so they keep tradition. Most were instituted many years ago out of necessity, when technology wasn't as sophisticated as it is today. Yet labels still attempt to apply them, though your lawyer can negotiate them out of your contract. According to George Stein, an entertainment lawyer in New York City:

You should never accept it when someone says, "The deal is standard." There are only general standards, most of which are negotiable. A red flag should go up if someone insists you sign a so-called standard agreement.

Finding ways to pay you less royalties benefits the record label. They'll always try keeping these "customary" provisions of a contract. But they can be toned down or eliminated. The deciding factor is how badly you want the deal versus how badly the label wants you. Unfortunately, the ball is usually in the label's court. Unless your act is so hot that people are clamoring for it, you'll probably be the more anxious party. A good lawyer knows what's worth fighting for. Attorney Micheline Levine says:

A lot of points aren't worth fighting tooth and nail over. You've got to learn and hopefully choose an attorney who is able to be not only a good attorney in terms of legal analytical skills, but a good negotiator as well. This entails seeing the forest from the trees, which is one of the most difficult tasks for most attorneys

I've encountered. Some can't let go of a point, and you have to determine which points are worth fighting for and how to let go of the ones that aren't worth it.

POINTS ABOUT POINTS

When you sign a recording contract, you agree to accept a certain number of *points* as the base for calculating your royalty for making the record. *Points* means a percentage of sales. Usually the rate is based on retail prices. Micheline Levine says, "In an all-in deal, the average royalty is between twelve and fourteen points, twelve being fair and fourteen just a little on the high end for a beginning artist."

When you have a ten-point deal on a retail agreement, it technically means that you're getting 10 percent of the retail selling price of your recording. But beware: Record labels ain't giving it up so fast! I said that *technically* 10 percent should go to you, but that's just the base for calculating what you get. Labels have all sorts of deductions that can be legally taken. Your lawyer can attempt to negotiate some of these out of your contract. For example, the record company always retains anywhere from 10 to 25 percent of the retail selling price, depending on the format, to cover the cost of packaging. This is usually more than packaging really costs, so in actuality it's a way for labels to save money.

Many deductions are based on outdated reasoning. For instance, some companies still only pay on 90 percent of sales to cover breakage because records used to break easily in the old days. The CD rate is another provision that record labels alter to their advantage. The CD rate is often lower than the rate paid on other formats because there were problems with CDs when they first came out. The problems no longer exist, yet the tradition remains. Lawyers fight harder against this deduction these days because it's absurd.

Record labels may also deduct a portion of your royalties as *free goods*, another tradition that works in the label's favor. This means they increase the wholesale price of each recording so that the price of eighty-five records is now what the price of one hundred records was. They bill for eighty-five records at the inflated price and say they're giving the stores fifteen out of one hundred pieces for free. Record labels make the same amount of money wholesale. You get no royalties on the 15 percent of records that are supposedly given for free. Since they pay you on retail price, rather than take into account the inflated wholesale price, this means you get less royalties. Record labels get more money on their wholesale price but you get none of it. In a way it's a legal scam, and everyone knows it.

Another provision to watch for is the number of records the label holds as a "reserve." This reserve postpones paying you part of your royalty to cover any returns. Record labels have very liberal return policies. Having run a label myself, I know that it's a difficult situation for them. Stores can wait to return products, so as much as 35 to 50 percent of what has been shipped may be held like an insurance policy against returns. Your contract should have limits on how much can be held as well as a time limit on when this money is released to you.

Issues such as these are negotiable, and it's up to your attorney to strike the best deal possible. Labels try to pay as little as they can. It takes a good attorney to make sure you give up only what's necessary to seal the deal. This is a business of pennies. For a hit record, a few cents can mean a lot of extra money in someone's pocket. For example, if a record sells 300,000 copies, one penny extra means a difference of $3,000. A dime yields an extra $30,000. That's why there's so much haggling about pennies between the record label and the artist's attorney. You want those pennies in *your* pocket, not the record label's.

So you're not dependent on royalties, ask for a decent advance—that way, there'll be at least something to show for your recording efforts. Enter a recording agreement with a realistic attitude, not expecting big bucks in a few months. Don't set yourself up for disappointment.

ALL-IN DEALS

Record labels often give an artist an all-in deal, which means that they set aside a fund for recording costs from which all expenses are deducted. The A & R person monitors the spending of the fund as the album is produced. The record company doesn't hand the fund over to the artist. They pay the bills out of it. When the recording is finished to the satisfaction of the record label, the artist can keep as an advance whatever money was not spent from this recording fund. Attorney George Stein adds:

> *When talking about "common" standards in record deals, you can really only refer to the deals offered by the majors. This is because deals with independent labels are all over the place in terms of the length of the deal, the advances, if any, and royalties.*

As for deals with the majors, the royalties are in the 12 percent to 15 percent range for the first album, with bumps of one-half point for U.S. sales of 500,000 (gold) and one million (platinum). There are usually—but not always—bumps of one-half point for each subsequent album. As for the recording "fund" for each album, the typical range to start for a rock or pop artist is $250,000 to $400,000. The fund includes the artist advance and recording budget. For example, a fund of $300,000 might break down to a $50,000 advance to the artist and a recording budget of $250,000. Like royalties, the minimum fund for each subsequent album is often—but not always—$25,000 to $50,000 higher than the previous fund. There is usually a so-called "mini/max" formula built into the deal, which allows for the minimum negotiated advance to be doubled if sales of the previous album take off.

Most smart artists budget their spending on a recording so they have a reasonable amount left over when all bills are paid. I've seen artists with large budgets get carried away on fancy studios, top-name producers, and other nonessential recording splurges. They end up regretting it when there's nothing left as an advance. Being prudent about spending assures you of some cash at the end. Don't forget that every expense comes out of your pocket.

If your producer is entitled to points on your album, they'll come out of yours. Artists don't always realize this when they agree to give a producer a nice chunk of points. Take into consideration whether the number being offered by the label will cover the producer's share and leave you with something fair. I hear less experienced musicians promising points to people such as the mixer or engineer, when there might not be that many to go around. The average rate for producers is two to four points. A big-name producer may want more because her name on the record can help it sell.

ROYALTY PAYMENTS

Royalties are paid twice a year, with the royalty periods ending on June 30th and December 31st. The record label then has from sixty to ninety days to calculate the royalties you've earned and to give you a statement explaining the amount. Sometimes these royalties are paid on what's called *on paper*. That's because you see the figures you've earned written down on paper, but they go back to the label as reimbursement for what are known as *recoupable expenses,* money the label is entitled to take from your earned royalties to reimburse itself for certain expenses. *Recoupable expenses* include things such as recording costs, advances, tour support (money spent to support you on a tour), equipment, at least part of if not the entire video, at least part if not all of the cost of hiring an independent promoter, and whatever else the label can justify. There can be other miscellaneous expenses. Thank goodness most expenses related to pressing, printing, advertising, publicity, and marketing are *non-recoupable.*

Very important: Be aware that when the label is spending money on you that seems generous, such as bringing food to the studio, buying new clothing for a TV appearance, or sending a limo for you, they will probably recoup these expenses later. That means you're paying for them yourself. And the price recouped may be much higher than if you bought them on your own. Keep this in mind when you're offered extras. Ask if they're recoupable expenses. If so, buy them yourself.

Once the royalties are finally computed and reduced by deductions, the record label will then deduct all recoupable expenses before you ever see a dime. The label keeps all artist's royalties (from the sales of the record only) until the designated recoupable expenses are paid back. Not until all of those costs have been recouped will the artist be entitled to collect royalties.

The system is simple. Let's say you earn $1,000 in royalties on your first royalty statement. Don't head for the mall yet, because the label will first repay itself for your recoupable expenses. Let's say these expenses are $100,000. So, *on paper* you have earned the $1,000, but it's deducted from the $100,000 you "owe" the label. Now you owe them $99,000 more. Six months later you've earned $10,000 *on paper*—you owe the label $89,000. It works like this until the money is fully recouped. If that doesn't happen, your debt (called the deficit) on the first album will be added to the amount to be *recouped* from the second album. This is called *cross collateralization.* But if you as the artist still "owe" the label money when you've completed your contract, you don't have to pay them back out of your own pocket.

The bottom line is that an artist should not expect to see royalties, especially at the beginning. Many artists never earn royalties that aren't just *on paper.* That's why it's important to go for a good advance. It may be the only money you get from the label. The only real money an artist may see after the advance is from doing live shows.

26

Songwriting Royalties: MAKING THE MOST *of Your* PUBLISHING OPTIONS

Myth:

It's best not to give up any of your publishing
to get a record deal.

● ● ●

Music publishing confuses many of my students. Over the years I've
heard countless misconceptions, some of which have actually stopped
young musicians from signing recording contracts that could have
advanced their careers. The responses of these individuals have usually
been along the lines of, "I'm not giving up 50 percent of my publishing
to a label. I wrote the song and 50 percent is too much."

The issue of giving up a portion of your publishing rights is well
worth careful consideration. If your song is earning steady royalties
because a record label or publishing company is doing its job, your 50
percent is probably worth a lot more than the royalties you might earn
if you tried to market the song yourself. Remember that 50 percent of a

substantial royalty is worth much more than 100 percent of nothing. Sometimes you have to give something away to get what you want in return. Keep in mind that if a label owns half of your publishing rights, it stands to make money too, so the company works to that end. Guess who gets taken along for the ride?

Publishing/songwriting royalties are where big money is made. Songwriters generally make more money than artists do. While the artist's royalties are recoupable, the songwriter's royalties are not. Because a songwriter earns royalties beginning with the first record sold, artists who write their own songs therefore stand to make more money than those who do not. If you don't write your own material, try to find someone to cowrite with you. A lot of big name singers have turned into songwriters by getting a good writer to work with them so they could share in the lucrative songwriting royalties.

MUSIC PUBLISHING DEFINED

The first step to make the most of your publishing options is to understand what publishing is. As a songwriter, putting your original song into a tangible form, such as on tape or on paper, automatically copyrights it. When you register your material with the Office of Copyright, in Washington, D.C. (contact them at (202) 707-3000 or (202) 707-9100 for more information), it gives you proof that you own your copyright. As a songwriter, you can file the PA (Performing Arts) form, which copyrights the lyrics and music, or you can file an SR (Sound Recording) form, which copyrights the actual sound as well as the lyrics and music. Either way the song is yours.

At this point, all of the songwriter's royalties are yours as well. If more than one person wrote the song, the royalties are shared equally, unless there's a separate written agreement indicating different percentages. Be careful about offering songwriting credit to someone who makes a small contribution to your song. I should know: I used to put my engineer's name on the copyright because he helped me to put my songs together. I write my own lyrics and create the melody, which technically is the song. But since I needed help, I'd put my engineer, producer, or a friend down on the copyright as a show of good faith. What I didn't realize was that this person owned 50 percent of the song, since I didn't specify otherwise, even though I created 90 percent of it. It was an expensive lesson.

Your next step is to get your song published, which means it's put into a form where it's available for purchase. At that point, it's considered published. That's when royalties come into play, and where confusion begins. Many people think of all songwriting royalties as publishing. That's why so many don't want to give up half of it. In actuality, *publishing* usually refers to only 50 percent of the total writer's royalty, known as the *publisher's share.* The other half is the *writer's share.* Are you with me so far?

The *writer's share* is, not surprisingly, allotted to the writer of the song. The *publisher's share* of songwriting royalties is considered an administrative fee for the music publisher, for taking care of the business end of songwriting. They usually have the copyright on songs assigned to them and issue licenses for others to use them. They market these songs on various levels, such as trying to get people to do cover versions and getting the songs into movies, TV shows, commercials, and other places where income can be earned. Publishers know where royalties come from. They know the going rate for licensing songs. Publishers collect the money and pay the writer.

Music publishing is a business. Established publishers have the business acumen that songwriters sometimes lack. And for that they often get 50 percent of the total songwriting royalties. Remember: publishing is where the big money can be made. It's a lucrative business. Songwriters aren't always businesspeople. Although my business skills are top notch, when I'm involved in a creative project I'd prefer not being bothered with the business end. A publisher may split the total royalty fifty-fifty so that the songwriter doesn't have to worry about business matters and can instead focus on what he does best—creating songs.

Music publishing today isn't what it used to be. In the past, a songwriter would sit in the publisher's office and bang out songs on the piano, which the publisher would then go out and sell to others. In those days, publishers were essential to getting songs marketed. Music publishers and songwriters did the fifty-fifty split on the royalties because they were both integral parts in making money from the song. Today, artists are writing more of their own material, so songs aren't as in demand as they were years ago. But publishers can be good to work with if you have marketable songs.

CO-PUBLISHING DEALS

If the artist is also the songwriter, many record labels, especially independent ones, want what's called a *co-publishing* arrangement. This means the label and songwriter each get 50 percent of the publishing rights. Larger labels sometimes take a smaller percentage. Almost all labels will want to control the copyright, though, so they can issue licenses for your songs to be used. Chances are that if you get a record deal, your label will want a piece of your publishing action.

Here's how it works when a label wants some of your publishing royalties. You start off owning the copyright of your song, so all the songwriting royalties are yours. (No one can take your publishing rights unless you designate otherwise, in writing.) Because it's the most common split, I'll show you an example of the writer and label each getting 50 percent.

WRITER'S SHARE — WRITER — PUBLISHER'S SHARE

WRITER / LABEL

Total Songwriter's Royalties

A co-publishing deal means that at least two people are sharing the publishing royalties for the song. The writer's share of royalties should always go to the writer. Anything else is unfair. In the above diagram, the publishing is split fifty-fifty. As you can see, the songwriter gets 50 percent of the publishing, for a total of 75 percent of the total royalties. The label gets 50 percent of the publishing, which is 25 percent of the total royalties. So when your friend is complaining he won't give up 50 percent of his publishing, explain to him that giving up 50 percent of his publishing means he'll still get 75 percent of the total songwriter's royalties. And with a label involved in the publishing, it could mean a larger royalty pot from which to get that 75 percent. In order to collect your share of the publishing royalties, you have to open a publishing company (more later in this chapter); such royalties can't be paid to you as an individual.

SOURCES OF SONGWRITING ROYALTIES

There are several sources of income available to you if you are a songwriter. Become familiar with the different ways in which your songs can earn songwriting royalties, and with the organizations that can help you with the collection of this income.

Mechanical Royalties

One source of income is from *mechanical royalties*. These are royalties paid by the record label to license the use of your song on their record. The publisher first issues a *mechanical license*, which gives the label permission to manufacture and distribute records, tapes, and CDs with one of their songs. As of this printing, the current mechanical royalty rate is eight cents per song on each record sold, but it increases periodically. The record label isn't supposed to cross-collateralize this royalty—in other words, to use this royalty to recoup money in the same way that artist's royalties are recouped. Some smaller labels may try to get away with this, however. While such an action is not illegal—provided you sign a contract allowing them to do so—you're supposed to get paid from the first record sold.

If you're concerned about your mechanical royalties, use the services of the Harry Fox Agency, a subsidiary of the NMPA (National Music Publisher's Association). One of the services it performs is to issue the mechanical licenses for the publisher. The agency also makes sure the correct mechanical royalties are paid, and provides an accounting for its clients. It regularly audits the record labels. In exchange for its services, the agency takes a small percentage of the royalties.

Performance Royalties

A second potential source of income is *performance royalties*. These are royalties paid for the license to use songs in public places. Most public places that play music must pay a royalty for its use. The obvious sources of income are television and radio, although royalties are also paid by restaurants, stores, clubs (for both the playing of musical recordings and live performances), and other public places that play music. The three performing rights societies—ASCAP (American Society of Composers, Authors and Publishers), BMI (Broadcast Music Incorporated), and SESAC—issue licenses for a song's use, collect the subsequent royalties, and pay the writers and publishers.

ASCAP and BMI are nonprofit and any writer can join. SESAC, a much smaller society, is privately owned and selective about who makes up its members. All three societies represent all genres of music. Each gives a *blanket license* to radio stations, TV stations, clubs, and other public venues where songs might be played. A fee is determined based on the establishment, and it entitles the venue to use all songs that are represented by the society issuing the license.

Which one should you join? I can't make that decision for you. I won't say that one is better than the other. There are pros and cons with each of them. They all benefit songwriters. If you live close enough to one of their branch offices, make an appointment with somebody at each society. Or talk with representatives on the phone. See where you feel more comfortable. Let someone at each society tell you why you should join theirs. You may like a representative at one so much that you'll choose that society. According to Frances Preston, president of BMI:

> *The BMI writer/publisher relations executive is often the first person a new songwriter or artist meets in his or her career and the BMI contract is often the first piece of paper the songwriter signs to prove he or she is a "professional." They come to rely on us, not just for our enthusiasm for their music, but for the good professional advice we are able to give them about the intricacies of the music business and their rights as creators. Those relationships, begun so early, can span entire careers and we are very proud of that.*

Marilyn Bergman, president of ASCAP as well as a renowned songwriter, says:

> *Why join ASCAP? As a songwriter, I am with ASCAP because it excels in what matters to me most—protection, reliability, and fairness. ASCAP is first in revenue collections, royalty distributions, and in negotiating the best license agreements with music-user groups. Just as importantly, ASCAP has championed the rights of music creators in the courts and in Congress since its inception in 1914 and continues to be the leader today as music use in cyberspace begins to take center stage. The royalties paid by ASCAP are based on uncompromising fairness—comparable performances are treated exactly the same way, whether the writer is a superstar or a newcomer.*

Linda Lorence, vice president of writer/publisher relations at SESAC, relates:

> SESAC is a privately owned organization whose owners are music industry veterans who have turned the organization around with a brand new vision to the future. Being the smallest of the three [societies], SESAC maintains its selectivity in order to offer a competitive payment structure and personalized service.

Speak to people at all three organizations and see what they offer. Since each provides assistance to songwriters, don't hesitate to approach the people on staff to get advice on what to do with your songs. This service is free to members. Take advantage of it. Once you affiliate with (join) one of them, they'll be available to give you assistance in making money with your songs. After all, they make money when you do. The people at these societies may have good contacts with the labels, too.

Once you're a published writer (remember, this means your song is on a format that's offered for sale), become a member of one of these three societies. You may join before being published, though at that point there are no royalties to collect. As a songwriter, however, you can join only one society, as opposed to being able to open a publishing company with all three. All your songs should be registered. Your society will send you accounting statements after each royalty period.

You need serious airplay to see performance royalties. What may seem like a lot of airplay to you may not be enough to earn anything. Real publishers are better at handling these collections, which is why a co-publishing deal with a good company can be worth the piece you give up. They keep a more accurate record of what monies are due. And they know the avenues to pursue when you're being shortchanged.

Synchronization Royalties

A third source of income is *synchronization royalties,* which are paid when your song is used on television shows, in movies, etc. The license issued for this kind of use is called a *synchronization license,* known as a *sync* for short. It's a license to use your song in a situation where it's used *in sync* with visual images. The royalties paid for these kinds of uses vary dramatically. It's up to the publisher to negotiate a fair licensing fee. Fees vary according to the budget, the length of the movie or program, and how much of the song is used. Publishers know how to tap into these sources. The Harry Fox Agency can issue sync licenses for you.

OPENING YOUR OWN
PUBLISHING COMPANY

Writers must open their own publishing companies to collect the publishing royalties. To do this, submit three potential company names to the performing rights society you're affiliated with as a songwriter. It will check to see which name you've proposed hasn't been used. Once a name has been cleared, fill out the appropriate forms, wait for acceptance, and you're a publisher. Very simple!

Once your publishing company is accepted, you can get a business certificate and open a bank account so you can cash your royalty checks. If you're going to publish other artists' songs as well as your own, you'll need a publishing company established with all the affiliates that other writers use.

27

SAMPLING:

What It Is, and

WHAT IT CAN

Cost You

Myth:

I can legally sample from a record as long
as I take only a small amount.

● ● ●

Sampling is the use of copyrighted sound from someone else's recording
for your own use. Some musicians sample beats. Some sample sounds.
Some sample actual vocals. Whatever is ultimately taken, sampling is
done by playing the original recording into a digital sampler, which
duplicates the sound. That sound can then be played on a keyboard so
that a *sample* can be added to any part of your recording.

Authorized sampling involves getting permission from the owner
of the sound recording copyright (usually the record label) to use a
piece of the song. A record label can issue you a license to use the sample as a courtesy or for a fee. Unauthorized sampling is stealing, an
infringement of copyright law. It's illegal, even if the writer of the
song gives you permission.

WHY SAMPLE?

I've been told that sampling became popular when hip-hop music first began. Many young rappers couldn't afford to hire someone to play an instrument or make a drum machine available. It became a common practice for them to sample a drumbeat and loop it for the base of their rap. If they wanted guitar chords, they'd simply sample them and use them in their songs. Without getting technical, sampling opens the door to having a multitude of sounds, instruments, and beats for a minimum of money. People sample beats, bass lines, etc. and mix them together as the base of a song. For someone who can't play an instrument or program a drum machine, sampling offers options.

Many producers and writers enjoy listening to lots of records, often old or obscure ones, to find new and interesting sounds to sample onto their own recordings. Kids listen for these sounds when recordings come out. When I was working with dance music and hip-hop, the guys producing and writing for me sampled all the time, much to my chagrin. They loved doing it and refused to acknowledge the liability it involved. "Everybody does it," was what I heard in answer to my fears.

THE HIGH COST OF SAMPLING

In my classes, I'm always asked about the minimum amount of bars/notes/seconds of other artists' recordings you can get away with using as samples without getting written permission. Zero. Nada. Not one recognizable note! I've asked several lawyers about this and have been told that if the owner of the copyright for the sound recording recognizes one second of their song, you're at risk. Of course, many musicians get away with it, as artists on my label liked to remind me. But the fact is, using even small bits of a song is illegal. If it's proven that you stole a sample of another artist's recording, no matter how small, you can be in serious financial hot water. Copyright infringement is a federal offense.

Yes, samples can be camouflaged. If they're covered and buried by other music, they may not be as recognizable and you may not get caught. Yes, you may blatantly sample and still get away with it. But it's a serious risk. According to musicologist Sandy Wilbur, president of Musicdata, "If someone takes a lipstick and doesn't get caught, it's still considered stealing. Sampling without permission, no matter how small or how disguised, is also stealing." If you get caught, you may pay big consequences.

There are ways to prove that you've sampled. Wilbur says that, "When someone believes a sample of their work has been taken without permission, a musicologist can often examine the two works with forensic thoroughness. Analytic skills and new technology can be used to show if they came from the same source."

Most record labels have clauses in their artists' contracts specifying that the artist warrants that there's nothing in their finished product that will infringe on anyone's copyright. The artists must sign it, leaving them legally responsible for using an uncleared sample. When I ran my label, my artists had something similar in their contracts. My lawyer included a clause stating that the artist would be responsible for any lawsuits claiming copyright infringement.

If you get caught sampling illegally, you can lose all your income, royalties, and more, if the record label holds you liable—and it will. Since most copyright disputes are settled quietly out of court, it's hard to say what the penalty might run you if you're found guilty. But if you do get caught with an uncleared sample, lawyers alone cost a fortune. So even if you win the case, you may lose a lot of money. Losing the case is an extremely expensive ordeal. The actual penalty for copyright infringement can exceed $100,000. This depends on how much money you're making from the song with the illegal sample. Sometimes when you lose, you may also have to pay the legal fees for the other side. Sampling is a dangerous gamble. While the odds may seem in your favor, if you get caught you may lose everything you own, now and in the future.

SEEKING PERMISSION TO SAMPLE

When you use samples there are two separate concerns. One is the owner of the copyright on the song itself; the other is the owner of the sound recording copyright. Many people are under the misconception that if the writer of the song says it's okay to sample, they're in the clear. The writer may not even own the copyright and, consequently, might not have the power to allow you to use it. Besides, the bigger liability lies in not getting clearance from the record label. That's where so many musicians get into trouble.

The owner of the song's copyright is usually the publisher and/or writer. Whether you can use the sample may not be your biggest consideration; what needs to be worked out, preferably before the song is released, is what percentage of the royalties you're going to give the copyright owner. If you use ten seconds of a song, what's it worth to you? If you negotiate this before your record is released, you've got a better chance of giving the copyright owner a reasonable percentage. If you wait until your record is in the stores, he may decide he wants more. At that point, how do you get any leverage?

The sound coming off of a record is copyrighted as well. The copyright owner of the sound recording, usually the record label, can be the harder party to negotiate with. A flat licensing fee, rather than a percentage of royalties, is most commonly the deal. While there's a limit with the publisher (the maximum usually being no more than 100 percent of songwriting royalties), there's no limit on the licensing fee for a sound recording. Again, negotiate a deal before you release the record. Once your product is for sale, you're in infringement of copyright and will either pay a lot more or get sued.

I cannot emphasize this enough: get everything cleared before the record is released! The first step is to contact the record label and ask for the legal department or the person handling copyright clearances. Deborah Mannis-Gardner, a licensing and clearance agent with her own private clearance company, dmg, inc., recommends submitting a letter of request along with recorded copies of the songs to the appropriate copyright holders. She also advises having some patience, as they may not respond right away. Your other option is to go to a music clearance company. For a fee, these companies will approach the record label for you to request the use of a sample. They know the going rates, whom to ask, and how to negotiate.

If you like the way a sample sounds but you don't want to go through the hassle and expense of clearing it, try reproducing the sound. You'll still have to work out an agreement with the music publisher for a percentage of royalties, but you won't have to clear it with the record label. Reproducing the sound means going into the studio and recording the track, as close to the way it is on the record, yourself. Then sample your recording, and use that sample in your project. I know it's not quite the same as taking the original, but it's a lot safer. And cheaper.

SOME FINAL WORDS

Even if you're on the right track, you'll get run
over if you just sit there.   —Will Rogers

• • •

I implore you to not give up if you believe in yourself. Life's tough and the music industry is worse. But if you want to make it your life, polish your balls and persist! Here are things to keep in mind on the road to a record deal.

Don't stop getting better!
You can never hone your craft too much. Don't sit around waiting for a record deal to happen. Improve your live performance by doing gigs regularly. Go to songwriter workshops. Don't think you're so good you don't need improvement. Keep striving to be the best you can be, looking for opportunities to have your music heard, and networking your ass off. This can only make you more marketable and increase your potential for making money from your music.

Keep a healthy attitude about drugs and alcohol!
I don't want to get preachy here, but if you respect what I've said in the rest of the book, please respect me now. Partying has been a partner to the music scene for too many years. When I began in the music industry, I felt

like a freak because I didn't do drugs and enjoyed alcohol in moderation. I've been in situations where I was the only one who didn't share in the coke lines being passed around, as I watched talented musicians turn to mush. I've held a musician's hand while we cried together as he free-based crack, wishing he could end the pattern destroying his career. I've gone to rehab with musicians who struggled to regain control over their lives. I've watched talented musicians lose their precision playing their instruments, their ability to create good songs, and their desire for a life. Drugs and alcohol seem exciting on the surface; how glamorous do you think Jimi Hendrix felt dying in his own vomit?

Chris Jones, manager of the band Blind Melon, did whatever he could to help singer Shannon Hoon get over his drug addiction and ultimately watched him die. He told me, "No matter how strong you think you are, the drugs are always stronger. The passion you have for your music will be destroyed by the drugs and the addiction to them." Chuck D added, "Underneath the streets is jail and death. Too many times the streets are marketed as this fantastic place of creativity where we come to reflect. The streets were thrust on us. It's up to us to elevate past the status and bring our people up." Drugs and alcohol kill, if only your soul. They do not enhance creativity on a long-term basis.

Respect yourself by not poisoning your body with excessive use of drugs and alcohol. Trust me, the rush of the moment isn't worth the consequences of long-term addiction, which you'll pay for with the rest of your life. Pursue your career on a healthier level! More and more labels are concerned about signing acts that party too hardy. The trend is now toward a healthy attitude about drugs and alcohol.

Prepare yourself on a mental level.
Be prepared to deal with a tough industry. A healthy attitude is essential for staying on track. The road to fame and fortune gets discouraging. You need determination to keep going. Don't take rejection or criticism too personally. Many people in higher positions have no clue about what will sell. If your material is good, someone will recognize it, if you hang in there. Remember, you need only ONE person to give you that break.

Keep believing in yourself and your music.
When people don't treat you fairly or things don't go your way, use the energy behind your anger to work harder. Don't wallow in obstacles or look for excuses for not succeeding. Forge ahead! For the best chance of getting signed to a record label, believe in yourself and your music with

all your heart. It's hard to keep going when people put up walls in front of your face. Get that positive revenge, as I did when I opened Revenge Records. Nobody believed a schoolteacher with no experience in the industry could make a success of a record label. Nobody but me.

Build a strong foundation.
Do everything you can to create a buzz. Most "overnight successes" paid dues for many years. The pieces—a good recording, a large following, write-ups in music publications, radio play, industry relationships, etc.—take time. It's like climbing steps: one piece leads to the next. The foundation needs to be very strong before you're ready for a record deal. Have patience to wait until you've built it for the best chance of attracting an A & R person's attention. A strong foundation gives you confidence to move forward. You'll succeed, IF you have talent *and* strong material. When your foundation is strong enough, labels come to you.

Be positive in your approach to life.
I truly believe with all my heart that we attract what we give out. A negative attitude attracts negative people. Positive vibes fulfill our dreams so much more. This includes always trying to be courteous. Publicist Terrie Williams believes we should always try to do the right thing, even with those who don't do unto us. Good or bad, it comes back to you. When you get turned down, thank the person anyway. Be gracious. Your attitude can influence that person to help you on another occasion.

Fight the fear!
You've dared to dream. You're trying for a career. That's a success right there! Don't let fear of failure stop you. You're NEVER a failure until you stop trying. There are enough obstacles in this business—don't create others. Take risks! Tap into your spiritual power for support. I've learned to close my eyes and ask for whatever I need and usually get it. It may not come exactly when I want, but it does come. Fear is normal. No one likes to feel like a loser and that's what rejection does to us, IF we let it. When you're scared, sit down and close your eyes. Think about your music and why you believe you should have a deal or whatever it is you want at that moment. Reinforce the reasons out loud if you can. Over and over, tell yourself why your music merits the deal/gig/publicity. When fear comes up, squelch it with thoughts of how great your music is. You can get past fear to what you need. Fight that fear. Think winner!

Never stop having fun while doing your music.
You can get so fed up pursuing the record deal that you lose perspective as to why you're doing music in the first place. Keep the pleasure of creating and performing at the top of your priorities. Even if a deal takes awhile, enjoy the road to getting it. Didn't you get involved with music because you love it? Love it with or without a deal. If you keep nurturing your music career, you'll make money doing what you love.

Be specific about what you need.
Keep putting your needs out there and you'll eventually find someone who leads you to answers. As part of your mental business plan, have specific goals as you move forward. Decide which contacts you need first. Just asking for help with a record deal is less productive than knowing what you want. Keep your options open, but be prepared to ask for specific things that might be more doable than a carte blanche "I want a record deal."

● ● ●

I'll end with this thought: Whenever you're trying to figure out the how, where, who, etc. of something you need, say to yourself, "Seek and ye shall find; knock and it shall be opened unto you" (New Testament, *Matthew, VII, 7*). I live by the intention behind this quote. I've repeated it to myself at times when I didn't know where to turn for what I needed and then found the answers.

I'll again say that the only failure is someone who stops trying! Let your belief in your music guide your heart and your energy in the right direction. Keep the faith. A little spirituality won't hurt you!

I wish you all successful record deals. Please let me know how you liked the book by e-mailing me at daylle@erols.com and visit my website at www.daylle.com.

APPENDIX 1
Advice From Recording Artists

PHOEBE SNOW
You have to be a self-starter. This is something I've found after twenty-plus years in the industry—no one's gonna do it for me. Nobody is going to really make that difference and be the special, persistent kind of force that an artist needs to keep people interested in them. Although, yeah, you do need a good team, and you do need people who are running interference for you and working for labels. But you need the belief in yourself. This is a hard lesson that I learned, but it's definitely a viable one: no one is going to hand me my career on a silver platter. I have to really kind of be the nucleus of whatever's happening. I have to make others want to be interested in me. That's the only secret that I know. Obviously, if you're talented, that's 75 percent. I wish it was 100 percent—that everybody who's talented just automatically gets settled somewhere and gets a label gig. But, that ain't the reality. It's really belief in oneself. [There are] people who are generally regarded as not being predominantly musicians, but as being "entertainers," who are now worth tens of millions of dollars, if not hundreds, because they are self-generating. They're their own best PR people, their own best hype

machine. The minute they get out on stage or get onto a CD, what they're doing is promoting themselves. For a lot of people that's an unsavory side of the business: "I don't want to sit there and talk about myself all night. I don't want to get in people's faces all the time." I'm the kind of person who really doesn't want to do that, but there are ways to do it. If you love music, you'll do anything to make music the center of your universe, if you love it that much. I finally figured it out, and for young artists, I hope it doesn't take as long.

SHAWN MULLINS

Concentrate on being the best you can be, and get as much feedback from other people about what you need to do to make it better. Don't hog the ears on it. You need ears on it! Don't wait on that deal. Do it yourself. That's what worked for me. Get damn good at what you do and then you have the choice of staying independent or getting a record deal.

SARA HICKMAN

I pretty much believe that wherever you live you make your own kingdom. I could be living anywhere and I wouldn't have a problem becoming the biggest fish in the sea because I think that's what you're supposed to do. You make things happen for yourself. If you approach things very smiley and open-hearted and with a lot of integrity, I think people will open doors for you and want to help you. Wherever you live, the best thing is to develop a following and get the press to write about you. If I wanted to speak to the president of the United States, I believe I'd get to him. It's a matter of taking action. Take your time and really discover who you are and what you like and don't like. I don't just mean artistically. I mean about your lifestyle, because it could change very suddenly. You need to explore your relationships with friends. Be full of conviction. In the music industry, a lot of people will tell you how to change or be better. Nine out of ten people will tell you that what you do isn't quite right, but it's that tenth person you need to listen to and that you would listen to, and that needs to be you. Some people may look at you like you're crazy, but that's how we got Leonard Cohen and Van Gogh—all these people who stood up and said, "This is what I am." What if Bob Dylan had changed if they had said he should be more like the Beatles? It wouldn't be Bob Dylan. He did what he had to do and the cake got the icing. Know yourself and your craft and have a vision. If you start getting muddled and confused, keep a journal. You need to reassure yourself. It's very hard. I don't give up. There's this little voice in me that says, "Just keep doing it." Success for me is just a lifestyle.

CHUCK D
Make sure that you gather information about the different occupations that make up the music business. Learn the names of every record company and important personnel within [them], and submit not only a tape but a presentable package (photo and bio info). This can be obtained by acquiring trade magazines and books consisting of history, facts, and know-how of the music business.

SHIRLEY MANSON (lead singer with the rock band Garbage)
I can only speak from personal experience, but my advice would be as follows: If your music is your passion, then guard it ferociously and do not be afraid of failure. Go forth and commit to it. Out of commitment comes surprise and magic. In relation to the industry, however—be afraid, be very afraid! Take responsibility for your business and watch it like a hawk.

LEANN RIMES
Sing as much as you can for experience and exposure, record a good demo album, and send it to friends and acquaintances who can get it into the right hands of major record companies. I sang on stages in Dallas and at various sports functions, and recorded an album on a small independent label in Dallas. The album attracted attention from a couple of record executives, and they came to see me perform live. Before I knew it, I had an official recording contract.

?UESTLOVE (with the rap group The Roots)
You have to have a hustler's attitude. I don't think you should prostitute yourself like some people do. Nepotism is definitely the name of the game in this industry. We're the rare exception. No one of note put us on. We took the back entrance.

JERRY JEFF WALKER
Start your own company!

FISHER

When you are absolutely convinced that you have the two to three hit songs necessary to get you whatever deal you are looking for or that would break you at radio, make yourself a CD with a few songs each from huge acts in your genre and mix your songs in between—like you'd hear on a radio station. Your material better at the very least match the vibe, energy, and sound. If it does, then perhaps you're really ready to be introduced to the world.

PAT GREEN

If you're in college, stay there. Soak up any education you can. This business isn't any different from any other business in that people will take advantage of you if you're stupid. If you don't dot your i's and cross your t's, you'll get screwed. Somebody will screw you anyway. I considered myself a business from the very first gig—we got paid $86.

JO DAVIDSON

Create your own opportunities. Don't wait for people to bring things to you, because they won't.

JOHNNY CLEGG (international recording artist from South Africa)

Believe in what you do and this will win through.

KAREN MATHESON (singer with the Celtic band Capercaillie)

The record company will still come to me to wear this or that. Do I listen? Never! I never felt it was relevant to our music.

APPENDIX 2
Resources

BOOKS

There are many books written about breaking into the music industry. What follows are those that I have found to be extremely useful. Check your local bookstores and online stores to see what else is available. You can never acquire enough knowledge about the music industry.

Schwartz, Daylle Deanna. *Start & Run Your Own Record Label*. New York: Billboard Books, 1998.

> *I'll toot my own horn. If you're going to go the route of pressing up a CD, I highly recommend your reading my other book. It gives many valuable details about getting your business in order, putting your material into a format that can be sold, and developing marketing and promotion strategies.*

Shemel, Sidney, and M. William Krasilovsky. *This Business of Music*. 8th ed. New York: Billboard Books, 2000.

> *When I first got into the business, this book was recommended to me as the bible of the music industry. It has retained this status over many years due to its thorough coverage of topics relating to the business end of music. It's an excellent reference for anyone*

wanting to fully understand the music industry's structure and standards. A must for all bookshelves.

Passman, Donald. *All You Need to Know about the Music Business.* Rev. ed. New York: Simon & Schuster, 2000.

Passman presents a comprehensive picture of how the music industry functions on a business level, including the most important issues a musician needs to understand when seeking a deal. The writing is light, making often difficult topics more easily understood. This book is a necessary part of your education!

Schulenberg, Richard. *Legal Aspects of the Music Industry.* New York: Billboard Books, 1999.

A detailed look at the various legal mumbo-jumbo issues and contracts, with clear explanations. This book is thorough in its presentation of most of the main legal aspects of the industry you may encounter. It breaks contracts down into understandable documents. I highly recommend you increase your savvy about the specifics of the legal end of the music business with this book. It's a great reference for all aspects of music.

Butler, Joy R. *The Musician's Guide Through the Legal Jungle: Answers to Frequently Asked Questions about Music Law.* Arlington, Va.: Sachay Communications, LLC, 2000.

For those of you who hate reading (and everyone else, too!), this is a treat, as it's on a cassette. It's the easiest way to learn the basics of the legal aspects of the biz. Attorney Joy R. Butler has made complicated topics very accessible. A written booklet comes with it. It can be ordered at www.LegalJungleGuide.com or by calling (877) 995-8645.

Blume, Jason. *6 Steps to Songwriting Success.* New York: Billboard Books, 1999.

If you write your own songs, this book is a great source of information. It explains the ins and outs of the business of songwriting and contains information necessary to getting your songs published. Read it through once to get an overall picture of the songwriting business, and use it later as a reference when marketing your songs. Blume is a very successful songwriter and was very generous in sharing his insider info on making money from your songs.

Schock, Harriet. *Becoming Remarkable.* Nevada City, Calif.: Blue Dolphin Publishing, Inc., 1999.

> *As a successful songwriter and inspirational songwriting teacher, Schock has taken her experience, knowledge, and positive attitude and constructed a book for everyone looking to have a career as a songwriter or anyone looking for a creative shot in the arm. There is valuable info on the specifics of songwriting, but Schock also delves into the subject on a deeper level as she speaks from personal experience. It can be ordered at www.harrietschock.com.*

Lathrop, Tad, and Jim Pettigrew Jr. *Music Marketing and Promotion.* New York: Billboard Books, 1999.

> *A guide to marketing your music, with details for putting together a successful marketing campaign. It includes specific steps for hands-on marketing and promotion. There are several good chapters about marketing your music on the Internet.*

Nevue, David. *How to Promote Your Music Successfully on the Internet.* Eugene, Oreg.: Midnight Rain Productions, 2002.

> *This step-by-step guide to creating an online presence for promoting your music provides basic knowledge for selling music on the Internet. It's filled with online music marketing ideas that work and a variety of ways to use the Internet to your best advantage. This good resource is updated at least once a year. It can be ordered at www.musicbizacademy.com/bookstore.*

Goldstein, Jeri. *How to Be Your Own Booking Agent.* Charlottesville, Va.: The New Music Times, Inc., 2000.

> *If you want to take your touring business seriously, read this fantastic resource. It's jam-packed with info about how to book your own gigs and alternative venues where you can make money performing. It includes invaluable info and resources for handling the business end of touring, including how to set career goals, negotiate contracts, run your own business, and set up a tour, including details that I haven't seen anywhere else. It can be ordered at www.nmtinc.com.*

Galper, Hal. *The Touring Musician.* New York: Billboard Books, 2000.

> *If you want to make touring your business, this book can help you get to the next level. It contains a wealth of information about touring, with an emphasis on treating it as a business.*

Frascogna, Xavier M., and H. Lee Hetherington. *This Business of Artist Management*. 3rd ed. New York: Billboard Books, 1997.

> *The standard reference on management in the music and entertainment business, it includes the latest information pertaining to management-related issues and features case studies and interviews with industry insiders and successful performers. The approach isn't sugarcoated, so you'll get a realistic view of what management is all about.*

Williams, Terrie. *The Personal Touch*. New York: Warner Books, 1996.

> *Publicist Terrie Williams shares her story and her principles on developing social skills and showing personal consideration toward others. The tools Williams provides are essential in building and maintaining those all-important relationships.*

DIRECTORIES

Here's a listing of directories that I've found to be extremely useful. I'm not including prices because they change too quickly. Contact the company to get specific information. Some will take your order over the phone with a credit card.

THE INDIE BIBLE

The Indie Bible *is the ultimate Web resource. It contains listings of thousands of e-zines that will review your music, radio stations that will play your music, and online vendors that will sell your music. All genres are covered. If you want to encompass every avenue for marketing your music on the Internet, this book will take you there. It's reasonably priced and updated regularly, and can be ordered at www.indiecontact bible.com.*

THE MUSICIAN'S ATLAS

This resource is a must-have for any artist who wants to tour or get exposure in cities around the country. It lists contact information for numerous resources—clubs, radio stations, press, record stores, and colleges. It also includes listings of conferences and festivals, organizations, record labels, publishers, and much more. It can be ordered at www.musiciansatlas.com.

SRS PUBLISHING
Ritch Esra, owner of SRS Publishing, has compiled or made available the following directories. They can be ordered by calling (800) 377-7411. All of the SRS directories are available on disk.

A & R REGISTRY
This lists the entire A & R staff, with direct-dial numbers and names of assistants, for most major and independent labels in New York, Los Angeles, Nashville, and London. It's updated every eight weeks and is available by subscription. A trial issue can be purchased.

MUSIC PUBLISHER REGISTRY
This lists all major music publishers and significant independents in New York, Los Angeles, Nashville, and London, with their direct-dial numbers and names of their assistants.

FILM/TV MUSIC GUIDE
A directory for those looking to get their music into film or television.

ATTORNEY, LEGAL & BUSINESS AFFAIRS
Lists most of the legal and business affairs people in the music industry, with all contact info.

ALL ACCESS®
Marketed by Measurement Arts, LLC, this music database on CD-ROM is not cheap. But if you're ready to take your career to the next level, it's a worthwhile investment. ALL ACCESS features contact info for over 10,000 music industry pros, including A & R people, music supervisors, radio stations, music publications, distribution and licensing companies, and many more. It also contains valuable resources, including "My Virtual Attorney," with templates for contracts and budgets. (If you use one of the contracts, please show it to a real-life lawyer when it's prepared.) For more info, go to www.label servicenetwork.com or call (310) 283-7131. If you mention my name, you get a 20 percent discount.

BILLBOARD
Billboard has a variety of directories and publications for sale. They can be ordered by calling (800) 247-2160.

BILLBOARD RECORD RETAILING DIRECTORY
A comprehensive directory of music stores, including both chain stores and those independently operated. It's published every March.

BILLBOARD INTERNATIONAL BUYERS GUIDE
Contains a listing of worldwide contacts covering every phase of the music and video industry. It's published every January.

BILLBOARD INTERNATIONAL TALENT & TOURING DIRECTORY
This directory has listings for U.S. and international talent, booking agencies, facilities, services, and products. It's published every October.

BILLBOARD INTERNATIONAL LATIN MUSIC BUYER'S GUIDE
This guide contains resources for finding contacts for breaking into the Latin music marketplace. It's published every August.

THE RADIO POWER BOOK
This is a comprehensive guide to radio and record promotion. It lists all key radio stations and record company promotion personnel.

PERFORMANCE GUIDE SERIES
Performance publishes a series of guides for the concert industry. You can get a full listing of what's offered at the magazine's website, www.performancemagazine.com.

POLLSTAR
Besides its regular publication, Pollstar puts out a wonderful series of contact directories, published biannually. You can get a full listing of everything they have available on their website at www.pollstar.com, or by calling (800) 344-7383 or (209) 271-7900.

RECORD COMPANY ROSTERS
Contains a complete artist roster and list of executive contacts for every major label and almost every independent label in the business. It includes listings of all A & R, artist relations, public relations, legal, and promotion staff, along with other key personnel.

AGENCY ROSTERS
This booking contact directory contains over 6,750 artists.

TALENT BUYERS & CLUBS
Lists every major concert promoter, nightclub, fair, festival, and theme park booking touring artists. It includes college buyers as well.

CONCERT VENUES
Contains booking and contact information for every venue used by major touring artists.

MUSIC CONFERENCES/TRADE SHOWS

Music conferences and trade shows are wonderful places to network and meet like-minded people. Most offer opportunities to showcase new music. Here's a list of some of the most popular ones. (Most are listed in the *Billboard* calendar section.) If possible, attend those that are targeted toward your music, rather than just a general music seminar. This way, you have the best chance of meeting the most people who are involved in what you're doing. Some seminars are held in different cities from year to year. Some vary the time of year they are held. I've tried to get as specific as possible for those that have fixed times and locations. Call the ones you're interested in for a brochure.

AES (AUDIO ENGINEERING
SOCIETY) CONVENTION
(212) 661-8528
60 East 42nd Street
New York, NY 10165
www.aes.org
Convention and exhibition for professional audio manufacturers and engineers; in New York or Los Angeles

ASSOCIATION FOR INDEPENDENT
MUSIC (AFIM)
(606) 633-0946
147 East Main Street
Whitesburg, KY 41858
www.afim.org
Conference for indie and artist-run record labels

ATLANTIS MUSIC CONFERENCE
(770) 499-8600
3015 Canton Road, Suite 3
Marietta, GA 30066
www.atlantismusic.com
A general music conference held the first week in August

CANADIAN MUSIC WEEK
(905) 858-4747
5355 Vail Court
Mississauga, ON
Canada L5M 6G9
www.cmw.net
Conference and music festival

CMJ MUSIC MARATHON
(877) 633-7848
151 West 25th Street, 12th Floor
New York, NY 10001
www.cmj.com
Alternative music/college radio convention; held in New York City in the fall

CUTTING EDGE MUSIC
CONFERENCE
(504) 945-1800
1524 Claiborne Avenue
New Orleans, LA 70118
www.jass.com/cuttingedge
Trade show, panels, and showcases; held in August

GAVIN CONVENTION
(415) 495-1990
140 2nd Street
San Francisco, CA 94105
www.gavin.com
Radio/record promoters conference

IAJE INTERNATIONAL (INTERNA-
TIONAL ASSOCIATION OF JAZZ
EDUCATORS) CONFERENCE
(785) 776-8744
P.O. Box 724
Manhattan, KS 66505
www.iaje.org
A gathering of jazz music educators, musi-cians, students, and industry people

IBMA (INTERNATIONAL
BLUEGRASS MUSIC ASSOCIATION)
WORLD OF BLUEGRASS
(270) 684-9025
1620 Frederica Street
Owensboro, KY 42301
www.ibma.org
Seminars, trade show, and showcases

INTERNATIONAL DJ EXPO
(516) 767-2500
25 Willowdale Drive
Port Washington, NY 11050
For club owners and club/radio/mobile DJs; held in Atlantic City in August

MIDEM
(212) 370-7470
125 Park Avenue South
New York, NY 10017
www.midem.com
International licensing/publishing/distri-bution; held in January in Cannes, France

MILLENIUM MUSIC CONFERENCE
(717) 221-1124
P.O. Box 1012
Harrisburg, PA 17108-1012
www.musicconference.net
Rock 'n' roll showcases and a symposium with panels, workshops, clinics, and a trade show

NEW MUSIC WEST
(604) 684-9338
1062 Homer Street, Suite 300
Vancouver, BC
Canada V6B 2W9
www.newmusicwest.com
A general music conference

NEMO
(781) 306-0441
Zero Governors Avenue, Suite 6
Medford, MA 02155
www.nemoboston.com
Showcases, panels, and trade show

NORTH BY NORTHEAST
(co-sponsored by SXSW)
(512) 467-7979
P.O. Box 4999
Austin, TX 78765
www.nxne.com
*Showcases, panels, and trade show;
held in Portland, Oregon*

SOUTH BY SOUTHWEST (SXSW)
(512) 467-7979
P.O. Box 4999
Austin, TX 78765
www.sxsw.com
*Music business seminar/trade show/show-
casing event for industry and independent
artists; held in March*

WINTER MUSIC CONFERENCE
(954) 563-4444
3450 NE 12th Terrace
Fort Lauderdale, FL 33334
www.wmcon.com
*Industry conference featuring dance music
and rap; held in the Miami area*

MUSIC-BUSINESS-RELATED
ORGANIZATIONS/ASSOCIATIONS

Joining organizations can be a great source of networking opportunities.
Below are some of the major organizations and associations. Many of
these organizations have local chapters in large cities. Call any that
sound interesting to find out or to get some literature.

ACADEMY OF COUNTRY MUSIC
(323) 462-2351
6255 Sunset Boulevard, Suite 923
Hollywood, CA 90028
www.acmcountry.com

AMERICAN SOCIETY OF
COMPOSERS, AUTHORS,
& PUBLISHERS (ASCAP)
(212) 621-6000
One Lincoln Plaza
New York, NY 10023
www.ascap.com

ASSOCIATION FOR
INDEPENDENT MUSIC (AFIM)
(606) 633-0946
P.O. Box 988
147 East Main Street
Whitesburg, KY 41858
www.afim.org

ASSOCIATION OF
INDEPENDENT MUSIC
PUBLISHERS (AIMP)
(818) 842-6257
P.O. Box 1561
Burbank, CA 91507
www.aimp.org

AUDIO ENGINEERING SOCIETY (AES)
(212) 661-8528
60 East 42nd Street, Room 2520
New York, NY 10165
www.aes.org

BLACK ROCK COALITION (BRC)
(212) 713-5097
P.O. Box 1054
New York, NY 10276
www.blackrockcoalition.org

BROADCAST MUSIC
INCORPORATED (BMI)
(212) 586-2000
320 West 57th Street
New York, NY 10019
www.bmi.com

CANADIAN RECORDING INDUSTRY
ASSOCIATION
(416) 967-7272
890 Yonge Street
Toronto, ON
Canada M4W 3P4
www.cria.ca

COUNTRY MUSIC ASSOCIATION
(615) 244-2840
1 Music Circle South
Nashville, TN 37203
www.cmaworld.com

FOLK ALLIANCE
(301) 588-8185
962 Wayne Avenue, Suite 902
Silver Spring, MD 20910-4480
www.folk.org

GOSPEL MUSIC ASSOCIATION
(615) 242-0303
1205 Division Street
Nashville, TN 37203
www.gospelmusic.org

INTERNATIONAL BLUEGRASS
MUSIC ASSOCIATION
(270) 684-9025
1620 Frederica Street
Owensboro, KY 42301
www.ibma.org

LA WIM (LOS ANGELES
WOMEN IN MUSIC)
(213) 243-6440
P.O. Box 1817
Burbank, CA 91507
www.lawim.org

LOS ANGELES MUSIC NETWORK
(818) 769-6095
P.O. Box 8934
Universal City, CA 91618-8934
www.lamn.com

MUSICIANS CONTACT SERVICE
(818) 227-5915
P.O. Box 788
Woodland Hills, CA 91365
www.musicianscontact.com

NASHVILLE SONGWRITERS ASSOCI-
ATION INTERNATIONAL (NSAI)
(615) 256-3354
15 Music Square West
Nashville, TN 37203
www.nashvillesongwriters.com

NATIONAL ACADEMY
OF POPULAR MUSIC/
SONGWRITER'S HALL OF FAME
(212) 957-9230
330 West 58th Street, Suite 411
New York, NY 10019

NATIONAL ACADEMY
OF RECORDING ARTS
& SCIENCES (NARAS)
(310) 392-3777
3402 Pico Boulevard
Santa Monica, CA 90405
www.grammy.com

NATIONAL ASSOCIATION
FOR CAMPUS ACTIVITIES
(800) 845-2338
13 Harbison Way
Columbia, SC 29212-3401
www.naca.org

NATIONAL MUSIC PUBLISHER'S
ASSOCIATION and HARRY FOX
AGENCY (NMPA/HFA)
(212) 370-5330
711 Third Avenue
New York, NY 10017
www.harryfox.com

NORTHERN CALIFORNIA SONG-
WRITERS ASSOCIATION
(650) 654-3966
41724 Laurel Street, Suite 120
San Carlos, CA 94070
www.ncsasong.org

RECORDING INDUSTRY
ASSOCIATION OF AMERICA (RIAA)
(202) 775-0101
1020 19th Street NW, Suite 200
Washington DC 20036
www.riaa.com

RECORDING MUSICIANS
ASSOCIATION
(323) 462-4RMA
817 Vine Street, Suite 209
Hollywood, CA 90038
www.rmala.org

SESAC, INC.
(212) 586-3450
421 West 54th Street
New York, NY 10019
www.sesac.com

SONGWRITERS GUILD
OF AMERICA
(212) 768-7902
1560 Broadway, Suite 1306
New York, NY 10036

(323) 462-1108
6430 Sunset Boulevard, Suite 705
Hollywood, CA 90028

(615) 329 1782
1222 16th Avenue South, Suite 25
Nashville, TN 37212
www.songwriters.org

WASHINGTON AREA MUSIC
ASSOCIATION (WAMA)
(202) 338-1134
1101 17th Street NW, Suite 1100
Washington, DC 20036
www.wamadc.com

ORGANIZATIONS TO PROTECT YOUR RIGHTS

There are organizations all over the country that provide free or low-cost legal assistance for people involved in the arts. They vary in their fees and in their criteria to be eligible for their services. Some offer seminars or have publications available. All are dedicated to providing help with legal matters. Call the one nearest you for more information. They may know of others. Many of these organizations are run by volunteers, and the people I've spoken to have all been sincerely supportive. There's a nice vibe throughout the staffs, one of really wanting to help those in need of legal assistance. I'd like to congratulate the efforts of all the good people who make this list possible.

California
CALIFORNIA LAWYERS
FOR THE ARTS
(510) 444-6351
1212 Broadway Street, Suite 834
Oakland, CA 94612

(916) 442-6210
926 J Street, Suite 811
Sacramento, CA 95814

(415) 775-7200
Fort Mason Center
Building C, Room 255
San Francisco, CA 94123

(310) 998-5590
1641 18th Street
Santa Monica, CA 90404
www.calawyersforthearts.org

Colorado
COLORADO LAWYERS
FOR THE ARTS
(303) 722-7994
200 Grant Street, Suite B7
Denver, CO 80203

Connecticut
CONNECTICUT VOLUNTEER
LAWYERS FOR THE ARTS
(860) 566-4770
Connecticut Commission on the Arts
One Financial Plaza
755 Main Street
Hartford, CT 06103

District of Columbia
WASHINGTON AREA
LAWYERS FOR THE ARTS
(202) 393-2826
815 15th Street NW, Suite 900
Washington, DC 20005
www.thewala.com

Florida
ARTSERVE, INC./ VOLUNTEER
LAWYERS FOR THE ARTS
(954) 462-9191
1350 East Sunrise Boulevard
Fort Lauderdale, FL 33304

Georgia
GEORGIA VOLUNTEER
LAWYERS FOR THE ARTS
(404) 873 3011
675 Ponce De Leon Avenue NE, #550
Atlanta, GA 30308

Illinois
CHICAGO LAWYERS
FOR THE CREATIVE ARTS
(312) 649-4111
213 West Institute Place
Chicago, IL 60610
www.law-arts.org

Kentucky
FUND FOR THE ARTS
(502) 582-0100
623 West Main Street
Louisville, KY 40202

Louisiana
LOUISIANA VOLUNTEER
LAWYERS FOR THE ARTS
(504) 569-1544
143 North Rampart Street
New Orleans, LA 70112

Maine
MAINE VOLUNTEER
LAWYERS FOR THE ARTS
(207) 985-1199
P.O. Box 17797
Portland, ME 04112

Maryland
MARYLAND LAWYERS
FOR THE ARTS
(410) 752-1633
218 West Saratoga Street
Baltimore, MD 21201

Massachusetts
VOLUNTEER LAWYERS FOR THE
ARTS OF MASSACHUSETTS, INC.
(617) 523 1764 or (800) 861 0176
City Hall Plaza #716
P.O. Box 8784
Boston, MA 02114

Minnesota
RESOURCES AND
COUNSELING FOR THE ARTS
(651) 292-4381
308 Prince Street
St. Paul, MN 55101

Missouri
ST. LOUIS VOLUNTEER LAWYERS
AND ACCOUNTANTS FOR THE ARTS
(314) 652-2410
3540 Washington
St. Louis, MO 63103
www.vlaa.org

Montana
MONTANA ARTS COUNCIL
(406) 444-6430
316 N. Park Avenue
Helena, MT 59620

New Hampshire
LAWYERS FOR THE ARTS/
NEW HAMPSHIRE
(603) 224-8300
One Granite Place
Concord, NH 03301

New York
ALBANY/SCHENECTADY
LEAGUE OF ARTS INC.
(518) 449-5380
19 Clinton Avenue
Albany, NY 12207

VOLUNTEER LAWYERS
FOR THE ARTS
(212) 319-2787
1 East 53rd Street, 6th Floor
New York, NY 10022

North Carolina
NORTH CAROLINA VOLUNTEER
LAWYERS FOR THE ARTS
(919) 733-7897
P.O. Box 26513
Raleigh, NC 27611

Ohio
VOLUNTEER LAWYERS AND
ACCOUNTANTS FOR THE ARTS—
CLEVELAND
(216) 696-3525
c/o The Cleveland Bar Association
113 St. Clair Avenue, Suite 100
Cleveland, OH 44114

TOLEDO VOLUNTEER
LAWYERS AND ACCOUNTANTS
FOR THE ARTS
(419) 255-3344
608 Madison, Suite 1523
Toledo, OH 43604

Oregon
NORTHWEST LAWYERS & ARTISTS
(503) 295-2787
520 SW Yamhill, Suite 1031
Portland, OR 97204

Pennsylvania
PHILADELPHIA VOLUNTEER
LAWYERS FOR THE ARTS
(215) 545-3385
251 South 18th Street
Philadelphia, PA 19103

PROARTS
(412) 391-2060
425 Sixth Avenue, Suite 360
Pittsburgh, PA 15219-1819

Rhode Island
OCEAN STATE LAWYERS
FOR THE ARTS
(401) 789-5686
P.O. Box 19
Saunderstown, RI 02874

South Dakota
SOUTH DAKOTA ARTS COUNCIL
(605) 773-3131
800 Governors Drive
Pierre, SD 57501

Tennessee
TENNESSEE ART
COMMISSION
(615) 741-1701
c/o Bennet Tarleton
401 Charollette Avenue
Nashville, TN 37243-0780

Texas
TEXAS ACCOUNTANTS
AND LAWYERS FOR THE ARTS
(713) 526-4876 or (800) 526-8252
1540 Sul Ross
Houston, TX 77006
www.talarts.org

Utah
UTAH LAWYERS
FOR THE ARTS
(801) 482-5373
P.O. Box 652
Salt Lake City, UT 84110

Washington

WASHINGTON LAWYERS
FOR THE ARTS
(206) 328-7053
1634 11th Avenue
Seattle, WA 98122
www.wa-artlaw.org

Canada

CANADIAN ARTISTS'
REPRESENTATION ONTARIO
(CARO)
(416) 340-8850
Artist's Legal Advice Services
(ALAS Ontario)
401 Richmond Street West, Suite 440
Toronto, ON
Canada M5V 3A8
www.caro.ca

Index

BMG Music, 121
BMI, 120, 135, 228-29
Bobb, Merlin, 200-201, 205, 209
Bonham, Tracy, 181
booking agents *See* talent agents
bookstores, 163-64
Boyd, David, 137, 204, 208, 212
Branciforte, Rich, 83-84, 86
Braun, Cody, 138-39, 141, 152, 158-59
breakage, 220
Brickman, Jim, 141
Brown, Mark, 84, 85-86, 87
business, music, 1-15
 attitude and, 2-3, 62-63, 105-9, 120
 career development and, 3-5, 11-12
 creating your own company, 190
 creative people and, 1-2
 hard work and, 10, 16-17, 23,
  42, 121
 lawyers and, 8-9
 marketing plan and, 5-6
 materials for, 9-10
 positive attitude and, 10-11, 86
 self-education and, 7-8, 65, 68,
  191-94
 songwriting and, 120-22
business cards, 9, 11, 78
Butler, Joy R., 8-9, 139
buzz, 17, 238
 record deals and, 180, 185
 visibility and, 18-19

Capercaillie, 244
Capitol Records, 61, 185, 200
Caplan, Michael, 61, 140, 144, 146,
 147, 179, 190, 202, 205-6, 210
career development, 150-71
 audiences and, 42
 education and, 7-8, 22-23, 65,
  68, 191-94
 finding a style, 65-66
 image and, 70-73
 live performances and, 90-93

managers and, 26
patience and, 18
quality and, 6-7, 21-22
record deals and, 3-5, 11-12
setting goals, 6, 68, 112
talent agents and, 37
Carrasco, Angel, 203, 207, 211
CD Baby, 142
Cellar Door Entertainment, 37
Central Park SummerStage, 90
Chemical Brothers, 181
Chisolm, Lois, 61, 68, 73, 156-57,
 160-61, 167, 168, 169
Chiu, Lester, 13-14, 152-53, 158
Chuck D, 237, 243
Ciaccia, Peter, 26
Circle, The, 116
Clegg, Johnny, 244
clubs, 68-69, 114, 138
CMJ Music Conference, 93
CMJ Music Marathon & Musicfest,
 99
CMJ New Music Monthly, 100
CMJ New Music Report, 99, 181
college market, 93, 97-104
 club and concert circuit, 101-4
 power of, 98
 radio, 100-101
College Music Journal, 98, 99-100
Collins, Wallace, 45, 47, 186-88, 189,
 190
Coltrane, John, 209
commercials, music in, 170-71
conferences, 113-14, 128-29, 149,
 161, 251-53
 showcase concerts at, 93, 99
Conner, Monte, 202, 206, 210
contracts, 7, 219-22
 with manager, 32-33
 standard agreement, 219
 term of, 32, 41, 214-17
copyright, 225
 sampling and, 232-35